# Hellenism in the East

# HELLENISM IN THE EAST

The interaction of Greek and non-Greek
civilizations from Syria to Central Asia
after Alexander

edited by
Amélie Kuhrt and Susan Sherwin-White

Duckworth

First published in 1987 by
Gerald Duckworth & Co. Ltd.
The Old Piano Factory
43 Gloucester Crescent, London NW1

ISBN 0 7156 2125 4

**British Library Cataloguing in Publication Data**

Hellenism in the East: the interaction of
Greek and non-Greek civilizations from
Syria to Central Asia after Alexander.
1. Hellenism    2. Middle East ——
Antiquities    3. Middle East ——
Civilization —— Greek influence
I. Kuhrt, Amelie    II. Sherwin-White,
Susan
939'.4    DS56

ISBN 0–7156–2125–4

Typeset by Input Typesetting Ltd.
and printed in Great Britain by
Unwin Brothers Limited, Old Woking

# Contents

# Plates

(between pp. 144 and 145)

# Figures

# Preface

The worldwide hegemony of Orientalism and all it stands for can now be challenged, if we can benefit properly from the general twentieth-century rise to political and historical awareness of so many of the earth's peoples.

(Said 1978, 328)

During the nineteenth and twentieth centuries archaeological excavation has revealed vast quantities of material relating to the different areas and civilisations of the peoples of the Near and Middle East. Yet this rich source of evidence has invariably been treated from a Europocentric perspective, and interdisciplinary co-operation between historians, Assyriologists and archaeologists has been almost totally absent. The narrowness of approach resulting from these failures in historical method characterises especially studies of the Near and Middle East after Alexander's conquest. The articles collected in this book represent an acknowledgement of the need to redress the balance by seeking the collaboration of scholars from a variety of fields concerned with different aspects of the Seleucid empire. Traditional approaches to the study of the hellenistic East after Alexander have been mainly hellenocentric and have selected as of prime importance the establishment and spread of Greek culture. Two recent contributions exemplify this bias: F. Walbank's *The Hellenistic World* (London 1981), and *Cambridge Ancient History* VII/1 (new edition: chs. 3, 5 and 11) in both of which the Near Eastern background, local traditions and cultures are grossly neglected. This is a serious lack which stems from the overriding significance attached to the classical tradition in which most scholars of the ancient world have been educated. One of the results of this is that where there is no *clear* Greek evidence a political, social and cultural vacuum is assumed. Another distorting factor has been the preoccupations of Roman historians who have tended (not unnaturally) to concentrate almost exclusively on those regions of the Seleucid empire which by the first century BC had become part of the Roman empire. This approach has led them to place a disproportionate emphasis on the importance of, for example, the role of Syria in the Seleucid empire as a whole, totally ignoring the central importance of the vast territories controlled by the Seleucids east of the Euphrates. A further methodological weakness has been the almost total failure of historians of this period to recognise the fundamental importance of the traditions and institutions of the Achaemenid empire for understanding the system of Macedonian rule in the East. This is the direct result of the traditional separation of disciplines whereby the Middle East before Alexander is usually studied exclusively by Assyriologists and Iranists and not deemed to fall within the scope of Graeco-Roman historians.

One important result of the development of Assyriology has been the publication of many more hellenistic period cuneiform texts and a growing interest in late Babylonian history. The new availability of this comparatively rich documentation has now made it possible to study Seleucid history and institutions in this particular area of the Seleucid empire on the basis of local sources instead of seeing them mainly through Greek and Roman eyes. The first three articles are thus devoted to different aspects of Babylonia and its culture under the Seleucids, which can now be recognised as the region of central importance for their empire (Sherwin-White; Kuhrt; van der Spek). This fact is also well reflected in Salles' article demonstrating the strong Seleucid presence and strategic and economic interest in the Gulf on the model of the Achaemenids. The impact of Greek rule in Syria is subjected to sceptical scrutiny by Millar, whose merit is to caution against exaggerating the influence and presence of Greeks and Macedonians in this area. However, his careful examination of a scattered body of material is susceptible to a more positive interpretation than he himself allows and the strength of Seleucid imperial rule there cannot be denied. A conspectus of Greek and non-Greek art and architecture of the Near and Middle East is presented by Colledge, who is one of the few archaeologists to emphasise the importance of early Greek contacts with the cultures of the East before Alexander, during the Achaemenid empire, and traces the subsequent development of Greek and existing non-Greek art forms and the gradual emergence of a new art combining Greek and non-Greek (primarily Iranian and Mesopotamian) features.

The results of these contributions suggest that there is an urgent need for Graeco-Roman historians to perceive correctly the geopolitical limitations of their particular sources (cf. Sherwin-White) and refrain from equating them with historical reality. What is required is a shifting of their focus to the Middle East if progress in understanding the Seleucid empire is to be made. Antidotes to the prevailing view are to be more aware of the existence and significance of what may appear to them to be tiny pieces of contemporary archaeological evidence from places such as eastern Iran, Afghanistan, Soviet Central Asia and North India and to realise the importance of trying to integrate this material into their accounts of Seleucid imperialism. This would be a fruitful method for fundamentally re-evaluating the dynamics of the Seleucid empire in a way that has been singularly lacking in past treatments and has been profitably applied in the following chapters.

Another new direction for research suggested by this volume (Sherwin-White; Salles; Colledge) is the application of this methodology to a serious re-analysis of the Parthian and Mauryan empires. The Mauryan empire has been so disregarded by Graeco-Roman historians as to be virtually invisible, in spite of the major work of Romila Thapar (see, for example, Thapar 1966 and 1981) and Fussman 1982, as well as the now significant archaeological remains. Despite some re-evaluation of Parthian imperialism by Soviet scholars, the prevailing view remains that of, for example, E. J. Keall (in Young and Levine (eds.), *Mountains and Lowlands*, Malibu 1977) by which the Parthians are characterised (or rather caricatured) as 'the political clowns of the millennium' (p. 81). And this of a people who successfully ruled an empire stretching from the Euphrates to Central Asia for about four hundred years and whom Strabo ranked with the Romans as the most powerful people of his time.

A further aspect clearly illustrated by most of the contributions (Sherwin-White; Kuhrt; van der Spek; Salles; Colledge) is the huge importance of the Achaemenid empire and its legacy and influence on the formulation and development of the Seleucid empire. This has been illuminated by much recent work on the Persians (cf. particularly Sherwin-White and Kuhrt) but has as yet to make an appreciable impact on standard views of the Achaemenids (cf., for example, Cook 1983).

An urgent need for furthering and implementing these studies is a full and critical analysis of Megasthenes' work on India in the manner achieved for Berossus by Burstein 1978 and Kuhrt (this volume) and for Hecataeus of Abdera by Murray 1970. It is, after all, one of the very few partially preserved examples of hellenistic historiography concerned with a non-Greek kingdom seen through the eyes of a Greek in Seleucid imperial service.

This volume represents a beginning to what we hope will lead to further fruitful collaboration between Assyriologists, archaeologists and ancient historians. The articles collected here originated in papers given in the seminar series *The Seleucid Empire: Sources and Problems*, organised by the editors and held in Autumn 1984 at the Institute of Classical Studies, London University. We are grateful to the Director, Professor John Barron, and the staff of the Institute for their support and help. We would like to thank Professor Fergus Millar for first suggesting that we should co-operate on this stimulating subject. We express our gratitude to the British Academy which, by awarding a visiting fellowship to Jean-François Salles, made possible his participation in the seminar. Thanks should also be given to the Institute for Jewish Studies for facilitating Bert van der Spek's visit and thus his contribution to the seminar. Finally we must thank warmly, for the help that we have received in preparing the articles for publication, Sarah Oliver, Department of Classics, Royal Holloway and Bedford New College, and Katie Edwards, Department of History, University College.

A.K.
S.S.-W.

# Contributors

Malcolm Colledge, Professor of Classical Archaeology, Westfield College, University of London

Amélie Kuhrt, Lecturer in the History of the Ancient Near East, University College, University of London

Fergus Millar, Camden Professor of Ancient History, University of Oxford

Jean-François Salles, Maison de l'Orient Mediterranée, CNRS, University of Lyons and Director of the French excavations on Failaka, Kuwait

Susan Sherwin-White, formerly Lecturer in Ancient History, Royal Holloway and Bedford New College, University of London

Bert van der Spek, Lecturer in Ancient History, Vrije Universiteit, Amsterdam

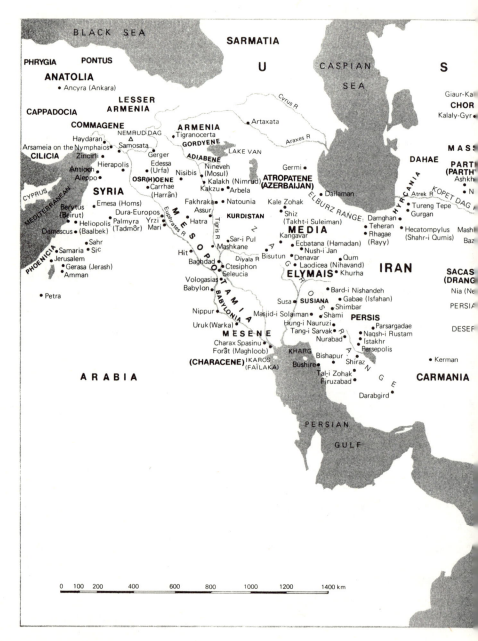

Map of the Seleucid empire in the Near and Middle East and surrounding territories [From Colledge 1977]

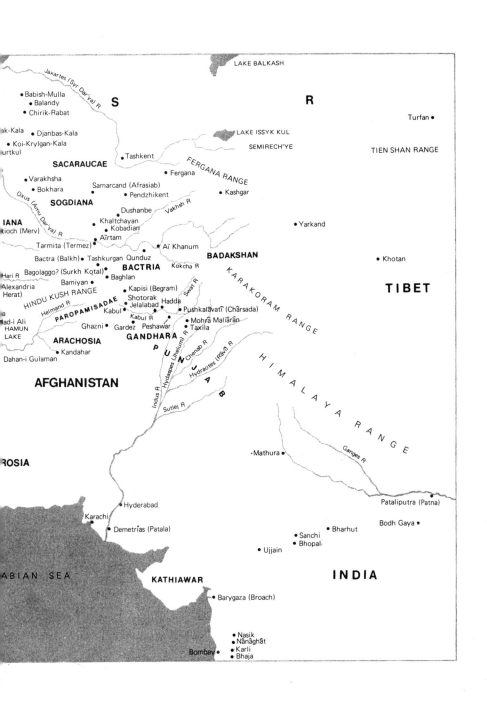

CHAPTER ONE

# Seleucid Babylonia: a case-study for the installation and development of Greek rule

## Susan Sherwin-White

The title of this chapter resembles the inscribed acclamations of the Graeco-Roman world – victory to Apollonius, Dionysius or Serapion. Like them it refers to something desirable and possible, not yet actual. It *is* true that Babylonia is the only region of the Seleucid empire, apart from second-century Judaea, where Greek and – vitally – non-Greek evidence (archaeological, documentary, numismatic) survives in any quantity; the bonus in the case of Babylonia is that the material spans the whole two centuries of Greek rule in the Fertile Crescent and, what is more, continues into the Parthian period.[1] Here, if anywhere, there is a prospect of analysing the establishment and impact of Greek domination on a non-Greek society and culture – a chance of coming closer to understanding what a part of the hellenistic world was like. This is one reason why Babylonia and its cities featured so much in the programme of seminars on the Seleucid empire upon which this book is based.

From Babylonia enough Greek and non-Greek material seems to survive for a work on the model of Martin Hengel's excellent surveys of the political, social, economic and cultural history of hellenistic Palestine (1974; 1980). Hengel is able to set the interaction of Greek and non-Greek and the barriers to this process in the context of the contemporary Palestinian hellenistic environment. But it is important to emphasise that research in this field is in a transitional phase. There are two main reasons for this; the first is that only in the last few years have Assyriologists begun a more systematic publication of unpublished Seleucid period cuneiform texts and begun to use them historically (van Dijk and Mayer 1980; Doty 1977; Funck 1984; *CT* 49; McEwan 1981b, *OECT* IX; Sarkisian 1964. For historical studies

---

1. For general studies of hellenistic Babylonia see Meuleau 1968; cf. also Pallis 1956; Rostovtzeff 1928 (*CAH* VII, ch. 5), 1933, 1951. For basic older collections of hellenistic period cuneiform texts see *BRM* II; Falkenstein 1941; Krückmann 1931; Rutten 1935. For recent publication of Parthian period texts from Uruk and Babylon see Doty 1980; McEwan 1981a.

see especially Doty 1977 and Oelsner 1971, 1974, 1976, 1978, 1981).
One recent, excellent example serves to illustrate the devastating
impact of a single new text on the status quo: the text was published
in 1984 by Kessler (1984b). Until now, Uruk has been seen as an
exemplar of discontinuity in Babylonia on the transition from Seleucid
to Parthian rule in the 130s BC; destruction of the temples (associated
with the Parthian takeover) and the decline and depopulation of Uruk
for approximately a century and a half (e.g. Adams, Nissen 1972,
57–8; Adams 1981, 199; Doty 1977, 27–8). This reconstruction
depended upon the combination of three separate sets of data – the
Parthian occupation of Babylonia, the destruction by fire of the great
Seleucid period temple complex – the Reš and Irigal – attested by the
archaeological excavations (but not dated) and results of Adams'
survey of the Uruk countryside (Adams, Nissen 1972). The new cuneiform text, a contract, is dated to early 108 BC (Seleucid era year 203),
in the reign of the Parthian king Mithridates II; the Reš temple is
still intact and functioning as normal; propertied families active in
the Seleucid period are still *in situ*. There is a continuity. The modern
version has to be totally revised.

The second general reason for the transitional state of the subject
is a 'knock-on' effect from current revolutionary developments in the
historiography of the Achaemenid empire (Briant 1982, 1984a; 1984b;
Sancisi-Weerdenburg 1983; cf. Kuhrt 1983; 1987a). As understanding
grows of Achaemenid rule as a relatively successful imperial system
in the fourth century BC it becomes more and more obvious that study
of the Seleucid empire can no longer be isolated from that of the
Achaemenid period, although this is not appreciated in most recent
work on the Seleucid empire.[2] The Seleucids got (or could have got)
from the Achaemenids a much more sophisticated system of exploitation and domination than was formerly known, and the central
question of continuities in policy, in spite of changes of dynasty, is of
prime importance for scholars to investigate. Historians of the 'hellenistic East' cannot remain unaffected by progress in the historiography of the world of the Achaemenids.

Next, some general remarks about current debate on the character
of the Seleucid state are needed to indicate areas where views are also
changing on central problems. I personally accept what I term the
'strong view' of the early Seleucid kingdom (Musti 1977, 210ff (but
not 1984); Wolski, especially 1974, 1976, 1977, 1982, 1984) and reject
a prevalent approach – the 'weak view' which characterises (and dero-
gates) the Seleucid empire as a mere patchwork of separate 'nations'
or countries – without cohesive structure and therefore easily disinte-

---

2. Thus, to take a recent example, Musti's section (1984) on the Seleucid empire is
   unaffected by recent Achaemenid historiography.

grated (weak) – in fact in slow decline right from the death of its founder, Seleucus I, in 281 BC (e.g. Will 1979, 264ff; Walbank 1981, 123ff; Musti 1984). This approach is encapsulated in Tarn's description of the Seleucid kingdom as an 'outer shell' whose living force was (predictably) to be imported Greeks and Greek culture (Tarn 1951, 4ff). This dichotomy in approach is not to be explained as the product of miserable sources which admit contradictory interpretations, so familiar a problem in Greek history. The schism stems in fact from a basic problem of categorising the large composite empires of the ancient east – Achaemenid, Seleucid or Mauryan. Discourse (in the case of the Achaemenid empire) has tended to be articulated and to stick in exclusive terms: the state as centralist (and therefore strong), or decentralised (and therefore weak). Thapar (1981) and Fussman (1982) on the Mauryan empire in India and Briant (1985; 1987) on the Achaemenid empire argue rightly, I believe, that this is a false dichotomy misconstruing the structure of these states which were not monolithic; local autonomy can and does co-exist with vigorous supervision from the centre. The characteristic feature of most ancient empires – that the further in distance and time you go from the centre the greater the power and independence local representatives of the central authority can wield – may work at times (e.g. of dynastic problems, or invasion) as a centrifugal force, but can equally be a strength for considerable periods.

There is also a tendency in writing on the Seleucids, and on the hellenistic world in general, to concertina three whole centuries of history and assume (often unconsciously) that what is characteristic of one century, or of part of it, is equally true of the whole (this is, for example, notable in the work of Tarn (1952) and Veyne (1976); on the latter see Gauthier, 1985). 'Weakness' and 'failure' is read back from the second-century defeats the Seleucids sustained from Parthia and Rome and used to characterise the early period – the 'slow agony' approach. In fact for some fifty years the first two Seleucid kings ruled continuously an absolutely vast region – no less than seven modern nation states now occupy the territories this huge empire included (Turkey, Syria, Lebanon, Iraq, Kuwait, Afghanistan, Iran) and much of four Soviet Republics (Armenia, Tadjikistan, Uzbekistan, Turkmenistan). In Babylonia Seleucid rule lasted for nearly two hundred years. A more positive approach seems desirable, seeking what held the empire together for so long, rather than why it did not break up sooner. Seeing the Achaemenid empire as a working imperial system opens up other ways by which to approach the Seleucid empire: the 'knock-on factor'.

There are two other general points relevant to analysis of the character of Seleucid rule and to the whole question of the treatment by the central power of the subject peoples, especially non-Greek.

Firstly, there is a failure to recognise policies that seem simply characteristic of an imperial power (Seleucid, Achaemenid, Mauryan); instead these are seen as somehow peculiarly characteristic of Greek colonial rule in the east. For example, it is a tenet of some modern scholarship that the Greeks' interest in foreign cultures was limited (and often superficial) and that few bothered to learn foreign languages. With endearing ethnocentricity British scholars love to compare French cultural chauvinism in their delineation of what is seen as peculiarly characteristic of the ancient Greeks (Balsdon 1979, 125; Lloyd-Jones 1982, 67). Greek cultural isolationism apparently continued even after Alexander's conquests, reinforced by the cultural, economic and social cleavage generally characteristic of colonialism. The picture is neatly completed by Cleopatra VII, last of the Ptolemies and first to 'learn Egyptian' (Plut. *Antony* 27.4–5).

But is any of this correct? Are we even (in the case of the Seleucid empire) in a position to know? If part of the traditional view is right (the empire mainly exists to make the Seleucid rulers powerful), is it also correct to explain Greek distancing from foreign cultures only in terms of Greeks' experience of their own culture as 'superior'? After all, curiosity about other peoples, their beliefs and way of life has hardly been the norm in the relations of one civilisation to another, whereas the pattern of ignorance, suspicion and xenophobia has.[3] There is also a lurking suspicion that modern expectations of what the Greeks *should* have achieved during their empire in the 'Orient' have been shaped by the European invention of Orientalism (Said 1978), to which the colonial empires of Europe gave birth with their handful of often brilliant administrator scholars.

Other factors are relevant in accounting for the existence of limits to Greek (and any other) cultural interaction. First, the status and availability of language learning in society. In neither classical nor hellenistic Greek education did foreign languages have any place; nor was their acquisition prized. Only those would tend to learn whose profession or circumstances made it desirable; merchants, soldiers, doctors, travellers, frontiersmen, slaves might acquire basic vocabulary or more from necessity. See e.g. from Ptolemaic Egypt the letter (*UPZ* I 148: ii BC) from a woman to her husband, who is learning Egyptian in order to teach it to Greek slaveboys learning the Egyptian medical technique of douches (*iatroklysteria*) from an Egyptian expert (Rémondon 1964); see also the Boeotian colony, uprooted by Xerxes (Herodotus 6.119) and settled in Sittakene (east of the Tigris), which in Alexander's reign still remembered its 'traditional customs' (*patrioi nomoi*). Diodorus (17.110.4–5) states that they were bilingual

---

3. See J. D. Gurney, *TLS*, March 11 1983, 241, reviewing Bernard Lewis, *The Muslim Discovery of Europe* (1982).

(*diphonoi*), 'like the indigenous inhabitants in one language and in the other they preserved most Greek words and keep some Greek practices'. The second-century BC explorer Eudoxus, blown off course 'beyond Ethiopia' met and shared food with 'natives', got water and pilots and 'made a list of some words of their speech' (Strabo 2.3.4: 99–100). Compare also the gloss in Hesychius s.v. *mamatrai* (Indian *mahamatra*) 'generals among the Indians', which Benveniste suggested may have derived from a Greek source writing on officials in the administration of the Mauryan empire (Benveniste 1964, 151). The best example perhaps of translation by a Greek in the hellenistic period is the free translation made from the Indian original of an edict of Asoka surviving in the bilingual Greek/Aramaic rock inscription discovered near Kandahar in Afghanistan (Schlumberger/Robert/ Dupont-Sommer 1958; Filliozat 1961/2). The chief barrier to the translation of *literary* works was the rudimentary state of the study of grammar before the Roman development of the art of translation (Bickerman 1976a, 177–9).

There is nothing peculiarly Greek about rulers of empires (from Darius the Great to Queen Victoria) 'failing' to learn the languages of the peoples they rule. The Achaemenids (Cook 1983, 67; 133), like the Ottoman emperors, relied upon the traditional system of scribes and interpreters for official communications and correspondence in foreign languages. No one can seriously expect the Seleucids to have learned the many spoken languages of their vast empire. Like the Achaemenids they would not have seen the need. In addition, language learning was not regarded as a royal virtue in either Achaemenid or Greek hellenistic ideas on kingship (unlike Pharaonic: Peremans 1982, 144; Baines and Eyre 1983, 77ff).

The second methodological point is that the system of administration and the structure of the Seleucid empire made it inevitable that only a minority, whether Greek or non-Greek, needed more than a slight proficiency in other languages. It is often misleadingly stated that Greek became *the* official language of the Seleucid empire. This is not true. The Seleucids permitted local legal systems to continue and allowed the official use of local languages (see below for documentation). The need for the acquisition of other languages accordingly diminishes. If much is available in more than one language, if officials can be addressed and legal documents made out in your 'own language', then many people much of the time will not need languages other than their own. This tendency is naturally reinforced in cultures which also relied upon professional scribes, as did the 'hellenistic east'. The logic of a policy allowing more than one official language is that a large proportion of the different populations is likely to stick to its own language(s) (Grosjean 1982, chs. 1, 2). Official multilingualism fosters and permits individual monoligualism.

The logic of the old view of a monolingual Greek-speaking imperial staff is that only Greek or Greek speakers could be members of it. Thus, the eminent historian C. Habicht (1958) held that the Successors turned their backs upon Alexander's policy towards non-Greeks, elevating as a general rule only Greeks and Macedonians. This influential theory underlies many modern analyses of the character of the new hellenistic kingdoms. From it stems the conventional picture of a hermetically sealed Macedonian Greek minority, culturally impervious to their non-Greek environment and monolingual. The Seleucid kingdom is thought to offer a paradigm ever since Habicht calculated on the basis of a sample of about 250 names (spanning three centuries!) that only about 2.5 per cent of non-Greeks held positions of authority. Since the Seleucid empire embraced the greatest number of different cultures of any hellenistic kingdom the apparent neglect of non-Greek talent is interpreted as a deliberate resolve to monopolise exclusively the fruits of conquest.[4]

Recent studies drawing partly on new material are gradually revealing that in bureaucracy, in administration, in the court and in the armies, the early Seleucids and Ptolemies drew much more widely upon non-Greek personnel to fill responsible positions in the Seleucid kingdom and in Egypt than used to be believed. The famous 2.5 per cent of non-Greek personnel in the Seleucid empire is statistically worthless since the evidence then was (and still is) so incomplete and random geographically and chronologically. The sample was anyhow limited (by the selection of the mainly literary sources) to the highest level of army, bureaucracy and court. It is to be expected that top positions would be filled predominantly by Macedonians and Greeks as under the Achaemenids they had been by Iranians. This monopoly seems something generally imperial as opposed to characteristically Greek. What goes on at levels immediately below, and in the middle and lower ranks, reveals more of policy towards non-Greek subjects. It is here that the role of non-Greeks in high positions as city-governors, bureaucrats and army officers is being revealed (for Ptolemaic Egypt see Welles 1970, Samuel 1970, 443ff, 1983, 110ff; for Seleucid Babylonia see Musti 1977, 261ff, Sherwin-White 1983b, 268–9). The single most important new piece of evidence is a decree from Amyzon in Caria dated to 321 BC (J. and L. Robert 1983 no. 1). It not only contradicts the idea of the Successors' exclusion of non-Greeks but actually attests precisely the opposite trend – their elevation to key positions through the personal intervention of a Macedonian governor. At Amyzon the citizen assembly (the *dêmos*) rubber-stamps the proposal of Asander, the Macedonian satrap of Caria, for the appoint-

---

4. Habicht 1958; Walbank 1981. Bengtson (1951), drawing on the same material as Habicht, reached opposite conclusions!

ment of the Iranian Bagadates to the important position of *neokoros*, temple warden of the sanctuary of Artemis, and he and his family are given citizenship. Bagadates is permanently integrated in the community by the will of the satrap.

The thrust of this discussion is not invalidated by the fact that court and culture remained basically Greek throughout the history of the Seleucid dynasty. The need to learn Greek to get on at the Seleucid (or Ptolemaic) court is paralleled by the necessity of learning Persian for success at the Achaemenid court.[5] There is nothing inherently Greek about the logic of language hierarchy at royal courts. But although there is no reason to suppose that the Seleucid kings regarded personal multilingualism as necessary to their role as effective kings, the odds must be high that the second king, the half-Iranian Antiochus I, learned some words of his mother's language from the Bactrian Apama, daughter of Spitamenes and Darius III's satrap of Bactria. His father, Seleucus I, is generally viewed as 'the only Successor' known to have kept and recognised as his queen the bride he took at the mass marriage ceremony Alexander arranged at Susa (324 BC) to symbolise the union of Persian and Macedonian aristocracies in running his empire; however, when on Alexander's death Craterus made a politically advantageous new marriage alliance to get Phila, daughter of Antipater, he did not simply reject his Persian wife, Amestris daughter of Darius III's brother Oxathres, but arranged for her a marriage with Dionysius tyrant of Heraclea, well endowed with wealth, and on Dionysius' death the *Successor* Lysimachus married her (Memnon, *FGrHist.* 434 4.4–5, 9: 306/5 BC). In cases where we have no sources about the subsequent history of the Persian wives married off in 324, it is foolish automatically to assume that no other Macedonians kept their wives, or exploited the evident influence that attachment to female Iranian aristocracy brought: see now Briant 1985.

Not only was Seleucus' son by Apama half-Iranian, but his descendants adopted the policy of arranging dynastic marriages with contemporary Iranian dynasties of Anatolia, so that the Seleucids kept up a constant blood link with the Iranian classes surviving Alexander. This important feature of Seleucid policy is not always given due recognition, but is well documented.[6] The idea of the Seleucids as quintessentially kings on the Macedonian model makes no allowance for this non-Greek ingredient in their history. In a different context Paul Bernard was right to stress the mixed cultural environment that the Seleucid kings experienced, when discussing the Iranianised Mesopotamian palatial style of the architecture of the hellenistic

5. The classic example is Themistocles: Thuc. 1.138.1–2; Nepos *Them.* 10.1.
6. *Pace* Walbank 1981, 125; see Schmitt 1964, 10–31; Seibert 1967, ch. 3.

palace at the Greek city of Ai Khanum (Bernard 1976b, 255–7: for the use there of a Mesopotamian temple design see Colledge, below p. 142). It is easy to forget that Antiochus I grew up at Babylon in the Achaemenid palaces that Seleucus used. When he was associated as king in the rule of Seleucus and the empire east of the Euphrates, 'Central Asia received a king who had never known Greece and whose tastes and concerns were probably marked by the "Greek-Oriental" ambiance in which he had lived' (Bernard 1976b, 257).

## Early hellenistic Babylonia: from the Achaemenids to Alexander

The first transitional period comes with Alexander. The transfer from Achaemenid rule to that of Alexander has until recently seemed to constitute a sharp turning point in the fortunes of Babylonia (for the better). It is easier to see now that this (old) view resulted in part from a predominantly hellenocentric approach which was itself shaped by the Greek biases of our rich Greek sources. Furthermore the idea that Babylonia was so suppressed economically by the Achaemenids that it was in both cultural and economic decline in the earlier fourth century has been effectively criticised (Kuhrt 1987a): the almost total lack of business, literary and other documents – the foundation of the old view – is no longer true (van Driel 1987; Kuhrt 1987a). The vitality of Babylonian culture in the Seleucid period (Oelsner 1978) may then in part be not so much a revival as a continuation (cf. Strommenger 1964).

The probability is that the picture of the Achaemenids as politically oppressing Babylonia by contrast with Alexander's liberality is mere Greek myth. The current view is still that Achaemenid treatment of Babylonia (the empire's breadbasket) changed rapidly for the worse in the 480s when Xerxes punished the Babylonians fearfully for revolt, destroyed the great temple Esagila and, most frightful of all, actually removed the cult statue of the god Marduk; afterwards Xerxes terminated the prestigious local kingship of Babylon which the Achaemenid kings had inherited from the Neo-Babylonian dynasty they replaced and which they utilised to mediate their authority to the Babylonians. This is the basis of the traditional view which stars Alexander, in stark contrast, as 'restorer of Babylon', rebuilding temples and funding temple repairs and cleaning (the latter he did do: Sachs 1977); Antiochus I's later use of the title 'king of Babylon' is then seen as 'restoration' of the kingship which Xerxes had destroyed and is understood as a resumption of Alexander's own new policy. This is false history. It rests on a careless misreading of Herodotus who is the unique primary source (1.183). Herodotus says nothing about the destruction of temples or the removal of the cult image whose appearance impressed him and which he describes as *in situ*. He simply mentions a story alleging Xerxes' theft of another statue. And in 1984 the first cuneiform text was published in which *Artaxerxes* has the title 'king of Babylon' (Kessler 1984a; Kuhrt and Sherwin-White 1987). Xerxes left the cult image and the temple of Esagila intact and the kingship of Babylon intact too. The crude idea of abrupt change and discontinuity between Alexander and the Achaemenids in policy towards cult and kingship in Babylonia has to go as well.

The functions (and importance) of the kingship of Babylon for rulers (Achaemenid, Alexander or Seleucid) have not yet been much studied. It seems clear that Babylonian monarchy was a dynamic mechanism foreign rulers were careful to utilise. In the prevailing ideology in Babylonia (e.g. the early hellenistic dynastic prophecy: Grayson 1975b) the ruler was responsible for everything; he was central in the eyes of the Babylonians. The kingship and rituals associated with it gave both king and his subjects a framework to operate in. The Seleucids actively exploited the system (Sherwin-White 1983c). This process should probably not be viewed as a one-way system enabling only the king (or his representatives) to make his rule as palatable as possible (Sherwin-White 1983b, 265). The traditional duties of a Babylonian king, in temple-building, cult, as provider of peace and prosperity – the all-responsible ruler – equally gave his subjects, or the more powerful among them, a set of expectations of how a good king should rule and a basis for the exercise of pressure on the king.[7] Just as in the case of Greek sanctuaries, where Seleucid temple patronage can be traced to the pressure from influential Greeks at court (J. and L. Robert 1984), so in Babylonia the temple patronage that we hear of may at times also have been elicited by Babylonian groups or individuals.

To be related to this readiness of the king to make use of Babylonian tradition is the unfortunately garbled Greek account of the priests of Babylon setting in motion the ancient Babylonian ritual of the Substitute King when, shortly before Alexander in fact died, the omens were dire enough for the priests to set this ritual in motion (see Parpola 1983, who authoritatively sets the episode in its Babylonian context). The ruling king temporarily abandons his throne for a surrogate who having ruled his predicted period is put to death: the king then regains his throne. It seems clear from Alexander's ratification of the death sentence of the surrogate that he was cognisant of and approved the implementation of the ritual.

7. Compare, in the context of Roman autocracy, Fergus Millar's observation on how the Senate 'for all its apparent powerlessness did none the less embody and express a quite coherent set of demands and expectations which offered unmistakable guidelines that Emperors crossed at their peril': *TLS*, February 15 1985, 175, review of R. J. A. Talbert, *The Senate of Imperial Rome* (Princeton 1984).

It is easy to take for granted the Successors' ultimately successful grip on Alexander's empire after his death. Macedonian rule seems to have survived in spite, rather than because of the Macedonian high command, whose members fought each other in wars notoriously lasting the rest of the fourth century. Macedonian rule in the east continued largely perhaps because there was *at this time* no other foreign power left strong enough to intervene, a situation that lasted for over a century. Internally there seems at first sight little evidence of unrest among the subjugated peoples. This quietism is usually accepted as reality (e.g. Will 1979, 27–8; id. 1984, 29) and variously interpreted (apathy, 'a waiting game' (Iran), the thoroughness of Alexander's methods). The picture of comparative tranquillity is part myth created by the tunnel vision of our main sources which are Greek (Diodorus/Hieronymus) and whose overriding interest is the warfare between the Successors and only incidentally non-Greek affairs (Wolski 1977 and 1984); the best example of this blindness is Diodorus' omission of the struggle for Babylonia between Seleucus and Antigonus (311–308), attested uniquely in the Babylonian Chronicle known as the *Chronicle of the Diadochoi* (Grayson 1975a, no. 10: see below).

Babylon, centre of the Macedonian army (and Alexander's new fleet) had no chance of military action. It kept quiet. But signs of hostility to Alexander and to Macedonian rule are attested in Babylonian sources, expressed for the first time[8] in the Babylonian cuneiform text known as the Dynastic Prophecy (Grayson 1975b, ch. 3; Lambert 1978) – a prime source. It belongs to a category of Akkadian texts which consist of phoney predictions referring to a sequence of kings who are described by the number of years of their reigns and are apparently classified ultimately as good or bad. The text originally contained three columns on each side of the tablet. A translation of the text has been included to make this very important new document easily accessible. The reconstruction of the disposition of the text on the tablet is that of Lambert (1978), who recognised that the text originally contained three columns on each side of the tablet, not two as assumed in the editio princeps (Grayson 1975b); the column numbers are therefore different from those used by Grayson. What survive are cols. I, II, V and VI. The text begins on the obverse with the rise of the Neo-Babylonian kingdom and overthrow of the Assyrian empire (col. I); col. II contained the reigns of the last Neo-Babylonian kings, Neriglissar (col. II, vv. 1–10) and Nabonidus (vv. 11–16), and the overthrow of Nabonidus by the Achaemenid Cyrus (vv. 17–24); col. IV contained the reigns of the last two Achaemenid kings, Arses (vv. 1–5)

---

8. As remarked by A. Momigliano in his Creighton lecture, delivered in the University of London, 1980.

and Darius III (vv. 6–23). Lambert neatly solved the mystery of the missing Achaemenid kings from Darius to Artaxerxes, who could now be accommodated on the missing cols. III and IV. These were originally the right-hand column of the obverse and the right-hand column of the reverse, respectively, since, as Lambert put it 'columns on cuneiform tablets run from left to right on the obverse and from right to left on the reverse and tablets are turned from top to bottom' (Lambert 1978). Alexander's reign (col. V, vv. 9–23) is bad. Darius' reversal of Alexander's victory is 'predicted' and the people will afterwards prosper (vv. 18–23). There is reference to (?the hope of) tax exemption (*zakûtu*, v. 23), which is of interest: see below. Since at least one other reign is mentioned after Alexander on the tablet the text must be post-Alexander. The reversal of Darius' defeat should not be used (*pace* Grayson) to date the text before the death of Darius, assuming a genuine prophecy, because the function of texts such as these is not 'objective' history. The transformation of defeats into victories is well attested in 2 Maccabees (e.g. 2 Macc. 13:9–24). The former Shah of Iran would have understood very well; among his lesser sins was his refusal to recognise the Macedonian conquest of Iran – a political stance memorialised in David Stronach's use of the term post-Achaemenid to record – inoffensively – his Seleucid period finds in Iran under the Shah's regime. The point of the Dynastic Prophecy is not just to be rude about Alexander; the continuation of the text shows this. Since at least two other reigns were mentioned in the lacunary final column (VI, vv. 3, 4–6: IV, vv. 1–2 may contain the end of Darius, after the reference to Alexander) before the colophon ending the text (ibid. 7ff), there is every reason to suppose that the text is post Alexander, probably therefore from the early Seleucid period. The fact that reigns are added after Darius is clearly demonstrated by the traditional Babylonian scribal practice, which was observed by the scribe here, of separating different reigns by drawing horizontal lines across the tablet (see the translation below) in the appropriate places at the end of each reign. Ringren (1983) has suggested that the text is the work of a Babylonian wanting to support a new ruler, who is expected to restore order after a period regarded as an example of bad rule – the earlier reference to tax exemption hints what good rule should include. This would in an historical context be most likely to be an appeal to a Seleucid king – I would guess perhaps to Seleucus I after the terrible destruction and disorder wrought in Babylonia by Antigonus (Grayson 1975a, no. 10, *Chronicle of the Diadochoi*: see below).

*Dynastic Prophecy: Translation*

I

Lacuna
1–6 Too broken for translation

-------------------------------------------------------------------------

| | |
|---|---|
| 7 | [. . . . .] later time |
| 8 | [. . . . .] will be overthrown. |
| 9 | [. . . . .] will come to an end. |
| 10 | [. . . . . *ar*]*my* of Assyria |
| 11 | [. . . . .] . . . |
| 12 | [. . . . .] will attack and |
| 13 | [. . . . .] Babylon, will attack and |
| 14 | [. . . . .] will be overthrown. |
| 15 | [. . . . .] he will bear . . . and |
| 16 | [. . . . .] . . . he will come and |
| 17 | [. . . . .] he will seize. |
| 18 | [. . . . .] he will destroy. |
| 19 | [. . . . .] he will . . . |
| 20 | [. . . . .] he will bring [*exten*]*sive* [*booty*] into Babylon. |
| 21 | [. . . . . *Esagi*]*l* and Ezida |
| 22 | [. . . . .] he will decorate. |
| 23 | [. . . . .] he will build the palace of Babylon. |
| 24 | [. . . . .] . . . Nippur to Babylon |
| 25 | [for N year]s he will exercise sovereignty. |

II

Lacuna

| | |
|---|---|
| 1 | . . . [. . . . . .] |
| 2 | . . . [. . . . . .] |
| 3 | . . . [. . . . . .] |
| 4 | *will go up from* [. . . . . .] |
| 5 | will overthrow [. . . . . .] |
| 6 | For three years [he will exercise sovereignty]. |
| 7 | Borders and . . . [. . . . . .] |
| 8 | For his people he will [. . . . . .] |
| 9 | After his (death) his son will [ascend] the throne ([. . . . . .]) |
| 10 | (But) he will not [*be master of the land*]. |

| | |
|---|---|
| 11 | A re[bel] prince will arise ([. . . . . .]) |
| 12 | The dynasty of Harran [*he will establish*]. |
| 13 | For seventeen years [he will exercise sovereignty]. |
| 14 | He will oppress (lit. 'be stronger than') the land and the *festival* of *Esa*[*gil* he will *cancel*]. |
| 15 | A fortress in Babylon [he will build]. |
| 16 | He will plot evil against Akkad. |

| | |
|---|---|
| 17 | A king of Elam will arise, the sceptre . . . [. . . . . .] |
| 18 | He will remove him from his throne and ([. . . . . .]) |

19  He will take the throne and the king who arose ‹from› the throne
    ([. . . . . .])
20  The king of Elam will change his place ([. . . . . .])
21  He will settle him in another land ([. . . . . .])
22  That king will oppress (lit. 'be stronger than') the land an[d (. . .)]
23  All the lands [*will bring to him*] tribute.
24  During his reign Akkad [will not enjoy] a peaceful abode.

V

1   [. . .] . . . [. . . . . .]
2   . . . kings . . . [. . . . . .]
3   Which/of his father . . . [. . . . . .]
4   For two years [he will exercise sovereignty].
5   A eunuch [*will murder*] that king.
6   *Any* prince [*will arise*],
7   will attack and [seize] the thr[one].
8   For five years [he will exercise] sovereignty.
9   The army of the Hanaeans [. . .]
10  will attack . . . . . . [. . .]
11  [*The Hanaeans will bring about the defeat of*] his army.
12–14 They will plunder and rob him. Afterwards he (the king) will refit
    [his] army and ra[ise] his weapons.
15  Enlil, Shamash, and [*Marduk*]
16  will go at the side of his army [and]
17  the overthrow of the army of the Hanaean he will [bring about].
18  He will carry off his extensive booty and
19  [*bring (it)*] into his palace.
20  The people who had [*experienced*] misfortune
21  [*will enjoy*] well-being.
22  The mood of the land [will be a happy one].
23  Tax exemption [. . . . . .]
Lacuna

VI

Lacuna (about six lines)
1   [. . . . . .] . . .
2   [*For* N *years*] he will exercise [*sovereignty*].

---

3   [. . . . . .] . . .

---

4   [. . . . . . *will attack*] and seize the land.
5   [. . . . . .]
6   [. . . . . .] will be extinguished.

---

7   [. . . . . . a secret/taboo of] the great gods
8   [You may show it to the initiated but to the uninitiat]ed you must
    not show (it).
9   [It is a secret/taboo of Marduk, lo]rd of the lands.

---

10  [. . . . . .] first, tablet
11  [. . . . . .] Munnabtum
12  [. . . . . .] written, collated

```
13    [.. .. ...] ...
14    [.. .. ...] ...
Lacuna
```

There is little to be sure about here except that the text continued
after Alexander, and in vv. 3, 4–6 probably, as the horizontal lines
show, mentioned two reigns, i.e. (1) Philip III and Alexander IV and
(2) ?Antigonus by whom cuneiform documents are dated in the period
of Seleucus' expulsion from Babylonia (315–312). It is worth pointing
out that since in v. 6 the verb can be read in the middle voice to mean
'They will rule', a reference to Seleucus' return and installation is a
possibility.[9] The Dynastic Prophecy began with the overthrow of the
Assyrian empire and the rise of the Neo-Babylonian kingdom. The
historic point at which it ends can only vaguely be glimpsed; it falls
after the end of Achaemenid rule, which is seen as a good thing, and
after a reign that should historically be Macedonian, in the context
of the establishment of a new dynasty or the termination of a bad
ruler (Antigonus?). Is a strand of the wishful message that the wheel
has come full circle from a first Babylonian kingdom to the second?
This would certainly fit the 'Babylonianization' of Seleucid policies.

## Seleucus and Babylonia

Seleucus' 'right' to Babylonia came originally from the slicing up of
Alexander's empire in 320 (Triparadisus: Errington 1970; Schober
1984). The satrapy of Babylonia was Seleucus' reward (and perhaps
price) for his help as one of the murderers of the regent Perdiccas the
previous year, whose removal had made the new carve-up necessary.
Seleucus' entry in office as satrap (319) is recorded in the fragment of
the Babylonian Chronicle known as the *Chronicle of the Diadochoi*
(Grayson 1975a, no. 10: a key text for the period).

New discoveries have demonstrated the remarkable longevity and
continuity of the tradition of chronicle writing in Babylon which,
though now merely represented by discontinuous texts thanks to the
chance of survival, lasted in spite of changes of dynasty (Neo-Babylonian, Achaemenid, Alexander's reign, the Seleucids). The 'corpus' of
Babylonian chronicles began in the reign of the Neo-Babylonian king
Nabonassar (747–734), lasted into the late Achaemenid period
(Grayson 1975a, nos. 8,9), into Alexander's reign (Sachs 1977) and
continued into the Seleucid period (Grayson 1975a, nos 10, 11–12, 13,
13a, 13b). The obverse of the *Chronicle of the Diadochoi*, the beginning
of which is not preserved, originally covered a number of years before
the first surviving entry (vv. 1ff = Seleucus' accession to the satrapy:

---

9. As noted by Andrew George in the seminar series, adding to the possible readings
   cited by Grayson 1975b, 36.

319). It originally began either with Alexander's death or its after-math,[10] a fact not hitherto recognised. Such questions as functions, audience, authorship and status of this genre still need much investigation which cannot be attempted here; what seems most relevant is to stress that foreign conquest and lack of political freedom did not stop this local tradition.

The Babylonian chronicles, which continue into the Seleucid period, present a Babylon-oriented view of the world. No. 10 does not question the validity of, or regard as illegal Seleucus' position as satrap, which is simply accepted by the author. This unnegative Babylonian attitude to the Macedonian conquest need not be left in limbo. In the period 319–315 Seleucus deliberately set about the creation of a system of political patronage to secure the support of the Babylonian population (or rather sectors of it). Seleucus was forced out of Babylonia by Antigonus in 315. In 312 he returned with a small task force (1500 men) and managed to reclaim his satrapy (approximately two-thirds the area of modern Iraq) which Antigonus had had no authority to remove from him. One important element of Seleucus' success against Antigonus' garrisons, which Diodorus (drawing upon Hieronymus, the contemporary historian) explicitly stresses, was the active support of the local *Babylonian* population (Diod. 19.91). This support (*eunoia*) reciprocated *euergesia* (patronage) from Seleucus in the earlier period of his satrapal rule: Seleucus had established a network of personal relationships based on favours binding Babylonians to him. What these were we are not told – land grants and tax immunities are obvious options. The classic text is Plutarch, *Eumenes*, 4: the grant by Eumenes to *Cappadocian* cavalry in his satrapy of tax immunities in 317 (Briant, 1982a). Besides immunities (note the reference to tax immunity – *zakûtu* – in the Dynastic Prophecy), Seleucus had land fiefs, used by the Achaemenids against military service, to dispose of or ratify.

Seleucus' ability to rely on Babylonian support was strengthened by Antigonus' behaviour towards the population. In the fighting for Babylonia that followed, attested uniquely in the *Chronicle of the Diadochoi* (Grayson 1975a, no. 10), Antigonus treated Babylonia as enemy territory, sacking towns, temples and countryside; though fragmentary, no. 10 gives vivid glimpses of the horror and suffering of the war (weeping and lamentation: 311/10–308). The destruction and upheaval of these years were ended by a final battle, datable to summer 308, which left Seleucus in control of Babylonia: Grayson 1975a, 25–6; Schober 1984, 133–9. The persistence of this struggle is

10. Grayson does not bring this point out in his description of the tablet and commentary on no. 10. The editors recognised this interesting fact in the course of preliminary work preparing a historical commentary on the chronicle fragments of the Seleucid period.

notable and needs to be explained, not skated over without comment; it presumably reflects recognition of the central importance of Babylonia as the key to control of Alexander's empire. Strategically, for the movement of goods and manpower and as a rich reservoir of agricultural resources and surpluses (Adams 1981) Babylonia was vital to any ancient power ruling, or aiming at an empire spanning the Middle East from the Iranian Plateau to Syria. Babylonia was valuable in itself and because it lies across the major routes. The function of the satrapy as a supplies redistribution centre for the Seleucid empire is well attested by a cuneiform text of the 270s (the so-called Astronomical Diary of the reign of Antiochus I: Smith 1924, ch. 6; Austin 1981, no. 141). The entry dating to February 275 reads: 'The governor of Akkad despatched a great quantity of silver, cloth stuffs, furniture(??) and gear from Babylon and from Seleucia, the city of royalty, and 20 elephants which the governor of Bactria had sent to the king, to Ebir-nari, to the king.' (Note the reference to Bactria in the perhaps earlier Seleucid chronicle fragment Grayson 1975a, no. 13). Babylonia was the key for tapping the resources of the 'outer satrapies'. This dynamic function of Babylonia in the imperial system requires emphasis because it has been under-rated, even ignored, by Aegean-oriented, hellenocentric historians, though it would be taken as read by historians of the ancient Near East.

It has been traditional to suppose that the easternmost parts of the Seleucid empire were less important in Seleucid thinking. Syria (and Antioch) tends to be seen as primary, partly because it was what Greek and Roman historians wrote about from the second century and what major wars and Roman diplomacy centred on (Musti 1984, 210ff; Will 1982). This old picture stems partly too from a perception of Antioch as sole capital of the Seleucid kingdom, although the concept of a single capital is inapplicable to the empire during the first one-and-a-half centuries of its existence. North Syria with its tetrapolis of Greek cities founded as part of Seleucus I's grand programme of city-building through his territorial conquests from Syria into Babylonia (Seyrig 1970b) only became the unique centre of Seleucid power during the second half of the second century. The Seleucid empire had no single 'capital' before the Parthians removed the Fertile Crescent (130s) and the Romans removed Asia Minor north of Taurus (188) from the Seleucids once and for all. Like the Achaemenids, several 'capitals' were used to house court, royal administration, army. The central authority, represented by the king, court and army was peripatetic, like the Achaemenids.

Strabo (16.1.5:738) stresses the Seleucids' focus on Seleucia-Tigris as a royal capital and also observes (11.13.5:524) the use by the Achaemenid, Seleucid and Parthian kings of Ecbatana as one of their royal residences; its situational value explained for Strabo the continuity of policy he observed of the succeeding dynasties ruling down to his own time. In the case of Susa, archaeology (Bernard 1976b, 255ff; Le Rider 1965), backed up by a Seleucid period Greek dedication relating to the court,[11] attest the Seleucids' continuing use of an Achaemenid palatial residence at Susa and their exploitation of one of the ancient Achaemenid administrative centres. The Achaemenid pattern is not destroyed before the second century BC. Wolski, in a stream of articles assimilating new material and reappraising old, has demonstrated that the third-century Seleucid kings took a far more active policy towards controlling Iran and the satrapies in Central Asia than has been admitted through their persistent wars and widespread city and fortification building (Wolski esp. 1977, 1982, 1984). Our frame of reference has been totally altered by archaeological work in Afghanistan in the 1960s and 70s and in the Arabian Gulf – especially at Failaka – continuing from the 60s (see Salles, below pp. 84–6). The building of a massive city like Ai Khanum, under the early Seleucids, the rebuilding of old foundations (Antioch Margiana; Alexandria Eschatê), the discovery of a Greek hellenistic level at Termez, in the hellenistic period fort of Kunduz, *exempli gratia*, all point to the premium placed by the Seleucids on the possession and defence of Bactria-Sogdiana, whose wealth in the former case and whose reputation as an effective power base were well appreciated in the period of the Successors (Diod. 18.7.1–4). In Iran, where no hellenistic site has been excavated for its own sake, stray finds, such as Antiochus III's edict attesting (*inter alia*) the location of the Seleucid city of Laodicea at Nehavand in Media, the third-century Greek *ostraka* from Seistan (Carratelli 1966), Bernard's recognition of a Seleucid garrison site in the remains at the Karafto caves in west Azarbaijan, situated by the frontiers of Seleucid Media (Bernard 1980b), Seleucid economic and political interests in the Arab Gulf (Salles, below, Chapter 4) may be disconnected pieces of evidence, but they are certainly tangible proofs of how actively the Seleucids sought to embrace these regions within their empire: tagging these areas as 'peripheral' is no longer on.

Seleucid power was located more squarely in the Middle East than is usually admitted and was also closer to the pattern of the Achaemenid empire of which the Seleucids were the inheritors. We should not be

---

11. *SEG* VII no. 4 (datable to the end of the third or early second century BC on the basis of lettering), a dedication from Susa by Leon and the officers under him for the daughter of the official in charge of 'the court (*aulê*) of the king'. I am grateful to Dr B. Leicknam, Conservateur of inscriptions in the Department of Oriental Antiquities, Louvre, for facilitating access to the hellenistic Greek inscriptions from Susa, and to the British Academy for a grant making study of them possible.

surprised that the Seleucids, like their Achaemenid predecessors, and like Alexander, had a global view of their imperial inheritance.

## Seleucus I and Babylon

The most visible change from Achaemenid times for any traveller in the hellenistic period was the foundation of Greek cities in the non-Greek world. At least two new cities were founded in the late fourth or third centuries, whose location in Babylonia is certain – Seleucia-Tigris below modern Baghdad on the west bank of the Tigris and Apamea-Silhu: *OGIS* 233; Seleucia-on-the-Red Sea was built somewhere on the Arab Gulf, perhaps in Babylonia (Cumont 1927; Roueché, Sherwin-White 1985, 30).

Seleucus I's foundation of Seleucia-Tigris at Tell Umar on the west bank of the Tigris (now known to be on the other side of the river from Opis) and the accompanying shift of 'capital', court and royal administration from Babylon has traditionally been used as a litmus test for the character of Macedonian rule and has, therefore, a general importance in assessing Seleucid policies towards the non-Greek inhabitants and communities of the empire. Is it right to take the foundation of Seleucia automatically as anti-Babylonian and as typifying the Seleucids as narrow colonialists in settlement policy?

It is difficult to find solid support for this view in the ancient sources. The main witness has been the Elder Pliny, although writing over three centuries later when Babylon offered little more than a deserted site of ancient monuments for tourists; Pliny described the city as a desert *in his time* (as did Strabo, again talking of the contemporary world of the early Roman empire: 16.1.5: 738) and flatly stated that Seleucia had been founded to empty Babylon (*NH* 6.122). Pliny's words have been taken surprisingly seriously as a statement of Seleucid policy and underlie several modern accounts (Eddy 1961; Newell 1941; Pallis 1956; Cohen 1978). His assertion can equally be read as simply a *post hoc ergo propter hoc* remark; it certainly needs corroboration before it can be taken at face value! Three whole centuries of Babylonian history cannot be compressed so drastically. Furthermore Babylon was not directly involved in serious warfare through the third and second centuries until the 120s. The Parthian ransacking of the city in 126 BC (Diod. 34/5.21) is one event that is relevant to our later accounts of Babylon in material decline in the early Roman empire.

It is also important to remember that Babylon was, after all, over forty miles distant from Seleucia-Tigris[12] – as far, for example, as Thebes from Athens. Before cars and buses this was, for example, a

---

12. The distance between the two cities tends not to be fully appreciated and is sometimes given wrongly; thus Newell 1938, 9, gives 40 miles and 60 miles at 99.

two-day ride for the well-equipped caravan of Rich in 1839. Besides distance, Babylon was of course on a different riverine system; the Euphrates carried the main trade from the Gulf in the Seleucid period (as in earlier periods) because of its easier navigability and course; goods could be conveyed not only to Seleucia-Tigris from the Euphrates but also to Syria (Salles below, pp. 90–1). Seleucia-Tigris could not *ipso facto* terminate or alter benefits Babylon gained from its position, nor could (or did) it affect the continuing function of Babylon as a local centre (social, religious, administrative) within its surrounding region. Independent evidence of economic, demographic and social decline in the early period is needed (and lacking) before such late testimony can be taken seriously as evidence.

Contrary to the gloomy pronouncements of modern ancient historians,[13] no Seleucid king put Babylon to death. Movements of population from Babylon are attested, but only at exceptional occasions – in war (the temporary evacuation of the Babylonian population for its protection from Demetrius by Patrocles: Diod. 19.100.5–6; the 'evacuation' to Seleucia-Tigris attested in the Astronomical Diary from the reign of Antiochus I under the year SE 36 (276/5 BC: Smith 1924, ch. 6; Austin 1981, no. 141)), and at the foundation of Seleucia-Tigris (Paus. loc. cit.). But no *total* or permanent population transfer is attested. In my view it is improbable that Babylon was merely a 'temple site with a skeleton staff of priests' through the third century. The Astronomical Diary itself continues to refer to Babylon among the other neighbouring Babylonian towns (Borsippa and Cutha) in the years after population was moved to Seleucia. Furthermore Babylon functioned as the centre of a Seleucid administrative district, forming perhaps one of the *pāhātu* into which Babylonia was probably divided for administrative purposes in the third century (Sherwin-White 1983b). Although it is true that the published cuneiform records from third-century Babylon refer, so far almost exclusively, to temple administration and temple business, because they happen to originate from the temples, the cross-section of society – craftsmen, builders, cooks etc. – point to the population living at Babylon, involved as in the past in servicing the cults and temples of its town (for the evidence see McEwan 1981b).

The Seleucid cuneiform texts document the continued existence and traditional vitality of Babylonian society and culture in Babylon (Oelsner 1978, 1981). It makes, perhaps, best sense to set the foundation of Seleucia-Tigris in the historical context of Seleucus' empire building, of his assumption of kingship (king in 305/4: King List, Sachs and Wiseman 1954), and royal image building. Seleucus

---

13. Cf. for example Newell's vivid words (1938, 99): 'Once the brains and most of the heart of the colossus had been removed, the life-blood flowed frm the stricken giant in an ever quickening stream.' Cf. Pallis 1956.

founded Seleucia-Tigris as king (Strabo 16.1.5 (738); Appian *Syr.* 58; Pausanias 1.16.3), probably at about the time of his 'accession'; thus Strabo's statement describing Seleucus as transferring his *basileion* (royal capital) from Babylon to Seleucia-Tigris suggests that Seleucia was founded to be the royal capital of Seleucus' *existing* empire, limited before the battle of Ipsus (301 BC) to satrapies from Babylonia eastwards. Hence Seleucia-Tigris, *alone* of the Seleucid Greek *poleis* named in cuneiform sources, was designated 'city of kingship' (*āl šarrūti*). This conforms to the practice of past Babylonian and Assyrian kings who used the formula *āl šarrūti* for their own new royal cities (Ikida 1979). Seleucus' foundation is presented in traditional Babylonian terms and is assimilated (Sherwin-White 1983b). The site itself was strategically well situated for control of Babylonia and for access to Seleucus' new empire in the east, near the age-old river crossing point of armies at Opis and the route via the Diyala valley up to Ecbatana and Media and connected with the Euphrates by a royal canal (Isidore of Charax, 1). It beautifully tapped all routes of importance.

It was the old and widespread idea that Antiochus IV turned Babylon into a *polis* which gave grist to the notion of Seleucid neglect of the city in the third century BC. The view should probably be modified since its main basis – a fragmentary dedicatory inscription in Greek to Antiochus IV which named the king as 'saviour of Asia' and 'founder of the *polis*' (*OGIS* 253) – has been shown to be of uncertain provenance from within Mesopotamia and probably a *pierre errante* (see Sherwin-White 1982, 65ff). There is, however, evidence of a Greek presence in Babylon in the early Seleucid period. An important Greek ostrakon, datable to the early third century, possibly to the second quarter, found in the German excavations of Babylon (Schmidt 1941, 815 no.1, fig.15; Wetzel, Schmidt, Mallwitz 1957, 50–1 no. 4, plate 40b; Sherwin-White, 1982, 54, plate 2a), directly attests the presence of military units at Babylon under Greek officers, which can be identified with a Seleucid garrison there in the early third century BC (Sherwin-White, 1982, 58ff). The Seleucids regularly posted garrisons in the citadels of cities under their control, as well as in the countryside at places of strategic or political importance (Bickerman 1938, 53–4). Babylon was garrisoned under Alexander and during the late-fourth-century struggle between Seleucus and Antigonus for control of Babylonia and the 'Upper Satrapies'. The stationing of Seleucid soldiers in the old Neo-Babylonian capital, whether on a temporary or permanent basis, is not surprising.

But there are other signs of Greek life in third-century Babylon besides the evidence of the Greek ostrakon. There is some archaeological evidence of a Greek presence after Alexander. This includes the famous Greek theatre dating from the early hellenistic period and refurbished several times under the Seleucids and later under the Parthians (Koldewey 1913, 293ff; Wetzel, Schmidt, Mallwitz 1957, 3–16, plates 4–9). The significance of the theatre, not normally thought to need comment, is that it presupposes a Greek/hellenised population of some size to use it. There is also Greek pottery (Wetzel, Schmidt, Mallwitz 1957, 52–5, 57), Greek amphora handles (ibid. 1957, 57 nos. 93–8 (Rhodian), 58 no. 99 (Thasian)), Greek glass 'pastes' (copies of engraved gems; ibid. 1957, 42–3 nos. 102–34) and many Greek terracottas (Koldewey 1913, 275ff). The theatre is in the central area of the part of the site known as Homera, which is situated inside the inner city walls on the east side of the city. This may have been the location of the Greek community – a Greek/Macedonian quarter.[14] Later attestation of an organised Greek/Macedonian community at Babylon is provided by a clay tablet inscribed in Greek (Haussoullier 1909, 352–3 no. 1 = *SEG* VII 39). The inscription, dated to 110/109 BC, comes from the period of Parthian control of Babylonia after Seleucid rule there had ended. It is a list of ephebes and *neoi* ('young men'), winners of various athletic competitions. The tablet reveals the operation of a gymnasium for Greeks and Macedonians who are named with Greek and Macedonian personal names and patronymics. The existence at Babylon of a Greek theatre, a gymnasium and an agora, which Diodorus mentions only in the context of its destruction by fire at the hands of the Parthian satrap Himerus (Diod. 34/5.21; Poseidonius, *FGrHist.* 87 F 13; Justin 42.1.3), probably does mean that the Greek community at Babylon was then organised as a *polis*, though there is no direct evidence of this. Since the link between Antiochus IV and the original foundation of a Greek *polis* at Babylon can be broken, a Greek foundation there could be considerably earlier, for example of the third century BC, when there is other evidence of a Greek presence and when the Seleucid kings carried out a very active colonising policy throughout their empire. The possibility is that as at Apamea-Silhu and Susa a Greek colony, possibly like these with the status of a *polis*, was juxtaposed in the third century alongside the local inhabitants who go their own way under Babylonian law, all however being subject to the will of the king:[15] Sherwin-White 1982, 67ff.

14. See Wetzel, Schmidt, Mallwitz 1957, 2–3; Koldewey 1913, 293–302. For plans of the site and for the location of Homera see Wetzel et al. plates 1–2. For the building phases of the theatre see ibid. 3–16 (plates 4–9). For the palaestra added to the theatre see ibid. 16–22 (plate 11a).
15. The third-century BC date for the foundation of Greek *poleis* at Susa (Seleucia-Eulaeus) and at the River Silhu (Apamea-Seleias) is established by the Greek inscription *OGIS* 233, lines 103–4, 108–9 (c. 205 BC). The precise date of their foundation is at present unknown. See Le Rider 1965, 260 n. 2 on the location of Apamea-Seleias.

## King and subject: patterns of relationship

Next, it is necessary to consider the question of the relations between the central power, the king, and his subjects – what is revealed about the glue holding the empire together? It is important, I think, to emphasise that for much of the first thirty years of Seleucid rule either the king or his son as crown prince, or as co-regent, put in regular periods of residence in Babylonia – and this seems to have continued (for example the brother of Seleucus III, the future Antiochus III, was in Babylon at the time of Seleucus III's death: Eusebius, *Chron.* (ed. Schöne) 1.253; Hieron. in Dan. 9.10) and Antiochus may be identified as the VIP arriving at Seleucia-Tigris to a traditional display of pomp and ceremony: Grayson 1975a, no. 13b, cf. Sherwin-White 1983b, 267–8.

From the king ran a set of separate lines of authority and administration. First the satrap, whose ethnic identity is rarely known and should not automatically be assumed to be invariably Macedonian or Greek, was governor of the southern half of what we know as the Fertile Crescent, except for an area around the Arabian Gulf (later Characene) which had been formed into a separate satrapy already by the accession of Antiochus III (Polyb. 5.48.13), but may have been created much earlier to facilitate Seleucid control (see Salles, below p. 97; Roueché, Sherwin-White 1985, 8 with note 16). Royal administration at local (city) level is now gradually becoming more visible, primarily because of the publication of new material (see van der Spek, below). As in earlier periods Babylonia seems to have been divided into smaller regions – *pāhātu* – ruled by royal officials, although at present this is documented only for Seleucia and Babylon and its district (Sherwin-White 1983b, 268 and note 26). It is notable that city officials – royal appointees – were not mere subordinates of the satrap in a descending chain of authority – king, satrap, city-officials. They are instead found taking orders directly from the king and even, in wartime, going to the king in Sardis (Astronomical Diary obv. vv. 15–17; Austin 1981, no. 141). It is they who pass on the king's orders to the local population, the Babylonians. Again it is the king who writes to the *shatammu* of Babylon, chief temple administrator, about royal sacrifices and gifts for the New Year Festival at Babylon (Grayson 1975a, no. 13b; Sherwin-White 1983c). There is direct communication, king to local administrators, Greek *or* Babylonian, in which the satrap has no part. It is possible, though the evidence is far from conclusive, that the Seleucids instituted some deliberate checks on the power of the satraps, as here. The Seleucid dossier from Scythopolis, in Palestine, tends to reinforce this suggestion (Landau 1966, with Bertrand 1982; Taylor 1983, 108–68). This new group of texts establishes that the new Seleucid satrap of the area, which had very recently been won from the Ptolemies by the campaigns of the king, Antiochus III, in 202 BC, had no authority over the Seleucid royal fiscal authorities (*oikonomos* and *dioiketês*), who, like the satrap, are directly subordinate to the king and, *inter alia*, were concerned with the administration of taxation and fiscal immunities even in the case of the satrap's fief. There is some evidence too that Seleucid garrisons were directly subordinate to the king, instead of to the satrap, though too little for any secure generalisation to be feasible.[16] But what does emerge clearly enough is that the king (or his secretariat) is plugged in directly to different branches of the regional administration (Greek and non-Greek), which are kept separate (at least when attested); he has, in theory and practice, much more direct control of local government and access to it than once appeared. The Scythopolis dossier shows too that the Seleucid bureaucracy was extremely complex and official correspondence extensive. What is important is that we now have the documentation which shows that, unsurprisingly, these characteristics were not peculiar to Ptolemaic Egypt (Taylor 1983, 147ff, 170–1; Roueché, Sherwin-White 1985, 35), any more than they had been to the Achaemenid empire.

But what about the language of the bureaucracy? Had the Seleucid administration been monolingual, using only Greek, it would have been severely disadvantaged in its work. In spite of an almost indestructible modern tradition to the contrary (cf. above p. 5), the Seleucids made use of a number of languages in their administration. First, there is evidence of the official use of bilinguals (Greek/Aramaic) from – notably – *both* the early and later Seleucid period.[17] Although a bilingual inscription of a Seleucid king has yet to be found, two bilingual versions of Seleucid inscriptions emanate from Iran. One is the Seleucid 'milestone' found within the Achaemenid citadel at Pasargadae in debris from the period after the destruction level of *c.* 280 BC (Lewis 1978; Bivar 1978). The Greek inscription is datable to within the early third century BC (Roueché, Sherwin-White 1985, 18). At Behistun in Media (between Kirmanshah and Hamadan), a relief sculpture of a Seleucid viceroy of the 'Upper Satrapies' sits at the foot of the cliff dominated by Darius the Great's famous relief (Robert 1963, 76; Kleiss 1970, 145–7, plate 66, fig. 11; Colledge, below pp. 157–8 and 1979). This Seleucid monument depicts Heracles reclining at ease, his club propped against a tree on which his bow and quiver are hung. It includes a dated inscription (June 148 BC) cut on a

16. Cf. Bickermann 1938, 53–4.
17. See Stronach 1978, 185 (plate 174f) for a sherd, again from the citadel hill, 'post-Achaemenian' (i.e. Seleucid) in date bearing letters written in Aramaic and in Greek script (but not a bilingual). For another hellenistic Aramaic inscription from Iran, on a silver plaque, interestingly recording the dedication of a fire altar to Gad, see Dupont-Sommer 1964. See Frye 1982 for demolition of the thesis that the name Seleucus, written in Aramaic, was inscribed on the tomb of Darius.

representation of a hellenistic stele with characteristic pediment. The Greek dedicatory inscription fills most of the surface of the mock stele, but below it traces of the start of an Aramaic inscription have been recently observed (Bivar 1978, 161), which it is possible to identify as the beginning of an abstract (unfinished) of the Greek text. There was not room for a full translation and the use of Aramaic for abstracts is well documented in the Achaemenid period.

The use of languages other than Greek for official purposes is also attested in Babylonia. There is the evidence of the use of Akkadian for the royal foundation inscription of Antiochus I (below p. 28), and now new evidence of the royal administration using cuneiform (below). There is direct and indirect evidence, old and new, of the continuing use of Aramaic for public inscriptions, administrative and legal records, and official communications under the Seleucids. The names of two Babylonians are stamped in Aramaic on Seleucid *bullae* from Uruk (Dougherty 1932). Since the same two names occur in contemporary cuneiform tablets as those of 'parchment scribes' it is possible to assume that this couple were scribes trained in Aramaic and that the original documents the *bullae* enclosed were *Aramaic*.[18] Besides a building inscription stamped on bricks in cuneiform (Falkenstein 1941, 6–8), Anu-uballiṭ-Cephalon, Seleucid governor of Uruk in the reign of Antiochus III, had his two personal names written in Aramaic on the wall of a cult room in the Seleucid period temple known as the 'Südbau' at Uruk (Bowman 1939). Another hellenistic inscription comes from Telloh, the Greek/Aramaic brick inscription of Hadad-nadin-ahe (*CIS* 2 no. 72). One of the Babylonian Chronicle fragments (Grayson 1975a, no. 13b v.4) and the Astronomical Diary from the reign of Antiochus I mention in their cuneiform texts official Seleucid communications on parchment (*šipištu*), in the first case from the king (Seleucus III) to the *shatammu* of Babylon (224 BC), and in the second from Seleucid royal officials (*lú paqdu ša šarri*) to the inhabitants of Babylon in 274 BC (Smith 1924, 155 v.16; Austin 1981, no. 141). The language of these communications must in this purely Babylonian context have been Aramaic. The king and his officials will have dictated in Greek to scribes of the Seleucid chancellery who wrote Aramaic. An analogous system was used by the Achaemenids whose Persian instructions were written in Aramaic by royal scribes and read off at the receiving end in the appropriate language (Polotsky 1932; Naveh and Greenfield 1984, 116 with n.3). It appears clear from this conspectus of material that the Seleucids 'allowed' Aramaic to continue to be used for administrative and legal purposes as an

---

18. See Dougherty 1932 for reference to several cuneiform tablets of the late fourth century BC with 'dockets' in Aramaic (i.e. 'notes in Aramaic script on the edge summarising the contents': Postgate 1976, 11).

'official' language and relied upon scribes and interpreters for non-Greek languages.[19]

The pragmatic approach of the Seleucids to government is well illustrated by a new (and neglected) piece of evidence. Under Antiochus I, a Babylonian crown official stamped and registered a contract in cuneiform of a slave sale at Uruk in 275 BC.[20] Below the impression of the official seal (the Seleucid symbols of horse protome and anchor) was a legend in cuneiform labelling the seal as that of either the *chreôphylax* of the king or of the 'ring' of the king (Doty 1979; McEwan 1982). It is worth emphasising the fact that this Seleucid official was equipped with an official royal seal bearing a *cuneiform* legend. Through trained local officials, no doubt drawn from Babylonian scribal families, the Seleucids equipped themselves to cope with the use of cuneiform and at this stage endorsed it to the extent of allowing officials to be issued with a royal seal actually 'franked' in cuneiform – an eye-opener for early Seleucid administrative practices, which admit a degree of continuity with regard to existing languages that few have suspected. Since the distribution of royal seals to subordinates in the satrapies was standard Achaemenid (not a Macedonian) practice (Hallock 1977, 127), it is very likely that here is another example of the survival of Achaemenid administrative institutions and practices under the early Seleucids. The Seleucids were not rabid monolinguals, nor was their administration as exclusively Greek as it is sometimes portrayed. They placed more reliance, at least in Babylonia (and no doubt elsewhere), upon the indigenous population in running the towns than is usually admitted.[21] There is every reason to suppose that the decisions and orders of Seleucid government could have been understood at the receiving end.

I turn next from the formal administrative system to another aspect of Seleucid rule in Babylonia: the question of the relationship between the king and the separate towns within the satrapy. Like the old Greek world, Babylonia was a region of separate cities – urban societies of great antiquity (and age-old rivalries). It is known that in the first millennium Assyrian (and Neo-Babylonian) kings made separate arrangements or 'charters' with individual towns under their suzer-

19. See Polybius 13.9, for Antiochus III's use of interpreters for the decipherment of a letter of the Gerrhaeans during his Arabian expedition in the Gulf, in 205 BC.
20. An example of dual recording, which did not result in the demise of the cuneiform copy, occurs in the reign of Antiochus III. A cuneiform contract from Uruk, concerning the sale of temple allotments, was registered both 'in the record (*šipištum*) of the *dioiketês* of the House of the King and in the document of the property of Anu of the temples of Uruk' (194 BC: *BRM* II no. 31, vv. 7ff). The Seleucid royal official, named here by his Greek title, is attested (sporadically) as an administrator operating in the satrapies both in the *chôra* (countryside) where he was concerned with the administration of royal land, and, as here, in towns of the Seleucid empire (Briant 1982a, 23–25).
21. See Sherwin-White 1983a, 212 n. 17; 1983b, 268–9.

ainty. This practice is reflected, for example, in the Babylonian 'wisdom' text known as *Advice to a Prince* (*c.* 1000–*c.* 700 BC: Lambert 1960). These arrangements agreed (or not) traditional privileges and statuses claimed by a town – e.g. immunity from the corvée, from taxes and so on. Obviously this system of relationship is potentially of great importance to the understanding of how the Seleucids dealt with the individual Babylonian towns. The question is whether the Seleucids followed this practice (see Kuhrt 1987b, for the Neo-Baby-lonian evidence and also below p. 49). I believe that they did. There is a brief but explicit statement in Pausanias (1.16.3) about Seleucus allowing the Chaldaeans to continue to dwell around the temple of Bēl at Babylon (in the context of the foundation of Seleucia-Tigris) and of permitting the fortifications of Babylon to remain; since in the same passage Seleucus is praised for his return to the Milesians of the bronze cult statue of Apollo removed by Xerxes (ibid.), it seems probable that here Pausanias is subject to the characteristic Greek anti-Persian attitudes and traditions about Xerxes (on the latter see Kuhrt in Kuhrt, Sherwin-White 1987). The best attested example of Seleucid charters is Antiochus III's famous 'charter' for Jerusalem, granting, *inter alia*, the Judaean *ethnos* ('nation') at Jerusalem the right to live under its own laws and as a community (Josephus *Antiq.* 12.138ff; Polyb. 16.39.5). A parallel in the Bible comes in Ezra with the refoundation of Jerusalem in the Achaemenid period. Did the Seleucid kings make individual arrangements with separate towns, granting such individual rights of autonomy as they (e.g. Babylon, Uruk) are independently known to possess and granting or with-holding privileges? What can perhaps safely be said is that there was an established framework (see Leemans 1946) for the Seleucids to use and some evidence, for example in the case of Babylon, that they did so, as had past rulers of Babylonia.

In the towns of Babylonia it should be possible to identify (and to a certain extent now is) groups and families within the towns as personal supporters of the new regime: notably crown appointees – Babylonian officials at Uruk and Babylon for example, who at Uruk are known from building inscriptions in cuneiform in which their attitude to the Seleucids is attested in loyalist formulae – dedications 'for the life of the king' (Sherwin-White 1983c, 158–9; 1983a, 214–18). Apart from named royal officials there is an important anonymous group: those possessing the privilege of an immunity (*ateleia*) from a specific tax. These people are indirectly attested by the stamped *bullae*, the pieces of clay originally used, like big rubber bands, to enclose documents written on parchment or papyrus (Rostovtzeff 1932). As texts they could hardly be briefer but they usually name (in Greek) town, record office and tax to which the individual(s) in the original contracts/documents were liable or immune. These persons may be anonymous but enough is known about grants of *ateleia* to know that they were people who as individuals of high standing, or as members of a social group, had been granted immunity by the crown (cf. e.g. the immunities granted to hundreds of temple personnel at Jerusalem by Antiochus III; Josephus *Antiq.* 12.138–43). The immunities system, personal grants by a king to an individual or to a group (Greek *and* non-Greek), was a mechanism widely used for support building by the kings to consolidate their rule.

In several respects the reign of Antiochus I, the second Seleucid king, marks a time of transition to a tighter imperial system under a kingship gradually being institutionalised and whose image as a dynastic system was now emphasised – the *progonoi* (ancestors) of the royal house are now mentioned in royal documents, a coinage which was probably meant to broadcast both the 'traditional' and dynastic aspect of Seleucid rule. It was also Antiochus I who, to hellenistic historians' great relief, took the unique step (among the Macedonian kings) of authorising at his accession the continuing use of his father's regnal era instead of starting his own, as every precedent suggested – royal time now had continuity and was *Seleucid*, not an individual king's.

It was in Antiochus' reign that royal taxes were re-organised in Babylonia and their administration revised. Doty (1977, 151ff, 308ff) has correlated changes in the pattern of what was documented in cuneiform with a change in royal fiscal system – the imposition of new taxes. From about 270 BC transactions involving the sale of arable land had to be registered with the Seleucid registry official (*chreô-phylax*). *Bullae* from Uruk (and Seleucia-Tigris), which are later (from the reign of Antiochus III for the most part: Rostovtzeff 1932; McDowell 1935; Invernizzi 1968; 1976, 169), show that contracts for the sale of slaves had also to be registered with the *chreôphylax* and a slaves tax and a general sales tax paid. Doty put together the different data and neatly explained them in terms of changes in royal fiscal policy – Antiochus I imposed a new tax on slave sales and a general sales tax applicable to the sale of arable land (but not to urban land which continued to be recorded in cuneiform and *not* taxed). Contracts for the sale of slaves and arable land had instead to be filed with the *chreôphylax* (in Aramaic or Greek). This certainly represents a tightening up and an increase of taxation. This change should perhaps not be seen only as a result of the sporadic warfare against Ptolemy II in the 270s, but as part of a more general consolidation of Seleucid rule in this second generation (see above). One of the most significant results of Doty's work is that it has destroyed Aymard's theory of the privileged status of Babylonian temples – a theory based on the non-appearance of royal taxes in cuneiform documents (Aymard

1938) – which has dominated approaches to Seleucid policies towards Babylonian towns and temples.

The Babylonian evidence is especially precious in allowing us to inspect Greek rule from the underside, from a Babylonian viewpoint, or at least through the eyes of the portion of the population producing the cuneiform texts. This is thanks to the work of the authors of a range of cuneiform texts: king lists, chronicles (now fragmentary), building inscriptions such as the famous cylinder foundation of Antiochus I as restorer of the temples of Esagila at Babylon and Ezida at Borsippa (Weissbach 1911, 132–5; Pritchard 1969, 317; Austin 1981, no. 189). There are many problems about the use of these texts as sources, which cannot be raised here – the questions, for example, of audience, circulation, authorship (they are mostly anonymous) and status (public/official, as is clear in the case of building inscriptions, or private?). But for present purposes I take it that they were composed and written by men whose professional training in cuneiform places them at the centre of Babylonian culture and society, members of a section of the population which had a fundamental role in religious and secular administration (for the scribal families see McEwan 1981b, 25ff). Antiochus' building inscription reproduces the traditional form of Neo-Babylonian building inscriptions which begin with royal titulature, continue with an account of the king's pious acts and conclude with the king's prayer for beneficence from the god of the temple under construction (Ellis 1968, 20–6), here Nabû of Borsippa, hence the emphasis upon Nabû rather than upon Bēl-Marduk. Antiochus' cylinder documents and reproduces basic Babylonian ideas on the king's political and religious role in society – in external relations the conquest of enemies and preservation of enduring prosperity, internally promoter of justice, peace, a long reign and a stable succession. Booty was to be used for the glorification of the gods. This is not 'just' image and propaganda; Antiochus was responsive to Babylonian traditions, which required a king to be involved personally (when possible) in the rituals concerning temple-building (for example Antiochus' symbolic brick-making for the temples of Nabû and Marduk and his direct participation in laying the foundation in the new building of Ezida at Borsippa (Pritchard 1969, 317; Austin 1981, no. 189). This and other Babylonian hellenistic texts present a coherent picture of the Seleucids in which the king is no foreign enemy but a legitimate and just ruler in harmony with Babylonian gods, participating actively in Babylonian cult (cf. Grayson 1975b, 19–20 n.29; 1975a, 278 n.2; Sherwin-White 1983c, 158–9). Like the continuation of traditional Babylonian architectural styles for temple building at Uruk and Babylon – as the evidence stands at present – the traditional character of all this is striking. As is familiar, scholars of modern colonialism in the era of decolonisation, notably Bourdieu, have recognised that traditionalism is encouraged by colonial rule.[22] The upkeep or re-shaping of values and traditions of earlier days functions as an expression of cultural opposition to the values of the dominant and foreign power. This language of refusal has been read into the traditionalist character of Babylonian culture, and has been encouraged by the 'decline revival' approach to hellenistic Babylonia (Eddy 1961), now shown to be ill-founded (see above and Kuhrt 1987a). It is not clear to me, and the texts will not reveal whether this is what they signify, or whether on the other hand Seleucid rule really did seem to some (at least in the successes of the third century) like a new Babylonian age. Certainly the Seleucids used the opportunity that being kings of Babylon provided for making their rule as Babylonian as possible and therefore as easy as possible for Babylonians to experience. This, plus cultural patronage was *actively* promoted by the kings and must greatly have helped their grasp of Babylonia (see Kuhrt, below pp. 52; 55–6), which was vital to their control of other regions.

Alongside this very Babylonian texture of Seleucid rule lies its Greek side. It is necessary to limit the investigation here to the question of royal encouragement of Greekness in non-Greek contexts. The only example that I can find in Babylonia (since there is no solid evidence that either Babylon or Uruk became 'Greek *poleis*' under the Seleucids (see van der Spek, below pp. 68; 73) is the king's practice of name-giving. The sole surviving testimonium from Seleucid Babylonia is the cuneiform building inscription of Anu-uballiṭ Nicarchus, city-governor of Uruk (244 BC), named as 'Anu-uballiṭ son of Anu-iqṣur, descendant of Ah'utu, *šaknu* (governor) of Uruk, whom Antiochus, king of the lands, gave as his other name Nikiqaarqusu' (YOS I 81–4 no. 52; Falkenstein 1941, 1–5). Rutten gave the best gloss on the process with her citation of the paradigmatic passage in Genesis where Pharaoh's rewards to Joseph included the grant of an Egyptian personal name (41.45; Rutten 1935, 70). Analogously, the programme of Nebuchadnezzar II for the assimilation of members of the royalty and nobility of Judah included the bestowal of new (Babylonian) names (Daniel 1.7: Coogan 1974, 11; 1976, 119ff). The purpose is the same: to reward and to assimilate – a primarily political purpose. Anu-uballiṭ Nicarchus, a Babylonian, governor of Uruk and in charge of building the central temple of Seleucid Uruk, was clearly a comparatively important figure for the Seleucids in Babylonia. He is the only individual specifically known to have got a Greek name from the king, but there is no reason to suppose that he was necessarily unique. The practice had stopped by the early second century mainly because of the evolution at court of a hierarchy of rank, with a system of graded

22. Cf. also Said 1978; Wachtel 1977.

titles, and a set of desirable distinctions for awarding to non-Greeks (as well as to Greeks), as I Maccabees well attests (cf. Bickermann 1938, 40ff). Secondly, however little impact hellenism may have had on culture in some non-Greek places and on the non-Greek country-side, Greek names had caught on in non-Greek circles, as the names borne by some of the orthodox families of the Maccabean party in Jerusalem strikingly reveal (Sherwin-White 1983a, 214–16). In such circumstances the grant of a personal name lost value.

I do, however, think that there is more evidence of Seleucid promotion of Greek culture (or of some elements of it) in non-Greek contexts than is at present admitted. The Seleucids' imposition of specifically Greek cultural traditions to create a recognisably Greek cultural activity for Greek and hellenised inhabitants of their empire is beautifully encapsulated in the Seleucid dossier from Failaka, in which the Seleucid governor puts into operation royal orders for cele-brating an *agôn* (festival) on this tiny island off the Arabian Gulf (Roueché, Sherwin-White 1985, 32–4). The *agôn* is for the (free) inhabitants, who appear to have included Greeks and non-Greeks. The Greek and non-Greek cultural traditions of the Seleucid settle-ments on Failaka are reflected in the material finds (cf. Salles, below e.g. pp. 142–4; for Ai Khanum see Colledge, below pp. 85–6). The case of Failaka provides an important counter example to a current view of the relationship between Greeks and non-Greeks in areas under Macedonian rule as one of juxtaposition and segregation.[23] This model is much too simple to apply *in toto* to the settlements of the Seleucid empire, where such variants as manpower, function and place combined to produce different patterns.

\*

There are several points that require emphasis in approaching the study of the Seleucid empire. The first, perhaps, is that the Seleucid kings inherited and, as necessary, re-shaped a relatively sophisticated imperial system in which non-Greeks were employed in responsible positions. Secondly, what has often been seen as symptomatic of Greek/

23. A new cuneiform document is relevant to this question in the case of Babylonia as it seems indirectly to attest Greek journeying between a Greek *polis* (Seleucia-Tigris) and a Babylonian town and the return home (Doty 1978/9). The text, dated to 225/4 BC, was found in the Italian excavations of the Seleucid level of Tell Umar (Seleucia-Tigris). It records the dedication of a slave as a temple oblate in a sanctuary of Nergal, probably at Cutha. The name and patronymic of the principal are Greek. The text seems to offer one model of how the operation of Greeks in Babylonian places worked; Greeks visited a Babylonian town for business (or for other purposes) but lived in a Greek community; see Sherwin-White 1983a, 219–20, for another pattern at Uruk – evidence perhaps attesting the absorption into the indigenous community of a few of the comparatively small number of 'Greeks' attested at Uruk.

Macedonian colonialism is best regarded instead as simply imperial, rather than specifically Greek. Thirdly, the Seleucid kings are attuned to local conditions, especially in Babylonia (where the evidence is most prolific), using and allowing the use of local languages (Aramaic; even cuneiform to start with) in their administration, activists in the promotion of their control of the region. Fourthly, the Seleucid focus on Babylonia is probably not the result of the chance survival of evidence, but directly reflects the fact that the Seleucids recognised Babylonia as the hub of their empire, as it had been for the Achaemenids.

# CHAPTER TWO

# Berossus' *Babyloniaka* and Seleucid Rule in Babylonia*

## *Amélie Kuhrt*

The impact of hellenism on the Near and Middle Eastern world might have been expected to result in more systematic investigation of some of the areas only known through a few Greek historians who had had the opportunity to travel in the Persian empire or had talked to people who had visited its various regions. With Alexander's conquest, the establishment of Macedonian kingdoms, creation of Greek *poleis* and founding of colonies, Greeks had an excellent opportunity of, as well as interest in, amplifying and correcting what had been obscure or unsatisfactory in earlier accounts of the history of places such as India, Egypt, Persia and Assyria-Babylonia (Momigliano 1975, 7). The latter was particularly confused in existing accounts. Thus Herodotus thought Babylon was an important city of Assyria which somehow escaped the Median destruction of the Assyrian empire and continued to flourish briefly under its own rulers; but there is no attempt in his work to explain the political niceties of this situation. Ctesias (*FGrHist*. 4 F 1) to whom we owe the expansion of the figure of Ninus, legendary founder of Nineveh and the Assyrian Empire, and the romantic figure of Semiramis his wife, was primarily interested in Persia and thus its predecessors in the 'hegemony' of Asia, i.e. Media and Assyria. As, by definition, only one power could at any one time exercise this hegemony, the Neo-Babylonian Empire (626–539 BC), which had emerged as a result of a prolonged war against Assyria at the end of the seventh century and an alliance with the Medes, and thus co-existed with the 'Median empire' which according to Ctesias was heir to the Assyrian hegemony, presented a problem with which he (or his sources) dealt effectively: the leader of the Babylonians was described as an astrologer ('Chaldaean'); in return for correctly predicting the successful outcome of the Median king's attack on Nineveh he was granted Babylonia as a satrapy. This provided a neat solution to a logical problem: the Neo-Babylonian empire had never

* I would like to thank the Fondation Hardt, Switzerland, for inviting me to spend three weeks there in June 1982 in order to carry out some of the research for this chapter, and the British Academy for enabling me to accept the invitation.

existed – it was merely a province of the Median empire, ruled by a local person through the generosity of the Median king.

Although Greeks generally were quite satisfied with this explanation (and its persistence is well-attested: Kuhrt 1982), there were plenty of gaps in Ctesias' and Herodotus' accounts of Mesopotamia, and with the creation of the Seleucid state an opportunity existed for Greek ethnographers and historians to investigate the still flourishing city of Babylon, question the local inhabitants and encourage them to write their versions of their own history in a manner comprehensible to the governing group. That a certain amount of such ethnographic research was undertaken is clear, but the result tended to be an amalgam of rather garbled traditions shaped to fit Greek tastes in literary style, Greek preconceptions of the history of these areas and (as pointed out by Murray 1970 in relation to Hecataeus of Abdera) the propaganda/legitimising requirements of the newly established Macedonian dynasties. Whether the distortions of such works provoked a response from local savants such as Manetho in Egypt or Berossus in Babylonia, or whether their books were also written under royal patronage to provide a further strut in the structure of political propaganda is not known, given the fragmentary preservation of their books. One thing that is plain, however, is that they, with access to the ancient written sources of their native countries, actually wrote in Greek and thus made this material, or a selection of it, available to the new ruling élite with whom they now shared a certain identity of interest.

What is remarkable is that both Manetho and Berossus had curiously little impact: it was not their versions of the history of their own countries which came to form the basis of later classical views on oriental traditions. The dominant view continued to be basically the earlier Greek version with a certain amount of expansion as a result of contact with new areas. The immediate result of this is that recovering what such indigenous experts actually wrote so that one can then try to place their work in its contemporary political framework is extremely difficult; and in the case of Berossus, a specific nexus of problems has developed, which makes that task yet more arduous.

## 1. Reconstructing Berossus' *Babyloniaka*

According to Eusebius (*FGrHist.* 680 T 1), Berossus described himself as a contemporary of Alexander and wrote works based on records preserved in Babylon, while Tatian (ibid. T 2) added that he was a priest of Marduk (*Bēlos*) who drew up a Chaldean history in three books for Antiochus I. The title of Berossus' work is not given consistently: *Babyloniaka* (ibid. F 1 (1), F 2) appears as well as *Chaldaean*

*History* (or *Antiquities*) (ibid. T 2, 8b; F 8) and *Chaldaika* (ibid. T 8a, 7a, 11). Possibly the title *Babyloniaka* is the more authentic (cf. also Schnabel 1923, 16) as it would certainly be clear to any Babylonian with knowledge of, and access to, the records of the earlier history, that the Chaldaean tribes, while important and providing three major and very successful rulers of Babylonia, hardly constituted enough of a distinctive element for a work that covered the story of Babylonia from creation to Alexander to be entitled 'Chaldaean antiquities', 'history of the Chaldaeans' or 'Chaldaean matters/things'.[1] It is worth noting that any such characterisation appears to be entirely absent both in contemporary Babylonian records and Babylonian historiography.[2] One of the possible reasons for the confusion and variations in naming Berossus' work is the fact that Alexander Polyhistor[3] produced a work called *Chaldaika* which appears to have been little more than an epitome of Berossus' history continued into the Seleucid period by adding excerpts from the chronicle of ps.-Apollodorus of Athens and the third Sybilline Book.[4] It is possible that Polyhistor's convenient summary presentations of the history and main characteristics of precisely those peoples of the Eastern Mediterranean in whom the Romans were particularly interested in the first century BC, resulted in Berossus' own work becoming superfluous and practically vanishing from circulation. This has certainly been supposed by some, e.g. Schwartz (1897, 315) who suggested that Josephus took all his Berossus quotes not from the *Babyloniaka* themselves but from Polyhistor's digest, which would explain why he usually refers to Berossus' work as *Chaldaika* rather than by its more probable name. This argument is somewhat circular and certainly not provable in any irrefutable sense, and it should be remembered that Jacoby in his commentary on the relevant Polyhistor fragments (*FGrHist*. IIIA 288) denied that all Berossus quotes came via Polyhistor. As neither Polyhistor's *Chaldaika* nor the works of a number of his probable excerptors such

1. Although it is usual to consider Nabopolassar and thus his son, Nebuchadnezzar II, as Chaldaeans, the evidence for this is fairly slight: cf. Voigtlander 1963, 17.
2. No Babylonian king-lists or Babylonian royal inscriptions ever refer to any ruler at all in this way; chronicles may describe a Chaldaean by relating someone to his locality (which in turn relates to his specific tribe) as either centred on Bit Jakin, Dakurri, or Amukanni, but never distinguish a Chaldaean as such. This is primarily a designation used by Assyrian rulers who usually (in the ninth and eighth centuries BC) characterised their intervention in Babylonia as 'protecting' cities and their temples and the Babylonian kingship, chastising Aramaeans and exacting tribute from Chaldaeans. On the wealth and nature of the Chaldaean tribes and the absence of any conflict in racial terms between them and 'true' Babylonians cf. Brinkman 1968, 260–7.
3. Exact dates cannot be assigned: general opinion (e.g. *RE* I.2 s.v. Alexandros 88, col. 1449–52; *Der Kleine Pauly* I s.v. Alexandros 19, 252) both limit his *floruit* to 70–60 BC, whereas Jacoby (*FGrHist*. 3 A 273, 248–9) suggests he continued to be active into the forties and possibly even early thirties BC.
4. Cf. Jacoby *FGrHist*. 3 A, 288–9, commentary on FF 79–81.

as Juba of Mauretania,[5] Abydenus[6] and Julius Africanus[7] is preserved the question must remain unsolved. An additional confusing element is introduced by the fact that Bishop Eusebius (late third/early fourth century AD), one of the main sources for Berossus, relied for his chronographic and historical information not only on these later excerptors, but also appears to have used Alexander Polyhistor directly (cf. Schwartz 1897, 315); so that what appear at first sight to be three distinct sources in Eusebius' *Chronikoi Kanones* for Babylonian and Assyrian history, in fact turn out to be the same source used in three different versions. None of this would be quite so problematical if at least Eusebius' interesting chronographic work had been fully preserved, but unfortunately only fragments of the original Greek text are extant and one is dependent on an expanded text of the Chronicon in an Armenian version (Karst 1911), the work of the eighth-century monk Syncellus who appears to have borrowed large sections of Eusebius *in toto,* and the apologetic work *Praeparatio Evangelico* of which about half is preserved.

From the above it is clear that simply establishing the basic structure of Berossus' history constitutes in itself a major problem. A further point to be made is that by far the most important and fullest quotes from Berossus appear in the context of Jewish and Christian apologetic: Josephus[8] in the *contra Apionem* as well as the *Antiquities* (F 4c, 6, 7a and b, 8, 9a); Eusebius (*Chron.* and *Praep. Ev.*: F 1, 3, 4a, 5a, 7c, 9b, 10); Clemens Alexandrinus[9] (*Protrepticus*: F 11); Africanus (used by Eusebius: F 8c); Tatian[10] (T2; F 8b); while other users are completely obscure figures of whom virtually nothing is known, such as Abydenus, Simacus and Athenocles,[11] scholars not part of the mainstream of Graeco-Roman intellectual activity, e.g. Juba of Mauretania, or people with a virtuosity in obscure items of knowledge usually

---

5. *Fl.* Augustan period; one of his works appears to have been a history of Assyria in two books which made use of Berossus in part, possibly already through the epitome of Alexander Polyhistor; see T 2 and *RE* IX 2 s.v. Iuba 2, cols. 2384–95.
6. Generally dated into the second century AD on the basis of linguistic considerations (*RE* I.1 s.v. Abydenos col. 129). It is not clear what he wrote as Eusebius cites him as the author of a history of Chaldaea (see *FGrHist.* 685 F 2) while listing him as the author of an Assyrian and Median history in his source catalogue: ibid. 685 T 1.
7. Early third century AD, see *RE* X.1 s.v. Iulius 47, cols. 116–25.
8. First century AD; cf. generally Rajak 1983.
9. Christian philosopher, *c.* 150 AD, cf. *RE* IV.1 s.v. Clemens 9, cols. 11–20.
10. Christian apologist of the second century AD from Assyria who made use of Juba of Mauretania's work: *RE* IV. A 2 s.v. Tatianus 9, cols. 2468–71.
11. Cf. *FGrHist.* 683 and 682 respectively; they are referred to once in the curious and very late historical work of Agathias (the continuator of Procopius, who lived *c.* 536–582 AD) together with Berossus as historians of the antiquities of Assyria and Media.

not of a historical nature, such as Athenaeus[12] and Hesychius.[13] An important corollary to this is that the *same* type of material drawn from the *Babyloniaka* and confirming Biblical traditions and chronology is quoted over and over again, while material irrelevant to this exercise is extremely scantily preserved.

## 2. Berossus and astronomy

So far I have only considered Berossus' historical work which, in order to avoid confusion and following the most convenient edition of the fragments in Jacoby (*FGrHist.* III C 680) I shall refer to as the *Babyloniaka*. The work appears to have consisted of a description of the origins of Babylonian culture and what Berossus knew or selected of its history down to Alexander. But was this all that was included and the sum total of what Berossus wrote? The reason why this question has to be asked, is that a number of further pieces of information are credited to Berossus, but they are of a completely different character: these are astronomical and astrological items quoted by a varied assortment of philosophers with an especial interest in the natural sciences.[14] Save for one reference by Syncellus (*FGrHist.* 680 F 16a) referring to the supposed fact that Nabonassar (= the Babylonian king Nabu-naṣir, 747–734) had destroyed all records of earlier kings and that precise astronomical observations were kept from his own reign onwards (which was the reason for Ptolemy beginning his chronological tables at that point) – a fact to which both Alexander (presumably Polyhistor) and Berossus are said to testify – none of the other writers refer to any kind of historical work by Berossus nor do these sources coincide with those from whom the historical fragments are derived. On the basis of this discrepancy both in the character of the transmitters and the type of information transmitted in Berossus'

12. End of the second/beginning of the third century AD; cf. F 2 where an abstruse piece of knowledge on a Babylonian festival is attributed to Berossus, although it can only be reconciled with Babylonian sources by rather elaborate arguments (Langdon 1924).

13. Compiler of a lexicon in the fifth to sixth centuries AD; cf. F 13 where an explanation of a word as used by Berossus is preserved, though it makes no particular sense in terms of Babylonian source-material except by special pleading (Dossin 1971).

14. The natural sciences would, of course, include astronomy and by extension astrology; cf. Lloyd 1979 passim for discussion of astronomy and medicine as two fundamental ingredients in the development of 'exact science' in Greece. For a definition of the underlying motive for studying astronomy being the belief that it would help in foretelling future events on earth, cf. ibid. 169–200, esp. 200; for references to the Greek notion that divination itself was an important *technê*, ibid. 227.

name, Jacoby[15] defined in his edition of the fragments a pseudo-Berossus as the originator of this material.

The *testimonia* associated with this hypothetical pseudo-Berossus come primarily from Vitruvius (early Augustan period: T 5a–c), who said that the first of the 'Chaldaeans' to hand on knowledge of horoscopes was Berossus who founded a school on Cos and was followed in this art by, probably, two disciples,[16] and who had also heard that Berossus was supposed to have invented an instrument presumably associated with astronomical observations and calculations. By the time Pliny the Elder was writing he was able to report (T 6) that Berossus had had an official statue erected to him in the gymnasium of Athens with a gilt tongue because of his marvellous predictions. A further detail on Berossus is added by Pausanias (*fl. c.* 110–115) who records (T 7a) a belief developed among the Hebrews that a female oracle variously identified as either a Babylonian or Egyptian Sibyl had Berossus as her father. This last piece of information was repeated by ps.-Justin (T 7c)[17] and was not lost sight of even in the tenth century AD when it was faithfully recorded as an established fact by the compiler(s) of the *Suda* (T 7b). Other *testimonia* referring to this aspect of Berossus are Seneca (T 9), who characterises him as an 'interpreter of Bēlos' (Lambert 1976, 171–2) (i.e. Bel-Marduk) in the sense of one who interprets the significance of astronomical phenomena, Syncellus (T 10) and Moses of Chorene (T 4).

While some elements of this description arouse strong suspicion and have generally been rejected as fanciful elaboration – such as Berossus' parenthood of the Babylonian Sibyl – others have been taken much more seriously because of the well-known identification in the Graeco-Roman world of 'Chaldaeans' with astrologers and the frequently reiterated debt that Greek science owed to Babylonian astronomy and genethlialogy.[18] Where Schwartz (1897, 316) already expressed great doubt as to whether Berossus had settled on Cos and taught astronomy/astrology there and was completely sceptical of the statue in Athens having anything to do with the Berossus who wrote the *Babyloniaka*, a scepticism given its clearest expression in the (alas, uncommented) arrangement of the Berossus fragments by Jacoby (FF 15–22), and more recently upheld by Lambert (1976) on the basis of the Babylonian material (cf. also Kuhrt 1982, 547–8), other scholars have continued to link these two aspects of Berossus' work together

15. Unfortunately the precise arguments for his separation of genuine and pseudo-Berossus are not known as Jacoby died without publishing his commentary on this volume of fragments.

16. For the corrupt name, Athenodorus or Achinapolus, cf. Vitruvius *de arch.* (Loeb ed.) 9.6.2, note 1.

17. Probable date: late third century AD, cf. *RE* X.2 s.v. Iustinus 11, cols. 1334–6.

18. This is first attested in Hdt. 2.109, where *gnômon* and *polos* are supposed to have come to Greece from Babylonia.

and attempted variously to accommodate the astronomical excerpts either in Book I, with the description of Babylonia, the creation and origin of civilisation (Schnabel 1923, 17–19; Burstein 1978, 15–16; 31–2) or at the end of Book III after the history ends with Alexander (Drews 1975, 53).[19]

In order to clarify this problem, which is fundamental to evaluating Berossus' work, it must be examined more closely. The questions that have to be asked are: What exactly is Berossus supposed to have said on astronomy and astrology? Can these attributions be related to what is known of Babylonian astronomy and astrology? At what date is the notion of a 'Babylonian' source for Greek astronomy and hence astrology first attested? Finally, can such astronomical lore be accommodated in Berossus' *Babyloniaka* in terms of the structure of the work and the space available? If not, was there a separate work by Berossus in which he presented this material?

A persistent but quite general emphasis is given to the astrological calculations and the science of prediction of Berossus (a characteristic of 'Chaldaeans' in general) by Palchas (F 15) an astrologer of the late fifth century/early sixth century AD and the anonymous commentary on Aratus of Soli.[20] Two attributions concern the length of time over which Babylonian calculations have been kept and are available, one by Syncellus (F 16a) concerning the destruction of records earlier than Nabu-naṣir (747–734 BC) mentioned above; the other comes from Pliny (F 16b) who quotes contradictory opinions on this by Epigenes[21] on the one hand, and Berossus and Critodemus[22] on the other in the context of a discussion on the age of the 'alphabet'. Both Censorinus (F 22b; third century AD) and Pliny (F 22a) quote statements on the length of life-expectancy taken from Epigenes, Berossus and Petosiris and Nechepso.[23] The two most important items credited to Berossus on which a great deal of the argument hinges are of rather a different calibre. The first concerns the theory of the 'great year' when the final

19. Spoerri 1975 remains aloof from the discussion.
20. Aratus of Soli was a friend of Callimachus the younger and called to the Macedonian court in 277; only his 'scientific' poetical works have in some measure survived, but the traditions are extremely confused. Notions on the date of the anonymous commentary vary widely; see Maass 1958.
21. Epigenes of Byzantium is generally but uncertainly dated to the second century BC and should perhaps be dated earlier. He was an astrologer who, according to his own statement (ap. Seneca *NQ* 7.4.1), was taught by Chaldaeans; it is generally assumed that his work was transmitted by Poseidonius; cf. *RE* VI.1 s.v. Epigenes 17 col. 65–6.
22. Generally mentioned with astrologers of the second and first centuries BC and thus dated into this general period, cf. Schnabel 1923, 118–20.
23. The latter are an interesting pair of almost certainly fictitious Egyptians, invented possibly *c.* 150–120 BC, who were supposed to have translated or preserved the teachings of Hermes Trismegistos, particularly those connected with iatromathematics, i.e. astrologically based instructions on diseases and their cure; cf. *Der Kleine Pauly* IV s.v. Nechepso; Petosiris.

destruction of the world by one of the elements, usually water or fire (Lucretius *de r.n.* 5.380f; cf. Bailey 1947, III, 1375f) will take place. According to Seneca (*NQ* 3.29, 1 = F 21) Berossus maintained a very similar theory. The other notion credited to Berossus and mentioned by Cleomedes (= F 18),[24] Aëtius (F 19a–c)[25] and in greater detail by Vitruvius (F 20) is the theory that the moon consists of a half-fiery sphere thus explaining both its light and phases.

At this point it might be useful to put testimonia and fragments together and briefly consider the impression one has of Berossus from them. He enjoyed a considerable reputation for predicting events based on astronomical calculations and was regarded as the earliest Babylonian astrologer with whom the classical world had come into contact, primarily one imagines through his establishment of a school on Cos where the science of systematic astrology according to Babylonian methods was supposedly taught. The basis for this method was the precise Babylonian astronomical observations which had been kept over a period of thousands of years (or at least since the reign of Nabu-naṣir). Both the past and future could be explained by astrology, as could the expectation of individual human life. Apart from this Berossus also described the light and phases of the moon and explained the conditions under which the final destruction of the world would take place.

One of the first points to note is that it is extremely difficult to relate any of the more precise statements to anything so far attested in cuneiform records. Burstein (1978, 15 n.19; 16 n.21) maintains that both the 'great year' and the theory of the moon's light were taken by Berossus from descriptions contained in *Enūma Eliš*, the so-called Babylonian 'epic of creation' (Pritchard 1969, 60–72; 501–3), and thus do not reflect Babylonian scholarly astronomical theory but rather mythological explanations of how things are, cast into Greek philosophical terminology. This is certainly a possibility, but two objections can be raised: first, concerning the well-attested Stoic theory of *ekpurôsis* (Liddell and Scott s.v.; Spoerri 1959, 195–7), Berossus is by no means the earliest authority credited with this notion as it also appears in connection with Empedocles' name (Tzetzes *VS*; 31 A 66 p.295, 15f.), and certainly the Lucretius passage fits such a derivation better than Berossus (cf. Bailey loc. cit.); moreover, the significant element in Seneca's description of the *ekpurôsis* is the fact that Berossus calculated the events using an astrological method. In other words it represents, as Schwartz (1897, 316) pointed out, an existing Greek concept to which the 'typical' Babylonian method of astrological calculation has been applied; further, and this is important, one should

24. Dated to the end of the first century BC; student of Poseidonius, see *RE* XI.1 s.v. Kleomedes 3, cols. 679–94.
25. Doxographer writing *c.* 100 AD on natural history, see *RE* I.1 s.v. Aetios, col. 703.

note that the astrological process described uses the concept of planetary spheres which is Greek and not Babylonian (Lambert 1976, 172 n.5). Secondly, the idea that the moon shines with its own light may for all one knows indeed be a Babylonian idea, but it should be observed that it is *also* attributed to Anaximander and Xenophanes (cf. F 19b) by Aëtius as well as to Berossus; further it is attested quite independently for Antiphon (Diels 12 A 22, 87 B 27). In neither of these cases can one observe either a definite dependence on, or derivation from, Babylonian concepts or any clear attestation of either of these theories forming part of Babylonian astronomy. Finally, even if one allows that one or other of these concepts formed perhaps part of the Babylonian 'Weltanschauung' (i.e. separate from Babylonian astronomy), it would be difficult to maintain on purely chronological grounds that these concepts were passed to the Greek world through the medium of Berossus, as both Empedocles, Anaximander, Xenophanes and Antiphon lived around 200 years earlier.[26]

As we have seen, the contribution of Berossus to the Greek theory of *ekpurôsis* as described in Seneca appears to be the astrological element. Beyond this Berossus was credited more generally with astrological predictions (see above). Astrology, of course, was the one feature, above all, that was fairly consistently associated with the Babylonians (although not by Herodotus[27]). Ctesias (*c.* 400 BC) provided the first clear identification of Chaldaeans with predictions based on celestial phenomena (D.S. 2.24.1), and the identification of 'Chaldaeans' with astrologers and Babylonia as the home of astronomy and astrology becomes prominent in Greek thought during the fourth century: thus in the *Epinomis* 986ef, Plato (or more probably a pupil of his) said that Egyptians and Syrians initiated the observation of planets and made them available to Greeks, a fact also maintained by Aristotle (*Cael.* 292a7ff.; referring to Egyptians only, *Met.* 343b9 ff). As there is no evidence of Egyptian astronomical observations and elaborations of the type referred to in these passages until somewhat later (cf. Lloyd 1979, 177) whereas astronomical observations, some particularly connected with astrological omens,[28] are certainly attested in Babylonia from the Old Babylonian period (first half of second millennium BC) onwards, the Egyptian element in the Greek references is somewhat baffling. One explanation may well be that it was in Egypt that Greeks first came into contact with some aspects of Babylonian astronomy (cf. for example, Parker 1959) as a result of the closer cultural interconnections fostered by the Persian empire (cf.

---

26. This is not to insist that attributions of theories to pre-Socratic philosophers are automatically always correct; but it is enough to sow serious doubts.
27. The earliest reference to horoscopes is given by Hdt. 2.82 with reference to the Egyptians.
28. In particular the series *Enūma Anu Enlil*, see Weidner 1941/4; 1954/6; 1968/9.

Kuhrt 1987a). This would also help to account for the curious 'facts' of Eudoxus of Cnidus' life (*c.* 391–338; *Der Kleine Pauly*, cols. 407–10) who, with a recommendation from Agesilaos of Sparta in his pocket, travelled to the court of Nectanebo of Egypt and spent one-and-a-half years there, yet according to Cicero (*de div.* 1142. 87) was familiar enough with Chaldaean astrology to reject it as untrustworthy. This last fact also provides strong support for the fact that Babylonian astrology in some form played a fairly prominent role in Greek thought during the fourth century, although its systemisation did not develop until much later (cf. Lloyd 1979, 6 n.20). Enough has been said to indicate that, beginning in the latter half of the fifth century and becoming much more fully attested in the fourth century, Greeks were increasingly aware of the possibility of receiving answers to their astronomical (and connected) problems from the ancient cultures of the Near East and that, although their notions on the precise knowledge of these peoples was somewhat vague, it was particularly Babylonian astrology from which much was expected in this direction (cf. Momigliano 1975, 144–6).

We shall now look more closely at the developments in these sciences in Babylonia. Although various kinds of astronomical observations are attested from the Old Babylonian period onwards (cf. Neugebauer 1957, 94ff) and astronomical observations became more precise by 700 BC, no appreciable theoretical development took place until the fifth century BC, at what precise point being quite unclear. The only indications of the major development of the arithmetical methods used in Babylonian astronomy is the change from irregularly intercalated months, still used *c.* 480, to a regular system of nineteen-year intervals approximately one hundred years later. This in no way makes it anterior to Greek developments since Meton and Eudemon had almost certainly already arrived at the same principle by 430 BC (cf. Lloyd 1979, 171–3). The Babylonian development would thus seem to parallel the Greek one in this instance. Of central relevance to the Babylonian observation of astronomical phenomena was the underlying notion that on this basis future events could be predicted (Sachs 1952; Parpola 1983) which means that much astronomical observational materials should really be classed with omen literature. The kind of happenings envisaged in these omens as well as the scholarly reports on celestial signs are of a general rather than specific application – it was the general well-being of the country in terms of peace, plenty and well-being that was the area of concern of these omens and, given the political system of both Assyria and Babylonia, the only individuals who could be specifically affected by any ominous sign were the king or the royal family whose well-being guaranteed the stability and prosperity of the state. Interestingly, towards the end of the fifth century and probably connected with the development of a systematic mathematical theory one finds for the first time some personal horoscopes, i.e. the astrological omen of general relevance was adapted into something approaching a science with various possibilities calculated in relation to a single specific individual (Sachs 1952).

One further element has generally been thought to have been borrowed by the Greeks from Babylonian astronomy;[29] namely the mathematical parameters connected with lunar motion theory which is identical in both schools of astronomy. But two factors should be noted: first, this apparently borrowed material is late and not attested in a classical context before the first century BC; secondly, as Neugebauer has pointed out (1957, 157), none of the extant fragments associated with Berossus' name contain any reference to mathematical astronomy or show any sign of having been the medium by which basic Babylonian observational data could have been transmitted to the Greeks.

Several points of relevance to Berossus the astronomer emerge from this brief discussion: perhaps most important is the fact discussed last. If, as has often been suggested, Berossus was the medium through which Babylonian mathematical astronomy was transmitted to the Greeks, one would expect to find a trace of this in the fragments attributed to him; yet nothing of this sort is preserved. Further, on the assumption of Babylonian influence on Greek astronomy with Berossus as the transmitter, one would expect to see a significant shift in Greek astronomy during the third and early second century BC but, although often assumed, this now appears not to have been the case. Very important is the fact that where an example of a Berossian astrological description is given in some detail it appears to correspond to Greek astronomical concepts, not to Babylonian ones. Finally, although Greek and Babylonian astronomy appear to have developed quite independently and within different conceptual frameworks (though chronologically parallel), it is plain that, for a variety of reasons, Greeks from the late fifth century onwards imagined that the people 'of the East' generally, and in terms of astrology, Babylonians in particular, would provide the information they sought.

A different argument (Drews 1975) in favour of accepting the astronomical fragments as genuine Berossus, ignores the question of the specific character of the attributed information, and concentrates instead on the possible ultimate purpose of Babylonian historiography as represented by Babylonian chronicles. All chronicles, this argument posits, were compiled for purposes of prediction based on a cyclical view of history, and as Berossus did little more than provide a skeleton

29. In the hellenistic period through the medium of Hipparchus (second century BC) cf. Neugebauer 1957, 145; 157; 187.

history in Babylonian chronicle style, his purpose must have been the same; the astronomical information was added at the end of the work because it would, of course, be part and parcel of a Babylonian historian's craft. A central place in this argument is given to Berossus' use of the concept of *ekpurôsis* but, as Lambert (1976) pointed out, there is no evidence that anything was supposed to succeed this and it is therefore difficult to connect it with a vision of cyclically recurring patterns of events. Further, as shown above, it appears to have been an entirely Greek concept for which Berossus is simply supposed to have supplied a specific astrological calculation. Yet another factor is that there is no evidence that the Babylonians at any period ever held the view that there was a cyclical pattern to historical events. If Drews' argument of the relevance of astrology and related sciences in terms of Babylonian historiography cannot be maintained, the logic for including such material in a historic-ethnographical work disappears, and as there is in no testimony or fragment any reference to the composition of other books by Berossus apart from the *Babyloniaka/Chaldaika* in three volumes, it is difficult to see whence such material might have come.[30]

So far, I have argued, there is absolutely nothing in the astronomical/astrological fragments of Berossus that exhibits convincing Babylonian traits, with one possible exception: the Syncellus reference to Nabu-naṣir's destruction of earlier records and the beginning of some kind of new system of record-keeping from his reign onward. This fits in with some of the facts known of Babylonian chronicle compilation and should perhaps be accepted (Grayson 1975a, 13); but it hardly counts as astronomical lore. What I would suggest, instead, following Momigliano (1975, 148) is that the astrologer Berossus was created by Greeks using a figure who was known to have existed and possess exactly the right qualifications to provide the revelations they wanted: i.e. he was a priest of Bēl, a Babylonian, and writing in Greek a Babylonian history based on old records, but who had actually failed to do so. Some time in the first century BC when Babylonia formed a centrally important area of the Parthian empire and had shifted to the margins of the Graeco-Roman world, the testimonials for Berossus and his by then little known work were exploited and he was transposed to Cos,[31] where the hoary antiquity

30. I cannot agree with Drews' arguments on the question of room for the astronomical fragments which are dependent on assumptions concerning Berossus' literary style; cf. my discussion on this below pp. 46–8.

31. The placing of Berossus on Cos is very interesting: astronomy and astrology displayed very much of the same nexus of problems encountered in medicine of observation, theory and practice. One is tempted to speculate whether there was some attempt, related to the competition between Cos and Cnidus (Levine 1978), to perhaps rival the reputation of Eudoxus of Cnidus who, apart from his astronomical and generally wide expertise (doctor, philosopher, mathematician,

of his arcane material could be used to guarantee the genuineness of his predictions which may have consisted of little more than resuscitating out-of-date notions and adding an astrological element to existing ones.[32]

## 3. The structure and form of the *Babyloniaka*

Having sketched briefly some of the complex problems concerning Berossus the astronomer, it would be best for the present to omit this material in any consideration of Berossus the Babylonian 'priest', who wrote a work on Babylonian traditions and history in Greek for Antiochus I, and regard Jacoby's pseudo-Berossus of Cos as a distinct and separate entity, whence it is unlikely that any genuine Babylonian learning was transmitted to the Greeks. One might now consider the contents of the *Babyloniaka* (as defined above) by themselves. In spite of the problems of text preservation one is able to reconstruct a general framework of the history that relates quite reasonably to Babylonian material as at present known. Thus Berossus began with a *prooimion* containing a geographical description of Babylonia, followed by the information that at first people lived like beasts[33] until a fishman called Oannes emerged from the sea and

---

lawgiver) also wrote descriptive historical treatises on geography (Strabo 1.1). It should also be remembered that the casting of horoscopes in Babylonia appears to have been a limited practice and, though developed by the end of the fifth century, very rare before *c.* 200 BC (Neugebauer 1957, 168). It was primarily the Greeks who played the most important role in turning it into a universal system (Lloyd 1979, 230).

32. Drews 1975, 52 argues that the 'real' Berossus could not possibly have made his name worth exploiting and notes that Josephus (T 3) states that Berossus enjoyed a reputation because of his astronomical and philosophical knowledge. This argument ignores the fact that the important authenticating factor for a pseudepigrapher would be not the actual work of Berossus, but his testimonials as a genuine Babylonian priest, i.e. 'a Chaldaean'. (Similar factors operate in the case of Manetho, and there can certainly be nothing more spurious, but clearly quite convincing to sober authorities such as Pliny the Elder, than Nechepso and Petosiris, neither of whom seem ever to have existed; cf. Bouché-Leclerq 1899, 564–5). As to the Josephus passage, my interpretation of this would be that the Greek pseudepigrapher has to be used to recommend the genuine author because the latter was little known and less read. It might be interesting here just to note the appearance of a much later fifteenth-century pseudo-Berossus, brought out in Italy by Annius of Viterbo in 1498; see Piggott 1976, 58.

33. I cannot agree with Burstein's interpretation (1978, 13) of *ataktôs* as 'without laws'; it means 'in an undisciplined/irregular manner' (Liddell and Scott, s.v. *ataktos*) and this is confirmed by the immediately following phrase: 'like wild animals'. Such a presentation relates, in fact, much more closely to a concept one finds in a Sumerian text where 'beginnings' are described and mankind characterised as behaving like animals (cf. Komoróczy 1973, 140–1); this seems to fit the Greek sense of the passage much better than 'without laws' which would be a rendering of Greek *anomos* with an implied meaning of 'impiously'.

taught them day by day the arts of civilised life, and revealed how the world, mankind and cities had been created by the god Marduk, who had also been responsible for building a wall around the city of Babylon. The second book presented the ten kings before the flood, their incredibly long reigns, and the mention of the occasional fishman appearing down to Xisuthros, last king before the flood, the latter being described at length; the rest of the book described post-diluvian dynasties and occasional fishmen down to Nabu-naṣir (eighth century). Book 3 covered the period of Assyrian domination and conflict with Babylonia from Tiglath-pileser III (744–727) onward to the defeat of Sin-šar-iškun by Nabopolassar with the help of the Medes, the glorious reign of Nebuchadnezzar II (604–562) and his beautifying of Babylon, the fall of Babylon to the Persians (539) and their rule over Babylonia presumably down to their defeat by Alexander (F 10). Assyrian history was completely ignored except for those Assyrian kings who had ruled directly over Babylonia;[34] in this Berossus was clearly following the Babylonian chronicle tradition. Ninus and Semiramis were entirely absent, a fact at which Abydenus (almost certainly referring to Berossus) was amazed: 'In this way the Chaldaeans imagine the kings of their country from Alorus to Alexander: Ninus and Semiramis they do not take much notice of' (cf. Schnabel 1923, 275 no. 57). Some notion of the amount that has been lost can be gained from the occasional parallel quotes; for example, the lengthy quote from Berossus in Josephus' *contra Apionem* 1.131–41 (= F 8a) concerning Nebuchadnezzar II is paralleled by the briefest of references only in the *Antiquities* (10. 219). Similarly Josephus (*c.A.* 1.145–53) contains a much fuller description of the successors of Nebuchadnezzar II and the capture of Babylon by Cyrus (= F 9a) than the bald statement by Eusebius (*Chron.* Armenian Version p.15, 5–10 K 35 = F 9b) which covers the same events and simply gives lengths of reigns. Particularly instructive in this respect is a statement made by Eusebius concerning Persian rule in Babylonia (= F 10):

> And Cyrus ruled Babylonia for nine years. Then he was killed in a battle in the plain of Daas. After him Cambyses reigned eight years. And then Darius thirty-six years. After him Xerxes and further the remaining Persian kings. As, in summary, *Berossus relates in detail.*

That Berossus did indeed relate the Persian period in considerable detail[35] can be seen from the purely chance preservation of a bit of

---

34. These were Tiglath-pileser III (728–727), [Shalmaneser V (726–722), Sargon II (709–705) – nothing on these is preserved in the Berossus fragments], Assur-nadin-šumi (699–694), Sennacherib (688–681), Esarhaddon (680–669), Šamaš-šuma-ukin (667–648), Assurbanipal (648–?627).
35. The surviving fragmentary chronicle texts indicate that chronicles were compiled throughout the Achaemenid period; cf. Grayson 1975a nos. 8 and 9; Sachs 1977, 145–7.

Berossus in Clemens Alexandrinus' *Protrepticus* 5.65.2 (= F 11), in a
passage discussing Persian religion:

> (The Persians) . . . did not believe in wooden or stone images of the gods
> but in fire and water like the philosophers. Later, however, after many
> years they began to worship statues in human form, as Berossus reports
> in the third book of his *Chaldaika*. Artaxerxes, son of Darius, son of
> Ochus, introduced this practice. He was the first to set up an image of
> Aphrodite Anaitis in Babylon and to require such worship from the
> Susians, Ecbatanians, Persians, Bactrians and from Damascus and Sardis.

In the very few instances then, where a comparison of excerpts can
be made, it is clear that Berossus' history contained a wealth of
detailed and valuable information that was simply omitted by many
excerptors as irrelevant to their own particular interests or contexts.[36]

Confirmation of the genuineness of the traditions and the antiquity
of some of the material in Berossus has not been lacking (see generally
Komoróczy 1973; Burstein 1978). Berossus clearly narrated the
creation in a form close to one preserved (*Enūma Eliš*, cf. Pritchard
1969, 60–72; 501–3) and made use of a Sumerian version of the Flood
Story as he gives the name of the hero as Xisuthros, which must
reflect the Sumerian name, Ziusudra, whereas in the later Akkadian
version his name is Ut-napishtim. It also seems as though his more
detailed political history began with Nabu-naṣir in 747 which indicates his use of the excellent Babylonian chronicles, the typical and
precise form of which appear to begin with this ruler (Grayson 1975a,
12–14), and argues for accepting F 16a (see above) as possibly derived
from genuine Berossus. Particularly remarkable is the relatively
recent discovery of the cuneiform *apkallu*-list from Uruk (van Dijk
1962) which lists kings, including the antediluvians, together with
their sages (*apkallu*) starting with Oannes (cf. Reiner 1961). The publication by Finkel (1980, 65–72) of a new part of the so-called 'Dynastic
Chronicle' suggests that for the lengths of reigns of the first kings,
Berossus made use of a late recension of the text. The interesting
information that Nabonidus, king of Babylon at the time of its capture
by the Persians in 539 BC, was spared and settled in another country,
for which Berossus was for a long time the only source (F 9), has
recently been confirmed to be part and parcel of the Babylonian cuneiform tradition (Grayson 1975b, 28, 32 and 33, obv. ll.19–21).

In spite of this evidence for the pedigree of the Babylonian material
which formed Berossus' sources, too much weight should not be placed
on a supposed correspondence between the literary style of the cuneiform material and that of the *Babyloniaka* (*pace* Drews 1975; Murray

36. Note the interesting fact that Josephus (*AJ* 1.158) found a notice in book two of
the *Babyloniaka* of a wise man who lived ten generations after the flood and was
thus identified by him with Abraham.

1972, 208–9; Kuhrt 1982, 547). Attention should instead be paid to two remarkable facts: Berossus' description of the physical characteristics of Babylonia finds no correspondence in Mesopotamian literary tradition, but does fit well the canons of hellenistic ethnographies as defined by Hecataeus of Abdera, modelled on Herodotus and already practised in the Seleucid empire by Megasthenes (cf. Murray 1972, esp. 208–9). Thus Book 1: position, size, resources of Babylonia, creation and legends/myths; Book 2: ancient history to Nabu-naṣir (including flood); Book 3: more recent and fully recorded history to the point where Seleucus I first enters the scene.[37] Secondly, Berossus gave an allegorical interpretation of the creation-legend (F 1 section 7), a practice which is at no point attested in Babylonian literature, but formed part of the Greek reaction to the pre-Socratic rejection of the Homeric gods.[38] Further points indicating Berossus' awareness of Greek notions could be made: e.g. F 8 in which Berossus took issue with the erroneous Greek notions concerning Semiramis' founding of Babylon which he firmly corrected; F 7 contains an otherwise unknown battle between Greek and Assyrian forces in Cilicia in the reign of Sennacherib. It has been suggested (Momigliano 1934) that this was put in to interest Greek readers or (Burstein 1978, 24 n.80) that Berossus was consciously correcting Greek traditions; certainly the incident does not appear in any preserved records which, for Sennacherib, are reasonably full. Another interesting feature concerns the 'theory of world-empires' (Assyria-Media-Persia-Macedon-Rome). Swain (1940), in a well-known article, argued for an adoption of this model from 'the east' in 188/7 BC. This has recently (Mendels 1981) been vigorously and, in my view, rightly rejected. Mendels demonstrated that, in fact, this notion appears to be a primarily Greek one and it is certainly not one found in the preserved cuneiform corpus (cf. Tadmor 1981 *addendum*). In the extant portions of Berossus there are no references to this theory, but I would suggest that he knew of it from Greek writers and therefore attempted to counter it or, at least, modify it by showing (a) that there were empires preceding Assyria (though given the sad state of preservation of this work this must remain hypothetical) and (b) that the Assyrian empire was

---

37. The date at which the *Babyloniaka* ended is not totally certain beyond the brief reference drawn by Eusebius (*Chron.* (ed. Karst) 25.32–6.1) from Abydenus that 'in this way the Chaldaeans imagine the kings of their country from Alorus to Alexander' (cf. Schnabel 1923, 26).

38. The particular concept into which Berossus' treatment fits is that of *huponoia*, indicating the 'underlying/deeper' meaning of a myth; the term appears first in Theagenes of Rhegion (late sixth century BC) and Anaxagoras (early fifth century BC); in the hellenistic period, under the new name *allēgoria*, it formed a frequently attested Stoic principle, see *Der Kleine Pauly* I s.v. Allegorische Dichtererklärung, col. 274.

succeeded by the powerful Neo-Babylonian one,[39] at least as large as that of the Assyrians. Also worth noting is the list of equations of Iranian and Babylonian deities, with Greek ones drawn from Berossus, among others, and preserved by Agathias (= F 12; cf. Cameron 1969–1970, 95–7).

Though sparse, these pieces of evidence are of major importance for assessing both the form and thrust of Berossus' work. He must be credited with a familiarity not merely with the Greek language, but also its literary style as well as Greek philosophical concepts and the ability to reshape Babylonian records in accordance with the principles of hellenistic historiography.

To conclude this section, the few indications concerning Berossus' life may be pieced together. His name very probably reflects the Babylonian personal name, Bēl-rē'ušu, meaning '(the god) Bēl-Marduk is his shepherd' (Lehmann-Haupt 1937, 2a; Komoróczy 1973, 125). Save for the general time-span (from Alexander the Great to Antiochus I), his place of residence (Babylon) and his profession (priest of Bēl,[40] ap. T 2; writer ap. T 1), his life is completely unknown. The fact that he composed a history in Greek and was influenced by Greek literary models in its presentation, combined with the fact that the city of Babylon and its god appears to have been given a prominent place in the *Babyloniaka* and his access to genuine, sometimes very archaic, Babylonian material, would tend to suggest that Berossus occupied a fairly elevated position among the temple-personnel of Esagila and was thus probably an influential member of the *mār banê* group of Babylon, a term designating the, juridically, fully free inhabitants of certain Babylonian cities (Dandamaev 1981; Oelsner 1976, 134–5).

## 4. The political and cultural context

Berossus lived at a time which saw major and rapid changes on the political plane: Alexander's conquest and early death, the struggles among the successors, some of which were fought within Babylonia itself, and the establishment of the Seleucid empire, of which Babylonia as one of the intended centres of Alexander's realm (*contra* Schachermeyr 1970, 74–7) and then Seleucus' satrapy, formed the focal point (Sherwin-White above, pp. 15–16). How soon and in what aspects of life did these changes manifest themselves and how were they perceived by Babylonians?

It has been usual to see the surrender of Babylon to Alexander in 331 as indicating a willing acceptance by influential priestly groups

---

39. See Kuhrt 1982, 544–5 for the elimination of the Neo-Babylonian empire in Ctesias.
40. The definition of a priest in Mesopotamia is fraught with problems and probably neither comparable to a Greek *hiereus* nor our own concept of priest (see Kuhrt, forthcoming).

disaffected with Persian rule because of Xerxes' destruction of the Esagila temple in 482 (Burn 1951, 159–60; Lane Fox 1973, 247–9; Briant 1977, 96–7). Alexander's gratitude for their support was expressed by his orders to rebuild the sanctuary (Arrian *Anab.* 3.16.4). The immediate acceptance of Alexander after Gaugamela by the Babylonians is beyond question, but the motives for it somewhat different from those presented. Of prime importance, before examining this further, is the fact that the long-accepted Persian destruction of Esagila is now without support: it only appears in much later sources and there is no Babylonian evidence for it as had been assumed (Kuhrt, Sherwin-White 1987). The presumption must therefore be at present that the temple was still standing in 331, which makes it somewhat difficult to maintain the notion that 'priestly' disaffection with the Persian regime was a major motivating factor in Babylon's surrender, as well as appearing to make nonsense of Alexander's orders to rebuild the temples.

These apparent contradictions can, however, be resolved, if one sets the events within a Babylonian context. Babylon, as well as some other cities, claimed privileges from reigning kings (Leemans 1946) and sometimes negotiated terms of surrender with armed invaders in order to survive the not infrequent conquests. Such formal surrenders usually took place after a decisive battle had been fought and were formalised by a ceremonial welcome extended by the citizen-body to the conqueror[41] who was then accepted as the new king. Such a reception also imposed duties: a Babylonian king was obliged to make war on the country's enemies, respect the privileged status claimed by certain cities, build and maintain city walls and defences, ensure that temple rituals and festivals were correctly performed and adequately supplied, and repair, elaborate and care for temple building (Kuhrt 1987b). It is against this background that Alexander's actions in relation to Babylon may be understood. The victory at Gaugamela made it virtually certain that Babylonia would be attacked next before Alexander moved into Iran (Arrian *Anab.* 3.16.2); the example of Gaza (332) showed the awful fate awaiting a city which resisted and lost (Arrian *Anab.* 2.27.7). The obvious course was to negotiate a surrender and welcome the victor as the new king, a course already followed several times in the past (e.g. Cyrus' conquest in 539: Grayson 1975a, no. 7, iii, 15–20). Alexander's acceptance of this and the obligations it carried with it were expressed by his orders 'to rebuild' (repair? beautify? extend?) the Esagila temple as befitted a traditional pious Babylonian monarch.

The conquest of Alexander was thus in Babylonian terms not a

---

41. This general practice was not by any means peculiar to Mesopotamia, cf. Bickerman 1937/1979, 32–3.

major disruption – one foreign ruling group was, in part, ousted by another but there was no immediate or sudden change in political, cultural or religious life. Further evidence for the continuity from the Achaemenid period into the Seleucid is also provided by non-historiographic material and may be briefly mentioned (see in detail Sherwin-White, above pp. 24–6). The forms of economic transactions and their recording continued to be precisely the same as those of the later Achaemenid period until the 270s (Doty 1977, 311ff), which suggests that administrative changes wrought by Macedonian rule were only gradually introduced. Similarly, standard Babylonian house-styles, burials, figurines and pottery continued to be the norm almost throughout the Seleucid period (Oelsner 1978, 105; Colledge, below pp. 146; 155). Temple structures, too, which in some cases were built on a vast scale (at Uruk, cf. Falkenstein 1941; North 1957, 237ff; Lenzen 1974, 23; Doty 1977, 26–9; Oelsner 1978, 102–3; Colledge, below pp. 145–6; 154) continued to use long-established local building styles and plans. It has been thought by some (Falkenstein 1941, 2–3; 8–9; McEwan 1981b, 187) that the pre-eminence of the cult of the Babylonian sky-god Anu at Uruk developed only in the Seleucid period under Greek influence; but Oelsner (1978, 103; 1981, 44) has shown convincingly that this little understood shift in Babylonian religious practice had already taken place by the end of the fifth century BC. Again, the major developments in astronomy and astrology, particu-larly horoscopes, which were thought to have been developed in Baby-lonia as a result of Greek stimulus in the hellenistic period, had all been completed by the end of the fifth century BC (Neugebauer 1957; Sachs 1952; Oelsner 1978, 106–7 and n.26; Kuhrt 1987a). Of particular interest is the fact that the evidence for cultural continuity is not entirely confined to traditional Babylonian forms – there is some quantitatively small yet extremely significant material that bears testimony to Greek influence in Babylonia at the end of the fifth and the beginning of the fourth century BC. The material comes from two sources: one is a small archive from Babylon in which a number of texts are sealed with stamp-seals bearing totally Greek motifs (Athena), yet the named owners of the seals have purely Babylonian personal names (Jakob-Rost, Freydank 1972). The other is an early fourth-century coffin excavated at Ur containing *c.* 200 impressions on clay, demonstrating that there was a seal-cutter at work using Greek coins as models to make stamp seals for local use (Wolley 1932, 389–90; 1962, 103; Legrain 1951, nos. 701–832; Porada 1960). The widespread possession of seals by private individuals in Babylonia is a remarkable feature noted by Herodotus (1.195) and illustrating the extent to which its inhabitants must have 'participated in literacy' as Clanchy (1979, 2) has demonstrated, on the basis of comparable evidence, for medieval England; possession and use was not limited to officials of the administration but fairly widespread among Babylonians (Renger 1977) for private transactions. The implications of this must be that contacts with Greek artistic products were not limited to a small, governing, primarily Persian group, but had penetrated their Babylonian subjects at large. One would probably also be right in assuming that the seals are only the physically extant evidence of much more extensive contact with other aspects of Greek culture in Babylonia. None of this is really surprising considering not just the extensive evidence for Greeks in Persian royal service (doctors, mercenaries, masons) but also the Greek communities known to have been settled in Babylonia such as the Milesians at Ampe (Hdt. 6.20) and the Boeotians settled east of the Tigris by Xerxes (D.S. 17.110.4–5).

Despite the strong evidence for continuity and the slow and partial process of institutional changes, the establishment of the Seleucids in Babylonia marked a new beginning for the country in terms of peace and stability. Darius III's mustering of his huge force in Babylon to meet Alexander at Gaugamela in 331, his defeat and Alexander's entry shortly afterwards must surely have caused some upheavals, as did the presence of his large army in 323 at his death. By far the worst consequence for Babylonia of the Macedonian conquest was undoubtedly the long-drawn-out and disastrous wars fought between the *diadochi* in which Babylonia, which held Alexander's major financial reserves, was frequently the central arena. At the very briefest one must allow a span of almost twenty years for this extremely unstable situation which culminated between 311/10–308/7 in terrible ravages of the Babylonian countryside causing great suffering, as well as in the destruction of sacred buildings (Grayson 1975a no. 10 rev.; cf. Sherwin-White, above p. 15 for detailed discussion). The fact that Seleucus I was successful in effectively stopping this carnage was no mean achievement. As part of the re-establishment of normal conditions Antiochus I was appointed co-regent with responsibility for the eastern part of the empire of which Babylonia constituted the crucial fulcrum. Recognition of the central importance of the country is demonstrated by the early foundation of Seleucia-Tigris (Sherwin-White 1983b, 269–70), not in order to detract from the prominence and wealth of existing local cities, but to provide an independent royal administrative and military centre,[42] which controlled and protected the strategic routes and thus encouraged the resumption of trade which in turn stimulated the economy (cf. also Salles below, pp. 88–90).

A further aspect illustrating the fundamental importance which the

42. The founding of specific royal cities as dynastic centres has a long tradition in Mesopotamia cf. e.g. Agade, founded by Sargon of Agade *c.* 2330 BC and Dur Kurigalzu, founded in the Kassite period *c.* 1595–1157 BC.

region had for the Seleucids is the close involvement of Seleucid rulers, especially Antiochus I, with Babylonian ritual and symbolic values. The most striking evidence for this is the famous cylinder from Borsippa of Antiochus I (Weissbach 1911, Anhang II; Pritchard 1969, 317; Austin 1981 no. 189), virtually indistinguishable in its literary form from standard Neo-Babylonian royal inscriptions, which commemorates both his restoration work on the Ezida temple there, as well as that in Babylon on the Marduk temple, Esagila. Much of the serious damage that these temples may have suffered was very probably inflicted during the war between Antigonus and Seleucus I. In addition it is also known that Antiochus instituted offerings to the Moongod at Ur (Grayson 1975a, no. 11 obv. 6–9) and granted land to Babylonian cities (Smith 1924, 155 and 156 ll.17–18; Austin 1981 no. 141; cf. van der Spek, below, p. 66), while later Seleucid rulers supported activities such as the celebration of the New Year festival in Babylon (Grayson 1975a no. 13b 11.3–9) and the building and elaboration of the vast temple complexes at Uruk and probably elsewhere (Oelsner 1978, 102–3 (Uruk); 104 (Nippur)).

The conclusions to be drawn from this brief discussion are first that hellenistic rule did not usher in a brief renaissance for a moribund Babylonian culture; on the contrary all the evidence points to economic and cultural life flourishing before Alexander's conquest. Moreover, as a result of the specific configuration of the Persian empire, Babylonia had already had some contact with Greek culture, the extent of which is difficult to gauge precisely but may well have been greater than the limited evidence suggests at first sight.

The impression gained from Babylonian material, in which one should include the Dynastic Prophecy discussed by Sherwin-White (above pp. 10–14), is that Alexander's conquest was not experienced by the Babylonians as a liberation. Rather his early death and the subsequent period of warfare and confusion impressed itself as one of horror and chaos. This was the emotional and political climate within which Seleucid rule was finally successfully established. The most important figure in actively fostering stability and recreating economic prosperity by his personal involvement with the country and active patronage of the important local religious and urban institutions was Antiochus I. It is in his co-regency and reign that one sees the beginnings of a definite interaction of Macedonian rulers and indigenous Babylonian subjects on both the administrative and cultural plane. And one of the significant products of this interaction are the *Babyloniaka* of Berossus, himself a member of the élite urban group of Babylon, for whom the Esagila temple, the repairs on which were probably completed by Antiochus I, was a symbol of its traditional privileged status.

## 5. The purpose of the *Babyloniaka*

A question briefly raised earlier (see above p. 33) was what motivated writers such as Manetho and Berossus to compose the histories of their countries in Greek. The question has been little explored with regard to Berossus and is, indeed, a difficult one given the small amount of the *Babyloniaka* preserved. Yet various possibilities suggest themselves or have been mooted and may be considered here. One possibility is that Berossus felt impelled to set the record straight and counteract a kind of Greek cultural imperialism (Oelsner 1978, 113–14) as happened, for example, more recently among Indian historians reacting to European-centred explanations of their civilisation (Thapar 1966, 17–18). Some support for such a view might be found in Berossus' deliberate rejection of the figure of Ninus (see above p. 45), so popular with Greek audiences (Kuhrt 1982, 544 and 546), and in the explicit statement in Josephus *c.A.* 1.142 that in Book 3, 'Berossus censures the Greek historians for their deluded belief that Babylon was founded by the Assyrian Semiramis and their erroneous statements that its wonders were her creation'. This sounds at first sight as though Berossus was strenuously trying to correct current Greek views of Mesopotamian history. But one can also interpret it differently: the rejection of statements by earlier historians has been demonstrated by Murray (1972) to form a standard element of hellenistic historiography whereby earlier writers on the subject – usually Herodotus – were discredited in order to emphasise the author's own superior knowledge and access to relevant records. This view robs the statement of specific polemical intent and suggests that, instead, one should place it within the traditions of hellenistic historiography.

Rather than being directed against Greek historians it has been implied (Oesner 1978, 113–14) that the work may have been intended to remind those of Berossus' fellow countrymen anxious to embrace the *mores* of the new political élite of their own proud history and cultural identity. This would suggest a cultural confrontation and deliberately imposed hellenisation that flies in the face of the existing evidence which suggests on the one hand fairly extensive contacts between Babylonians and Greeks from the late fifth century onwards (see above pp. 50–1) and, on the other, documents the strong support given by the Seleucid rulers to those aspects of Babylonian civilisation which had very strong traditional symbolic value.

Another approach arguing that the *Babyloniaka* represented a subtly disguised expression of Babylonian opposition to Seleucid rule was presented by Drews (1975). By arguing that all Babylonian chronicles were compiled for purposes of prediction based on a cyclical concept of history and that Berossus faithfully reproduced the literary style of these chronicles, Drews concluded that his purpose was the

same as theirs. Implicitly, therefore, his work would predict the ultimate demise of the Seleucid dynasty. This interesting argument is,
however, vitiated by the absence of any evidence to support this view
of the chronicles or the concept of cyclical history (see above p 00);
furthermore there are a reasonable number of indications that
Berossus reworked the Babylonian material to fit Greek historio-
graphical and philosophical concepts (see above p. 43). This is not to
deny that there may well have been groups opposed to the Seleucid
control of the country, but the evidence indicates that one should
search for expressions of this in another context, such as the pro-
phecies. This would suggest that a more likely vehicle for giving vent
to dissatisfaction with the régime were traditional Akkadian literary
forms.

Yet another approach has been to see the work as an elaborately
cloaked plea to the king, presented to him in the guise of an
ethnography for his edification (Burstein 1978, 5). The suggestion is
that Berossus seized the opportunity presented by Antiochus I's
accession to offer him a history of Babylonia in the hope that it would
lead Antiochus I to pay more attention to the Babylonian cities which
had been 'degraded' by Seleucus I's foundation of Seleucia-Tigris. In
the form in which the argument is presented it is untenable as there
is little to support the idea that either Seleucus' motives for founding
Seleucia or the consequences of its foundation were of such a kind (cf.
Sherwin-White above, pp. 18–20 in detail). The concept, however, is
not without its attractions. It fits the dedication to Antiochus I and it
was he who, already while crown-prince, had taken it upon himself to
act like a traditional Babylonian monarch and was to continue to do
so. Was he inspired in this by Berossus? Did the work perhaps combine
the aspect of a 'thank offering' for what had already been done together
with the hope that he would do even more if he were more fully
informed of Babylonia's ancient past? If it is allowed that this could
have been the aim of the work, what specifically might Berossus have
been expected to achieve? One apparently striking element of the
*Babyloniaka* is its emphasis on the importance of the city of Babylon:
its walls were built by the great god Bēl-Marduk himself; it was
rebuilt straight after the flood; Sennacherib, the destroyer of Babylon,
was horribly murdered by one of his own sons; and the mighty Nebuchadnezzar beautified the city extensively. Might this not all be a reflection of a plea for recognition of the special status of the citizen-body
of Babylon? Could it be a kind of *Fürstenspiegel*, a type of text for
which there is some evidence at earlier periods (Lambert 1960, 110–15;
Diakonov 1965)? One consideration, unfortunately, mars this
attractive hypothesis, namely that the state of preservation of the
*Babyloniaka* is not sufficiently taken into account. As indicated above
(pp. 35–6), the main excerpts are the ones made by people trying to

find corroborative evidence for Biblical traditions. In this connection, of course, the city of Babylon which occupies a place of such symbolic importance in the Old and the New Testament, the unnatural death of the evil Sennacherib who had besieged Jerusalem, and the history of Nebuchadnezzar II who had destroyed Jerusalem and led the Jews into captivity – a turning point in their history – would all be bound to figure prominently. Yet, as was shown above, in the instances where a comparison of excerpts can be made, it is clear that Berossus' history contained a wealth of information that was simply omitted by many users as irrelevant to their own particular interests. In spite of its considerable attractions, this proposition had best be discarded as it seems to rest on a somewhat distorted picture of the original content of the *Babyloniaka*.

So far this brief discussion of a complex subject has considered Berossus' work as representing primarily a response to events, as part of a dialogue between Greek cultural and political domination and indigenous subjects. But what of the alternative possibility that Berossus wrote specifically under royal patronage – 'at royal command', as Tarn (1951, 64) put it – to provide the Seleucid dynasty with an ideological support? As emphasised repeatedly, the arrangement of Berossus' material and his literary style all fit the pattern of ethnography established by Hecataeus of Abdera in his propaganda work written for Ptolemy I (Murray 1970), which served as an instrument for fitting the new dynasty into the long line of earlier Egyptian kings. By adopting this line of approach it may be possible to offer a view both for the setting of Berossus' composition in Antiochus I's reign and its structure. In spite of initially close relations between Seleucus I and Ptolemy I, the two rulers in establishing themselves in their respective areas of rule were perforce in competition with each other over possession of frontier areas (such as Coele-Syria, Phoenicia, Cyprus) and control of Greek cities in Asia Minor. At the same time both needed to create viable and solid relations with the populations of their power bases in order to receive the economic-military and ideological support both for their rule within these countries and any expansionist aims which they might harbour. In Egypt this was achieved by a conscious modelling of the Ptolemaic kingship on earlier Pharaonic practices, and Hecataeus' history of Egypt played its part in this process: Egypt was presented as the ideal philosophical state, the source of all civilisation, and the figure of Sesostris III was reshaped into that of an ideal king and great world-conqueror (Murray 1970, 162–4).

The original core of the Seleucid realm was Babylonia; the establishing of Seleucid control over a larger territory was a gradual and relatively long drawn-out affair, achieved only by the time of Seleucus' death in 281 BC. It thus fell to Antiochus to consolidate Seleucid control over this vast territory, which he did extremely successfully. An integral element of this process of consolidation may well have been the composition of Berossus' *Babyloniaka*: in it he demonstrated the uniqueness and antiquity of Babylonian traditions and any claims that Hecataeus may have made, such as that 'the Chaldeans' had emigrated from Egypt to Babylonia, would have been shown to be a complete fantasy as well as a misunderstanding of the term. Even more significant were the figures of the first two rulers of the Neo-Babylonian dynasty, Nabopolassar and his son Nebuchadnezzar II; not only was the latter's magnificent rebuilding of Babylon obviously fully described, but Berossus also presented both of them as wielding control over Phoenicia, Coele-Syria and Egypt itself (F 8) – the last being historically quite incorrect. It seems as though the activities of these two famous rulers may have been expanded to function as a counter-balance to Sesostris III in Hecataeus' history. In this respect Berossus could have been building on the figure of Nebuchadnezzar II presented as a world-conqueror by Megasthenes in the *Indica* (*FGrHist.* 715 T 1) some years earlier. But more interesting and suggestive is the depiction of Nabopolassar, who rose from the position of governor to found the most glorious phase of Babylonian history and re-established order after a lengthy war of liberation (F 7); much of this was accomplished with the help of his son Nebuchadnezzar, whose consolidation and extension of his father's achievements after the latter's death culminated in the extensive programme of reconstruction within Babylonia (F 8). What better models than this famous father and son could be found to prefigure the activities of Seleucus I and his son and successor, Antiochus, almost exactly three hundred years later, who by their closely comparable behaviour could be presented as the direct heirs of Babylonia's greatest and most pious kings?[43]

The conclusion I would like to draw from this is that Hecataeus and Manetho in Egypt, on the one hand, and Berossus in Babylonia, on the other, helped to make accessible the local ideological repertoires and historical precedents for adaptation by the Macedonian dynasties, which resulted in the formation and definition of the distinctive political-cultural entities of Ptolemaic Egypt and the Seleucid empire.

43. The major and continued importance for Babylonians of the figure of Nabopolassar has been illustrated by the recent publication of the fragment of an epic concerning Nabopolassar's war of liberation and his subsequent coronation in a late Babylonian copy (Grayson 1975b, 78–86).

CHAPTER THREE

# The Babylonian City

## R. J. van der Spek

### The Greek *polis* and the ancient Near Eastern city

Much ink has been spilt on the question of the status of the city in the hellenistic empires. Most scholars have assumed that there was an essential difference between the Greek *polis* and the 'oriental' city. The discussion has centred on the Greek *polis*, the question being whether or not it could be viewed as a *polis* in traditional usage: a city-state possessing freedom and autonomy.[1]

I do not wish to re-embark on this discussion, although I cannot refrain from making a few remarks. It is, in fact, incorrect to make a distinction between the classical and the hellenistic age. In the classical period the majority of the Greek cities (*poleis*) were *not* free and autonomous. The great powers of those days, Sparta, Athens and Persia had many Greek cities in their leagues or empires, which were thus neither free nor autonomous. Further, it is highly misleading to speak in strict legal terms of the status of the Greek city in the hellenistic period. The treatment of Greek cities and cities in general was the object of a subtle policy dictated by the power of the central government at any given moment and the possibilities open to it. For this reason, and because of the sensibilities of the Greek cities, it was at times opportune to treat them as though they were independent, but the measure of real independence varied in time and place.

Naturally, non-Greek cities also had their own traditional prerogatives and the Seleucid rulers tried to respect them in the same way, as long as it did not hamper royal policy. The kings treated the Greek cities according to Greek traditions and non-Greek cities according to their own customs. Thus they sometimes presented themselves to Greek cities as allies proposing certain measures to the people and council of the city, instead of giving orders, while for example in Babylon it was quite natural, indeed preferable, to act like a Babylonian king, as an heir of Nebuchadnezzar II. The Babylonian cities

---

1. It is unnecessary to present a detailed discussion of this problem, cf. Tcherikover 1927; Heuss 1937; Bickerman 1939a; Jones 1940, 45ff; Magie 1950 I 56ff; 89–146; II 825ff; Préaux 1954; Ehrenberg 1969; Orth 1977; Versnel 1978, 13ff; Seibert 1983, 179ff.

too were used to certain privileges such as exemption from certain
types of taxes, receiving donations of royal gifts for temples and cults,
and royal iniatives in restoring temples and civic structures (see
Kuhrt, above p. 49). With some of these demands the Macedonian
kings complied. Alexander intended to make Babylon one of the capitals of his empire, and ordered the restoration of Esagila, the temple
of Marduk, which was continued by Seleucus I and Antiochus I. We
have a cuneiform inscription of the latter in which he styles himself
as a Babylonian king with traditional Babylonian titles, who
completed the restoration of Ezida, the Nabû-temple of Borsippa, and
Esagila in Babylon (Pritchard 1969, 317; Austin 1981 no. 189). Some
privileges such as exemption from taxation were not granted, but this
was also true for many of the Greek cities.

Modern scholars, in my opinion, have made too much fuss about the
term *polis*. It has often been maintained that the Greeks used the
word *polis* only for Greek independent city-states with a Greek type
of government and institutions. But this is not the case. The word was
used in two senses: town or city and state, and as Greeks wrote
primarily about themselves, they generally visualised the state in the
classical period as a city-state in which city (including city-land or
*chôra politikê*) and state were identical. Despite this, Greek authors
called Carthage, Nineveh, Babylon, Opis, Ecbatana and others *poleis*
(Hdt. 1.178–89; 2.150; Xen. *Anab.* 2.4.25). Aristotle's doubts on Babylon's status as a *polis* were caused by his false impressions of it: he
believed Babylon to be so large a city that the message of its capture
took three days to reach all the inhabitants (*Pol.* 1276a28).[2] Similarly,
he says, he would hardly call the Peloponnese a city if it were
surrounded by a wall. But his uncertainties about whether or not
Babylon could be called a city demonstrate that it was generally so
designated by his contemporaries.

Despite these observations on the definition of the term *polis*, I do
not wish to suggest that all cities were identical. The fact that Western
Asia had been conquered by foreign people, Macedonians and Greeks,
who had their own distinctive civilisation, must have left its marks.
The Greeks were conscious of their own customs and did not wish
merely to take over existing forms and become assimilated. They
tended to live according to their own traditions, wherever they settled,
while permitting the indigenous people to continue their way of life.
For the Greeks it was, of course, easiest to follow their customary way
of life in cities that had been Greek for centuries, especially in Western
Asia Minor, and in new cities founded by the Seleucid kings, such
as Seleucia-Tigris, Antioch and Apamea-Orontes. Problems became
greater when Greeks lived as a minority in indigenous cities. In some

---

2. Plato's definition (*Rep.* 2.11) is not specifically Greek either.

of those cities there seems to have existed a certain segregation between the different population groups. Sometimes the Greeks formed a special *politeuma* within a Near Eastern city, sometimes an existing city was reorganised on the Greek pattern. It received a new, usually dynastic, name; the official language became Greek; popular assembly, council and magistrates according to Greek principles formed the government; membership of the gymnasium and *ephebeion* were conditions of citizenship. Citizenship was open to the Greek inhabitants and to more or less hellenised non-Greeks, who mostly belonged to the upper strata of the society and possessed arable land, the possession of which was a condition of citizenship in most Greek cities. The less privileged inhabitants would continue to use their own language, religion, and styles in art and architecture. They had their own community and called their city by its local name (Bickerman 1937, 62; Briant 1982b; cf. Colledge, below).

In some cities Greek immigration did not take place on a grand scale, but nevertheless such communities gradually came to consider themselves Greek cities. They began to use Greek for some official documents and coins and stressed their relationship with the Greek past. Leading citizens learned Greek. This did not mean that these cities (especially in the interior of Asia Minor and on the Phoenician and Palestinian coast) became entirely Greek, as is shown by the Greek inscription from Sidon in which the city (*Sidôniôn hê polis*) honoured Diotimus, the judge (*dikastês*), which is presumably the translation of the Phoenician magistracy of *šofēt* (Bickerman 1939b; Millar 1983 and below pp. 123–4). Thus, although this inscription stresses Sidon's ties with Greece by the participation of Diotimus in the Olympic games and a common mythological past, Sidon retained its traditional structure. In the same way, the action by the high priest Jason to hellenise Jerusalem did not affect the government structure, even though a dynastic name was introduced (2 Macc. 4.9, 12, 14).[3]

But the appearance and the structure of the cities differed. Ancient authors therefore distinguished Greek cities (*poleis hellênides*), which included hellenised cities, existing non-Greek cities (e.g. Babylon and Susa – *polis persikê* (Steph. Byz. s.v.) – and Ecbatana before it became Epiphaneia) and mixed cities (*poleis mixobarbaroi*, e.g. Edessa, cf. Malalas 17.418). How should we view the ancient cities in Babylonia? Were they hellenised to some extent or not?

---

3. 2 Macc. 4:11 seems to suggest new government structures, but the later history reports only the presence of high priests and the council of priests and elders, as before.

## The Babylonian cities

When Alexander the Great conquered Babylonia he subdued cities which could glory in a history of thousands of years. These cities came under the sway of a political power whose culture had been spreading its influence to the east (and west) already before the days of Alexander, a process now furthered by direct political domination (see Colledge, below pp. 134–8). The question which now requires consideration is how far Babylonian cities were affected by hellenisation especially in their government structure, and the extent of Greek immigration. From two of these cities, Babylon and Uruk, we have a fair amount of textual (cuneiform) evidence, from others, Borsippa, Cutha, Ur, Kish, Marad and Larsa we have only a few texts. As most of our evidence comes from Babylon and Uruk, we should look at these cities first.

### Babylon

For hellenistic Babylon there are four different kinds of sources. Greek and Roman authors such as Strabo, Diodorus Siculus, Arrian, Appian, Stephanus of Byzantium, Pliny, Quintus Curtius and others provide more or less elaborate descriptions by outsiders. Cuneiform documents from Babylon itself constitute direct evidence, as do the monuments and other material remains which came to light during excavations. Some Greek inscriptions make it possible to hear the voice of Greek or hellenised inhabitants. From most of these sources it is clear that Babylon was a typical Mesopotamian city, living according to its own customs with the temple as a focal institution of the community. For classical writers it was the centre of Chaldaean astrology and learning (Appian *Syr.* 58; D.S. 2.9; Pliny *NH* 6.30.121–2; cf. Bidez 1935; Smelik 1979). Pausanias (1.16.3) tells us that, when Seleucus I founded Seleucia-Tigris, he moved Babylonians to this new capital, but left 'the Chaldaeans' in the old city. Pausanias mentions this fact in order to show that Seleucus I was a pious man, who respected Babylonian religion. No writer makes any allusion to an alternative Greek name for Babylon, to an extensive Greek population or to the introduction of Greek institutions. For the Greeks and Romans it was an eastern metropolis filled with marvels, although it declined in importance in time as a result of the presence of nearby Seleucia (Strabo 16.1.5; Pliny *NH* 6.30.121; Appian *Syr.* 58). The cuneiform tablets present a comparable picture. Nearly all of them have to do with the main temple, Esagila. The administrative texts, which continue into Parthian times (92 BC), give us a good insight into the organisation of the temple. Other texts, chronicles, astronomical diaries, horoscopes, which continued to be composed at least until AD 75 give additional information. There is no sign of Greek gods being revered in Babylon,[4] the temple-organisation was entirely in keeping with Babylonian practices, and was perhaps even reactionary in character, as McEwan concluded (1981b, 184–5). Given this view it is strange that McEwan elsewhere in his book argues that Babylon and Uruk were *poleis* in the Greek sense (ibid. 158). His main arguments are the use of the terms 'Babylonians' and 'Urukaeans' as designations for 'citizens', the existence of an 'assembly of Esagila', as a parallel to the Greek council (*boulê*) and the clan system in Uruk, which is supposed to be roughly the same as the *phylê* system in Greek cities. These institutions were, however, purely Babylonian and not at all the result of Greek influence.

It is necessary, therefore, to take a closer look at the information contained in the cuneiform texts on the government of Babylon. Within the administration of Babylon we have to distinguish between local and royal authorities. The former are represented by the ·*šatammu* (the chief administrator of the temple) and the board called 'the Babylonians, (of) the council of Esagila'. Thus they are in the first place temple authorities, which also appears to be the case from the activities of these persons. In chronicle no. 13b (Grayson 1975a, 283) an unnamed *šatammu* established, according to the written command of the king, a sum of money and sacrificial animals for the offerings to the gods and for a ritual concerning the Seleucid king. In a poorly preserved letter the *šatammu*, Bēl-uṣuršu, settled a question concerning astrologers.[5] In all other texts the *šatammu* acts in accordance with 'the Babylonians, (of) the council of Esagila'. This body, written with the cuneiform signs l ú. u k k i n, was interpreted by von Soden as ˡᵘ*kiništu* = 'Tempelkollegium' ('temple board'), not as *puhru* = 'assembly' as is usually done (*AHw* 480b; 877a; id. 1975, 461; 1977, 89; *CAD* K, 386a; Joannès 1982, 51). He had the following arguments for this reading: first, *puhru* never has the determinative *lú* (indicating a person or profession), while *kiništu* does; second, *puhru* is never written syllabically, while *kiništu* is, in some texts from Uruk. Further arguments might be the addition 'of Esagila' and the existence of a l ú. u k k i n of weavers (*CT* 49, 190:2) and one of exorcists (*CT* 49, 140:9–10; at Cutha, *BRM* I, 88:2). Sometimes single persons are described as *kiništu*, probably meaning membership of that body. In *OECT* IX.61:30 a witness bears the epithet, written syllabically (ˡᵘ*ki-niš-tu*), as does Kephalon in ideographical rendering (ˡᵘUKKIN) in van Dijk, Mayer 1980, 116:4'. As we shall see later, the board was very small, so that it could not have been a popular assembly, as argued

---

4. Except perhaps the Seleucid dynasty: Grayson 1975a, 283 no. 13b:7–8; cf. however Sherwin-White 1983c and van der Spek 1985.
5. *CT* 49, 192:1; the name is not Bēl-ibni (McEwan 1981b, 26) but ᵐu m u n. š e š-*šu* = Bēl-uṣuršu; date: probably some time before 185 SE = 127/126 BC.

by Funck (1984, 281ff). Furthermore, all texts, with one important exception, mentioning the *šatammu* and l ú. u k k i n are concerned with the temple administration. There are two categories of these texts: records of court proceedings in cases where certain persons claim income rights (*CT* 49, 115; 140; 144; 147; 149; Pinches 1890, 132; Lehmann 1892, 332) and letter orders to paymasters ordering the use of certain incomes for payment to temple personnel (*CT* 49, 118; 122= 123=182; 128).[6] To the last category belong three receipts of payments in accordance with such letters (*CT* 49, 132; 168; 170; (179?)). In a late astronomical diary (*LBAT* 516 r.15: 234 SE = 78/7 BC) they act in regard to sacrifices.

The one text in which the *šatammu* and the council of Esagila make statements that do not seem to concern the temple, is the so-called 'Lehmann' or Antiochus II text, partly published by Lehmann in 1892 and still awaiting full publication. It is a copy on clay composed under Antiochus IV (173/2 BC) of an inscribed stele containing a statement by the *šatammu* and council[7] of Esagila made in 236 BC in the reign of Seleucus II. The *šatammu* and council recall a land grant by Antiochus II to his wife Laodice and their sons Seleucus (II) and Antiochus (Hierax), who in turn gave it to 'the Babylonians, the Borsippaeans and Cuthaeans'; on the reverse they state that this land shall belong to all Babylonians, Borsippaeans and Cuthaeans forever. Lehmann's suggestion that the land was made the property of the temple is very doubtful. He argued from reverse l.2,[8] which he translated as 'they (= the Babylonians) declared (the arable land) as temple property'. This interpretation, however, must be wrong. According to the modern dictionaries the expression must mean something like 'Let the Babylonians plead for their own land' (cf. *CAD* 217a; *AHw* 1504b; 157b), which was followed by the plea mentioned above.

Thus the *šatammu* and council of Esagila took action in favour of the entire (?) population of Babylon, Borsippa and Cutha, which seem to have formed one political unit, although Borsippa and Cutha had their own *šatammus*. It seems, therefore, that this board was the highest local political and legal authority of the city and had power outside the temple too. This assumption is corroborated by the fact that neither the chronicles nor the diaries ever mention any other local authorities. It is, thus, unlikely that this is due to the accidental character of the evidence. Furthermore, there are parallels for such a situation. Landsberger (1965, 58–63) argued that the *šatammu* had political power in Neo-Assyrian times (seventh century BC) and in the Seleucid period we have parallels from elsewhere. Judaea was

---

6. *CT* 49, 160 is a contract in dialogue form concerning a lease of the right to administer an offering box, cf. McEwan 1981b, 127–8.
7. The sign must obviously be read LÚ.UKKIN instead of LÚ.SAR.
8. *Babilaia zêre-šu-nu dam-ka-tum li-iz-zak-ru* in Lehmann's transliteration.

governed by the high priest and the Council of Elders, which consisted mainly of priests (Jeremias 1962, 166ff). In the interior of Asia Minor several cities were under the leadership of high priests (e.g. Commana in Pontus: Strabo 12.2.3; Cappaodica: ibid. 5.3).

The autonomy of Babylon seems to have been restricted by several royal officials. In the first place one should mention 'the deputy of Nicanor' who acted together with the *šatammu* and the council (*CT* 49, 118; 122=123=182).[9] The texts in which he appears concern the spending of temple income. Who Nicanor was is not known. In another text (*CT* 49, 117:4) the same (?) Nicanor is mentioned, together with Mnesinous, a judge. The text deals with a complaint (?) by a Babylonian about the spending of money in connection with a letter from a certain Mūrānu, who was a paymaster, and the addressee of the letters mentioned above in which the deputy of Nicanor took action. Nicanor and Mnesinous, who bear Greek names without filiation, were presumably important royal officials, representatives of the central government. Nicanor could have been the satrap of Babylonia, the *epistatês* of Babylon, or the *prostatês* of the temple, Mnesinous a royal judge. The existence of royal judges in Babylon is shown by chronicle no. 13b (Grayson 1975a, 283, 1.9), although in that instance they should probably be regarded as a Babylonian, not Greek, institution (Sherwin-White 1983c).

According to an interesting text from the ninth year of Alexander IV (=308/7 BC) a 'governor of the royal treasury of Babylon' seems to have tried to expropriate the domains of the Ebabbar temple in Larsa.[10] In this he was unsuccessful: the temple's ownership of the land was recognised but the temple had to pay half its yield to the royal treasury. The treasurer was the servant of another 'governor', Intaphernes, whose full title is lost. The compromise agreement was worked out by yet another official of the treasury, whose precise title is also only partly preserved. The cuneiform tablets from the Parthian period also mention some royal officials. In an account-tablet of some cashboxes of the temple of Zamama and Ninlil 1¼ shekel of silver is spent for an offering sheep which was given to 'the governor (*pāhātu*) of Babylon' (date: 94 BC; *CT* 49, 156:12 ˡᵘ*pa-hat E.KI*). This title was possibly the equivalent of the *stratêgos kai epistatês tês poleôs* in an inscription in honour of this functionary (*OGIS* 254). Some support for the equation *pāhātu* = *epistatês* comes from a chronicle (Grayson

9. It is not an additional title of the *šatammu* (McEwan 1981b, 26) but a different person whose name is preserved, Bēl-šunu (*CT* 49, 122:3; 123:3) as noted by Oelsner 1971, 168.

10. Porter 1822, vol.2, pl. 77g:19, ˡᵘNAM *šá* É.LUGAL DIN.TIR.KI; É.LUGAL = *bīt šarri* does not mean 'royal palace' but 'royal taxation office' or 'royal treasury', cf. McEwan 1981b, 138. The tablet is transliterated and translated in van der Spek 1986.

1975a, no. 13 1.5) in which a *pāhātu* of Seleucia is mentioned.[11] That Seleucia had an *epistatês* is confirmed by Polybius 5.48.12.

Two temple officials of the Parthian period seem to have been royal nominees. In a well-known record of a court-proceeding of the *šatammu* and council of Esagila judgment was passed on a claim by the two sons of an astronomer, dated in the reign of the usurper king, Hyspaosines of Characene (127 BC: Pinches 1890, 132; cf. van der Spek 1985, cols. 548–551). The astronomer in question, Itti-Marduk-balaṭu, was also called the 'overseer of the temples', 'over-seer' being rendered by the Iranian word *uppudētu*. It seems that this Itti-Marduk-balaṭu came into the service of Hyspaosines and consequently lost his job as astronomer, so that his sons claimed (with success) the income of their father. Itti-Marduk-balaṭu had yet a third title, *rab banî (ša) muhhi āli*, which is often taken to be a city magistrate, but which was in fact no more than a temple functionary.[12] The Greek equivalent of *uppudētu* was presumably *prostatês*. This title occurs in a letter by an astronomer to one of the sons of Itti-Marduk-balaṭu saying that the latter received, or would receive, one third of his rights to income for 196 SE = 116/115 BC. This income was a part of the 'surplus' (?) of the *prostatês*.[13] In the light of the verdict a few years earlier it would seem that this *prostatês* was none other than Itti-Marduk-balaṭu, the *uppudētu* himself. The *prostatês/uppudētu* probably kept an eye on the properties of the temple, just like Simon, the *prostatês* in Jerusalem (2 Macc. 3.4) and the *prostatai* in Egypt (Preisigke 1931, 111:150).

The conclusion we may draw from the cuneiform tablets is that the temple in Babylon was governed by a *šatammu* and a council, and that this board formed, in fact, the highest local authority in the city as it also had power in civil matters. On the other hand royal officials, some of whom were Greek, some of Babylonian extraction, represented the central government and limited the autonomy of Babylon. Greek civic institutions are not attested.

The archaeological remains of the hellenistic period from Babylon show us a generally Babylonian city with some limited Greek influence (Schmidt 1941; Wetzel, Schmidt, Mallwitz 1957; Oelsner 1978; Sherwin-White above). The restoration of Esagila, ordered by Alexander and completed by Antiochus I, was carried out in traditional style. Houses were built in the local style, though one house has been found with a peristyle (Colledge 1977, 54). Since this

---

11. ᵐ*se-lu-ku* ˡᵘ*pa-hat* [ᵘʳᵘ*se-lu-ki-'-ia ana muh-hi* ᶦᵈIDI]GNA *u* ᶠD.LUGAL; the equivalent of the *epistatês* may, however, have been the *šaknu* (as in Uruk, see p. 71); note that a *šaknu*, possibly in Babylon, is attested in Grayson 1975a no.12, obv.7.
12. There are texts concerning rations for this group of persons, cf. Joannès 1982, 332–4. According to *CT* 49, 124:2 and 125:2 there was a paymaster of the *rab banîs*.
13. McEwan 1981a, 140–1 (*AB* 247:4); *i-tur* perhaps from the substantive *utru* 'surplus', 'extra income'; cf. *Nbn.* 169:22; *BE* VIII 51:8; *TCL* XII 40; *CT* 55, 306:17; 57, 124:4 (suggestion of M. Stol, Amsterdam).

house stood in an otherwise entirely Babylonian area within the city, it may have belonged to a more or less hellenised member of the indigenous élite. Some Greek influence is detectable in the royal palace (Oelsner 1978, 105), which must be the result of its occupation by Greek authorities and Alexander himself. Typically Greek, of course, is the theatre. The date of the building is difficult to establish. According to Mallwitz it was built in the days of Alexander and provided with a proscenium in the middle of the second century BC, while new additions were made later in the Parthian period as late as the second century AD (ap. Wetzel, Schmidt, Mallwitz 1957, 19–22). Greek ceramics, dating from the Mycenaean to the late hellenistic period, have been found, but this may reflect commercial connections with the Greek world rather than Greek occupation (but see Salles, below pp. 86–7). It is not surprising that Greek objects should be more numerous after the Macedonian conquest of Babylon (Wetzel, Schmidt, Mallwitz 1957, 51–8). The Greek inscriptions are, of course, indicators of some kind of Greek influence. I shall consider this evidence in the next section.

## Royal policy towards Babylon

Alexander the Great planned to make Babylon the capital of his empire (Strabo 15.2.10; Q.C. 5.1.42; Arrian *Anab.* 3.16.4; 7.17.2), which does not mean that he wanted to turn it into a Greek city, but rather that as heir to the Persian empire, a centrally located capital for his conquests was essential. He would probably have wished to embellish the city with Greek buildings, such as a gymnasium, or a theatre (as he may actually have done), but the Babylonian character of the city was to be retained by the rebuilding of Esagila in local style and the maintenance of Babylonian institutions. He would certainly have given the Greek inhabitants, who would have flocked to the new capital, citizen rights but these rights would not have been so important in a city where the king resided as he would have wished to limit the autonomy of a royal capital. The same was true of Alexandria under the Ptolemies (Fraser 1972, 99–100), Antioch under the Seleucids (Downey 1961, 112–18) and Pergamum under the Attalids (Rostovtzeff 1923; Allen 1983, 158–77).

Alexander died too soon to carry out his plan, but the idea of Babylon as one of the capitals of Asia was not immediately abandoned. The kings Philip Arrhidaeus and Alexander IV, and the regent Perdiccas, resided in Babylon until Perdiccas' death and the ensuing conference at Triparadisus (320 BC), when the kings were taken to Macedon by Antipater. The Asian part of the empire was under the control of Antigonus the One-eyed, the general of Asia, who entered Babylon in 316 BC and drove out the satrap, Seleucus. Antigonus also seems to have regarded Babylon as at least the capital of Asia, and wanted control of it. When Seleucus returned in 311 BC, Antigonus only surrendered his claims to Babylon after years of fighting in and near the city, which must have suffered extensively as a result of the warfare (Grayson 1975a, no. 10, rev.). But restoration work on Esagila was resumed by Seleucus and probably completed by Antiochus I (see Sherwin-White, above p. 28).

In 306/5 BC a new era began for Babylonia. Alexander's dynasty was at an end and the successors took royal titles. Until 306/5 Babylonian tablets continued to be dated by Alexander IV even after his death, but in that year a new dating system was introduced, the Seleucid Era, which reckoned as its starting point Seleucus' capture of Babylon in 311 BC (cf. Joannès 1979–80). This shows that Babylonia was seen as the centre of Seleucus' empire although he built new capitals, Seleucia-Tigris, Seleucia-Pieria and Antioch-Orontes. In this respect he may have wished to emulate the other successors who built royal capitals (Alexandria, Antigonia, Cassandria, Lysimachia). Whatever the reason, Seleucia was favoured at the expense of Babylon. The new city was populated with Greek settlers, but also with Babylonians. According to Pausanias 1.16.3, Seleucus I moved part of the Babylonian population to Seleucia and later in 273 BC Antiochus did the same, as attested by a Babylonian astronomical diary (Smith 1924, 155: 17–19; Austin 1981 no. 141). Both kings registered some Babylonian arable land as royal land, presumably as a consequence of these 'deportations'.[14] On the other hand, Babylon was not abandoned or destroyed in the way that Seleucus had demolished Antigonus' foundation, Antigonia near Antioch (Strabo 16.2.4). Pausanias (1.16.3) praised Seleucus for leaving 'the Chaldaeans' in Babylon. Esagila's restoration continued until the days of Antiochus I (Pritchard 1969, 317; Austin 1981 no.189). Thus Babylon remained a centre of Babylonian civilisation, while Seleucia was to function as the representative of the new order. This did not mean that Babylon suffered particularly: Antiochus I gave land to the Babylonians in the first year of his reign (although this was taken back in his sixth year (Smith 1924, 155: 17–19; Austin 1981, no.141; cf. Sherwin-White, above p. 19)[15]), Antiochus II gave expropriated land to his wife Laodice and her sons, who bestowed it on the Babylonians, Borsippaeans and Cuthaeans, which was then presumably reckoned as their private property under Seleucus II.[16]

Antiochus IV (175–164) seems actively to have fostered a colonising policy in Babylonia as he did in Media (Ecbatana) and Syria (Hamath).

---

14. Cf. Lehmann 1892, 330:4 'everything that Antiochus (I), his (= Antiochus II) father, and Seleucus (I), his grandfather, had registered as the arable land of their own house'; cf. van der Spek 1986.
15. For the correct dates, cf. Otto 1928; the events refer to year 38 SE.
16. The 'Lehmann Text', cf. above n.14; the text is discussed in van der Spek 1986.

He did not, however, turn Babylon into a Greek *polis* as has often been suggested. Babylon continued to be primarily a non-Greek city with traditional Babylonian government, although a Greek colony was established there, when by the late second century a gymnasium and agora are attested. This hypothesis cannot be proved, but a great deal of circumstantial evidence makes the suggestion tenable. At the end of the last century a Greek inscription (*OGIS* 253; cf. Bunge 1976) was purchased from a dealer in Baghdad, who declared that he had found the stone between Jumjuma (near Babylon) and Birs-Nimrud (Bersippa). It is therefore generally attributed to Babylon, but Köhler (1900, 1105) and, more recently, Sherwin-White (1982, 65f) have questioned the attribution. Their doubts are sound, but a provenance from Babylon is not impossible and Köhler's argument, that the dealer had named Babylon to give the stone value and because of the excavations at Babylon by the *Deutsche Orientgesellschaft, can* also be taken as an argument in favour of such an origin: i.e. the dealer could have purchased the inscription from a labourer on the excavations. The text is a dedication by a certain Philippos, son of Di[?. . .], probably a Greek, to Antiochus IV Epiphanes, who is called 'saviour of Asia and founder (*ktistês*) of the *polis*' in the date formula (146 SE = 167/6 BC), and mentions games and thank-offerings which *possibly* refer to the *pompê* at Daphne, as is assumed by Bunge 1976. But since Daphne is not mentioned in the text we cannot be certain of this. The expression '*ktistês* of the *polis*' in honorary inscriptions could be used in a variety of senses. It could refer to the founding of a city, but also to royal iniatives in building operations or other favours bestowed on the city (Le Rider 1965). In this instance it might refer to the foundation of a Greek community and some restoration of the theatre in Babylon. In the last line of the inscription mention is made of the year 144 SE, 169/8 BC according to Greek reckoning, which might have something to do with the offering or with Antiochus' victory in Egypt, as a result of which he was called saviour of Asia.

It is tempting to connect this Greek inscription with a Babylonian astronomical diary of the year 169/8 (= July to November 143 SE according to Babylonian reckoning), which was given in translation only by Pinches (1902, 480–1), but which can now be presented in transliteration, thanks to the courtesy of H. Hunger, Vienna. The relevant lines (15–16) are:

ᵐ*an* LUGAL *ina* u r u. m e š *šá* k u r *me-luh-ha šal-ta-niš* DU.DU-*ma* [. . .]
ˡᵘ*pu-li-ṭe-e pu-up-pe-e u ép-še-e-tú šá* GIM *ú-ṣur-tú ia-a-man-nu* x [. . .

King Antiochus entered victoriously into the cities of Egypt [. . .]
The *politai* [established] a *pompê* and a ritual (?)[17] according to a Greek design [. . .

17. Perhaps *panêgyris*; for a *pompê* as part of a *panêgyris* in Daphne, cf. Polybius

In my opinion this text refers to an activity of the Greek population in favour of Antiochus, the founder of their community, on the occasion of his victory during his first campaign against Egypt – his failure during his second one, in 168 BC, as a result of Roman intervention was not known at that time. It cannot refer to the *pompê* in Daphne which was held two years later.[18] *Pompê* is the usual Greek word for processions conducted in connection with religious festivals of Greek cities, normally accompanied by games, and in hellenistic times often held in honour of rulers. The Greek character of this *pompê* and ritual (?) was remarked upon by the Babylonians.

Although *politês* in itself can mean any citizen with citizen rights, in Babylonian terminology it seems to have been the designation for Greek or hellenised citizens. This supposition is corroborated by another astronomical diary of 234 SE (= 78/7 BC), according to which 'the *šatammu* of Esagila and the Babylonians' made an offering of two bulls and two sheep (*LBAT* 516: 15'), while the *politai* were fighting one another in the neighbourhood of a temple (ibid. 16'). Another peculiarity in the occurrence of *puliṭe* in the diaries can be observed. The word does not occur before 140 SE (= 172/1 BC).[19] Thus it seems that it indeed may have been Antiochus IV who introduced the *politai* into Babylon.[20] The date of this could be 139 SE (= 173/2 BC), the date of the Lehmann tablet mentioned above (n.14). This tablet was a copy of a stone slab dated 75 SE = 236 BC on which the rights of property on Babylonian territory had been requested and, presumably, accorded. The reason for the Babylonians making the copy may have been the king's desire to expropriate land in favour of the colonists, which would have been disputed by the Babylonian citizens.

The other evidence for Greek inhabitants in Babylon itself also points to the later period. Greek personal names in cuneiform tablets tend to occur in the earlier part of the third century or after 151 SE = 161 BC. These Greek names are evidence of Greek influence in the Babylonian community. The majority of people known with Greek names were certainly Babylonians, such as 'Marduk-erība, whose second name is Heliodorus' (*CT* 49, 138:5–6; 111:4; 118:6; 130:2; 138:9).

---

30.25.2; D.S. 31.16.1.

18. Some connection with the celebrations at Daphne was suggested to me by Gilbert McEwan who was worried by the dates of the diary. The only possible solutions are either that the diary is wrongly dated (which is extremely unlikely) or deals with preparations for the *pompê* in Daphne, as people from all over the inhabited world were invited. In that case the festivals celebrated by Aemilius Paulus after his victory over the Macedonians in 168 BC would not have inspired Antiochus' displays.

19. I owe this information to H. Hunger, Vienna, who is editing all the astronomical diaries.

20. Oelsner forthcoming, ch.3 had arrived independently at the same conclusion.

Many of them have fathers with purely Babylonian names.[21] The only persons who were certainly Greeks are Nicanor (see above p. 63), Nicostratus (*CT* 49, 29d) and Mnesinous (see above p. 63), who, however, were not Babylonians at all but representatives of the central government. Nicostratus did not even live in Babylon. Only three other persons appear who might be Greek; they are: Satyrus, son of Demias (undated tablet, *CT* 49, 193:23), Xenon, messenger of the governor of Babylonia (Parthian period, McEwan 1981a, 132–4: AB 244: 18), and Marion, an architect (Parthian period, *CT* 49, 154:14; 155:9; 157:8). This scarcity of Greeks in the tablets is quite understandable in the light of the fact that cuneiform material belonged to the Babylonian community. Some Babylonians, like Marduk-erība/ Heliodorus, might have become members of the Greek community.

The surviving Greek inscriptions present *mutatis mutandis* the same picture. They are all late, most of them Parthian (*OGIS* 253 is in fact the earliest), except one, the Ballarus-ostracon, which dates from the very beginning of Macedonian rule (Sherwin-White 1982). Finally, the archaeological evidence suggests building activity in Greek style in the same periods, the third century and later second century BC.

All these arguments taken together suggest that Babylon continued as a traditional Mesopotamian city with its own institutions. Because of the foundation of Seleucia-Tigris no colonisation appears to have taken place until the days of Antiochus IV. This colony did not affect Babylonian institutions. In the period between Seleucus I and Antiochus IV some Greeks may have lived in Babylon (perhaps without citizen rights). Dromon, son of Phanodemus, 'the Babylonian',

---

21. Temple personnel with Greek names and no patronymic were probably Babylonians not Greeks (cf. Zadok 1979):

Si-x-x-ar-su (=?), parchment scribe of Ti-du-... (=Theodoros?): *CT* 49, 5:7–8 (year 9 of Alexander III or IV)

La-mi-in-ni-' (= Laomenes) from Borsippa: *CT* 49, 54:3; 70:3; 89:3 (no date, Antigonus?)

Du-ru-um-mu (= Dromos/Dromon?), has a daughter and son-in-law with Semitic names: *CT* 49, 111:4 (42 SE)

Ti-bu-li-su (= Theoboulos?), son of Iddin-Bēl: *CT* 49, 118:6 (50 SE)

Ni²-ka²-nu-u-ru (= Nikanor?), son of Bēl-bulissu: *CT* 49, 130:2 (63 SE)

E-ru-tu-us (= Erotios), son of Marduk-*eriba*?: *CT* 49, 138:9 (151 SE)

E-ra-ak-li-de-e (= Herakleides): *CT* 49, 146:13 (209 SE)

Su-si-pa-tu-ru-us (= Sosipatros): *CT* 49, 150:38 (218 SE)

A-pu-ul-lu-du-ru-us (= Apollodoros) from Cutha: *CT* 49, 187:3' (no date)

As-ta-pa-nu (= Stephanos?): *CT* 49, 178:5' (no date, but 'staters of Antiochus' mentioned)

Di-pa-an-tu-us-su (= Diophantos) from Cutha: *CT* 49, 187:2' (no date)

It seems to me that the badly transliterated names are early and the clearly written ones late. That would suggest a late date for *CT* 49, 187 (Apollodoros and Diaphantos).

mentioned in an inscription from Andros of the third century BC was
perhaps one of these (*IG* XII.715; cf. Sherwin-White 1982, 67f.).

## Uruk

The situation in Uruk displays both similarities to and differences
from Babylon. Like Babylon, Uruk continued to function as a Mesopotamian community with the temple as its central institution. The
cuneiform tablets show us that the highest local authorities were those
of the temple, namely a temple-council headed by an administrative
official. This official was not called *šatammu* as in Babylon and pre-
hellenistic Uruk, but *rab ša rēš āli* (*ša bīt ilāni*) (*ša Uruk*), 'the leader
of the *ša-rēš-āli*s (of the temples) (of Uruk)'.[22] The meaning of this
title is difficult to establish.[23] The only profitable approach is to look
at the function of the *rab-ša-rēš-āli* which appears to be comparable
to that of the *šatammu* in Babylon. The fact that there was no longer
a *šatammu* in Uruk supports the view that the *rab-ša-rēš-āli* had
taken over the function of the *šatammu* of Eanna (temple of Ishtar)
of pre-hellenistic Uruk. As a result of a little understood change in
religious practice at Uruk Anu, the sky-god, had become the principal
deity in the late Achaemenid period, as shown by his preponderant
position in personal names there (Oelsner 1978, 103; 1981, 44; Kessler
1984a). The *šatammu* of Eanna, then, was replaced by the *rab-ša-rēš-
āli* (of the temples) and the *kiništu* of Eanna was replaced by the
'*kiništu* of the temples' or 'of the Reš-sanctuary'. All texts in which
the *rab-ša-rēš-āli* and council occur deal with temple property: temple
slaves and income connected with the holding of temple offices, often
called prebends. They acted as a court of justice and checked the
performance of duties connected with 'prebends' (Doty 1977, 15–18;
*BRM* II 17; 47; *OECT* IX 62).[24] That the *kiništu* was a small board and
not a popular assembly is proved by the record of a court proceeding
concerning a temple slave, published by Doty (1977, 15–18). 'The

22. *TCL* VI 1:57; Falkenstein 1941, 6–8; Sarkisian 1974b no. 23:12; *OECT* IX 42:6–7;
    Sarkisian 1982, 335 n.9, A 3678; *OECT* IX 62:28 (cf. McEwan 1981b, 68–71); *BRM*
    II 47:2 (the reading ᴸᵁ[SAG URU] – *i* seems certain in view of the parallel in *OECT*
    IX 62; Funck's reading (1984, 100), ᴸᵁGA[L.MEŠ *ša* É.]DINGIR.MEŠ is wrong and thus
    also his conclusions regarding this line (ibid. 280)).
23. There was a *hadru* (community of military fief-holders) of *ša-rēš-āli*s in Achaemenid
    Nippur (*TBER* pl. 51: AO 17641 = Joannès 1982, 38–9 no.2) and a council (lú.
    u k k i n) of *ša-rēš-āli*s in Seleucid Larsa, which dealt with the sale of a share of
    temple-income connected with rituals for the goddess Aja (*OECT* IX 26:13, 18). The
    literal meaning is something like 'city-heads'; but this must surely be misleading
    as it is hard to imagine that the 'city-heads' of Nippur were organised in a *hadru*.
    In this respect Oppenheim's (1949) discussion of the term *arad ekalli*, literally
    'palace slave', but in fact, 'builder', 'labourer' is instructive.
24. In Sarkisian 1955 no.8 it is the *paqdu* who acts with the council, see below pp.
    71–2.

council of the freemen' (l ú. u k k i n ˡᵘ*mār banî*) consisted only of 12 men, all mentioned by name. Although the board need not be complete, twelve is a small number for a popular assembly and the recording of the members name by name is certainly unusual for assemblies. Another remarkable feature of the list of names is that, of the members, only *two* had ancestral designations. It indicates that it was not necessary to claim an ancestor in order to be a free man or citizen.

That the *kiništu* was a small body is also apparent from a text of the fifth year of Cyrus (534 BC), in which it made a decision in respect of the admission of someone's adoptive son to the *ēreb-bītūtu* 'prebend' of the goddess Kanišurra (San Nicolò 1934, 48:15–16). The *kiništu* (written syllabically ˡᵘ*ki-niš-ti* É.AN.NA) consisted of seventeen members, all mentioned by name and subsumed as 'the *ēreb-bīti*, the headmen, the brewers, the bakers, the butchers, the Babylonians and Urukaeans of the *kiništu* of Eanna'. This looks like the phrase 'the Babylonians (of) the council of Esagila' in the texts from Babylon. It seems that the *kiništu* of Eanna, Esagila or Uruk (or the Reš-sanctuary) was a central temple-board with representatives of lower boards, such as the board of the weavers (*CT* 49, 190 (Babylon)) and of exorcists (*CT* 49, 140 (Babylon); *BRM* I 88 (Cutha)).[25] The formulation of the text of Cyrus' fifth year just mentioned suggests the same. The small size of the *kiništu* is further suggested by the epithet which some people (without clan-affiliation) bear, i.e. 'from the *kiništu* (written syllabically) of the temples' or 'the Reš-sanctuary' (*BRM* II 41:24, 32; 46:29; 47:3, 36; 48:14, 23; 50:1; Speleers 1925, 295:1; Sarkisian 1952, 71f.; 1955, 146 no.3:3).[26] That the board of the *rab-ša-rēš-āli* and *kiništu* was in the first place a temple institution is clear from the sources. Nevertheless, just like Babylon, Uruk does not seem to have had other city institutions so that this board also might have had civil authority. The *rab-ša-rēš-āli* was apparently the most important man in Uruk. The descendants of Anu-uballiṭ-Kephalon in the third generation were proud that their forefather bore the title (Sarkisian 1974b no.23:12). Anu-uballiṭ himself is known as the restorer of the Reš-sanctuary from building inscriptions (Falkenstein 1941, 6–8).

But, as in Babylon, the royal government had its officials and representatives in Uruk too. In the first place the *šaknu* (governor) should be mentioned; *šaknu* and *bēl-pīhāti* were in the Neo-Assyrian empire the regular terms for royal governors and in hellenistic Uruk the term seems to be used in the same way. The *šaknu* of Uruk was apparently an institution analogous to that of the *pāhātu* (or *šaknu*,

25. The witnesses called *bēl piqitti* in the text from Cutha seem to be the presidents of the lower *kiništu*s.
26. In *OECT* IX 61:30 a witness is simply called ˡᵘ*ki-niš-tu₄*; cf. ᴸᵁUKKIN in van Dijk, Mayer 1980, 116:4' as an epithet of Kephalon.

see n.11) of Babylon. The only *šaknu* we know of is Anu-uballiṭ who had received from Antiochus II his second name Nicarchus. His Greek title was probably *epistatês* (*YOS* I 52; Falkenstein 1941, 4–5; cf. Doty 1977, 24).

The second important royal representative was the *paqdu*, the deputy of the temples of Uruk. He seems to have exercised control over the exploitation of temple property, since we know him *inter alia* as the lessor of temple land in a lease contract (Sarkisian 1974b no.1).[27] Sarkisian 1982 had the idea that the *paqdu* and *rab-ša-rēš-āli* were in fact the same (the father of Anu-uballiṭ-Kephalon bore both titles: cf. Doty 1977, 22–5), but this view is now disproved by a new text according to which Kephalon was *rab-ša-rēš-āli* and his brother *paqdu* (*OECT* IX 42:6–7). The *paqdu* of hellenistic Uruk was presumably the continuation of the *rēš šarri bēl piqitti Eanna*, 'the royal commissioner, the deputy of Eanna' of the Neo-Babylonian and Achaemenid period (San Nicolò 1941, 9; 18–20) and had his equivalent in Babylon in the deputy of Nicanor and the *uppudētu* (*prostatês*) of Parthian times. This functionary was in the first place a temple-official as is evident from the addition 'of the temples' which is sometimes made (Sarkisian 1955 no. 8: 20–2; 1974b, 16; 29; 39; 51).[28] Other royal officials are attested by their Greek titles. The *dioikêtês* was the director of the royal office (*bīt šarri*) who registered the sales of rations of the temple personnel. The registration was probably connected with the Seleucid sales tax (*BRM* II 31:7; cf. Doty 1977, 259). The *chreô-phylax* was certainly a fiscal officer. His duties have been described by Rostovtzeff 1932 and Doty 1977, 316–35; 1979 (cf. McEwan 1982).

The conclusion we must draw from the cuneiform material is that the society of Uruk showed few signs of Greek influence. There is no indication that Uruk tried to behave like a Greek city. There is no trace of magistrates, council and popular assembly of a Greek type, despite efforts by Sarkisian, McEwan and Funck to find them. The clan system is quite un-Greek, but typical of some Near Eastern societies (cf. the clan-affiliations in Ezra 2), and has nothing to do with the 'tribes' (*phylai*) in Greek cities. There is no sign of Greek gods being revered in Uruk. The rituals and temple organisation were very traditional. Contracts were drawn up in accordance with Babylonian legal practices. The Reš-sanctuary was restored in typical Mesopotamian style (see Colledge, below pp. 145–6). Some slight Greek influence can be discerned in the adoption of Greek names by Urukaeans. Members of the family of Anu-uballiṭ-Kephalon especially

27. Funck's idea (1984, 281) that the *paqdu* was the *epistatês* is certainly wrong. It was a temple function as Funck himself admits. It is not likely that an *epistatês* would act as lessor of temple-territory.

28. Cf. *tetagmenos epi tôn hierôn* in Apollonia/Salbake in Caria; Robert 1954, 285 no. 166:13.

chose Greek names, as this family filled the higher positions in Uruk and because the mother of Kephalon was possibly Greek. Some of the persons with Greek names might actually have been Greeks. Sarkisian 1974a and Doty 1977, 155 assume that people with a Greek name and Greek patronymic but no clan affiliation were indeed Greeks. This is of course possible but not certain. It is to be expected that Urukaeans who chose a Greek name also gave their children Greek names, and, as we know (see above p. 71), not every citizen of Uruk had a clan affiliation. Thus, it is hazardous to infer a Greek-Urukaean 'civic and temple community' from the Greek names in the contracts, as Sarkisian does. Yet one might defend the hypothesis that Uruk had a Greek community like Babylon had. But the indications are scanty: no Greek inscriptions, no *puliṭē*, no Greek buildings, such as a theatre. The only evidence we have for the existence of a Greek community in Uruk is a cuneiform tablet of year 41 SE (270 BC) from 'Antioch-on-the-Ishtar-canal' (NCBT 1942:20 = Doty 1977, 193–4). Since the principals and the scribe of the contract are known people from Uruk with Babylonian names and since Uruk was situated on the Ishtar canal, this Antioch may have been the alternative name of Uruk for a while, but perhaps more generally used by Greek inhabitants (van der Spek 1980, 254a). This would explain the fact that this name only occurs once in cuneiform (the name 'Uruk' may have been erased in 1.19). The Greeks perhaps called themselves Antiochians in Uruk, for which parallels are known from other cities as well, e.g. Susa-Seleucia on the Eulaeus, Gaza-Seleucia (cf. Bickerman 1937, 62; Briant 1982b); the same may have been true for Uruk/Orcha[29] and Antioch. It is of course possible that the Urukaeans themselves chose Antioch as an alternative name, as the inhabitants of Jerusalem did in the days of Antiochus IV, but that practice seems to be late. We should recall that Greek names in Uruk occur with any frequency only during the reign of Antiochus III and later (Sarkisian 1974a) and that the earliest is the governor Anu-uballiṭ-Nicarchus in an inscription from 68 SE (244 BC) (*YOS* I 52; Falkenstein 1941, 4–5). A possible date for the introduction of a Greek community may have been 38 SE (274/3 BC), a year which was very eventful for Babylonia. It suffered severely from the first Syrian war, as we learn from the astronomical diary (Smith 1924, 154–7; Austin 1981 no.141). This text also informs us about the 'deportation' of Babylonians to Seleucia and the expropriation of arable land. Doty has demonstrated that in Uruk no sales of arable land and of slaves were recorded in cuneiform after that year. He argued that this was caused by the introduction of new taxes (Doty 1977, 308–35). Perhaps there was even more at stake in Uruk: arable

---

29. The name is apparently not Orchoi as usually assumed; most of the graecised names have neuter plurals ending in -*a*, e.g. Borsippa, Sousa, Doura, Koutha, Arbela.

land may have been expropriated in favour of the newcomers, and landed property had now to be treated in accordance with Greek law (but see Sherwin-White, above p. 27).

## Other cities

Not much cuneiform material of this period survives from other Babylonian cities. There is only a handful of texts from Ur (*UET* IV, 43), Larsa (*BRM* II 51:15 (ᵁᴰ¹.UNUG.KI); *OECT* IX 26; Porter 1822 pl.77g), Kish (Langdon, Watelin 1930, 20 no. 159), Marad (*CT* 49, 169), Cutha (*BRM* I 88; *CT* 49, 131) and Borsippa (*CT* 49, 7–9; 187). Cutha had a *šatammu* and a temple-council (*BRM* I 88:3; Grayson 1975a no.10, rev.5) and Larsa a *kiništu* (LÚ.UKKIN: *OECT* IX 26:13 and 8; Porter 1822 pl. 77g:15–16, 20: LÚ.UKKIN *ša* É.BABBAR.RA), so it seems that in these cities too Babylonian forms of government prevailed.

## Conclusion

The question, was Babylon (or Uruk) a *polis*, is, to my mind, irrelevant; it is more profitable to study the pattern of city-life in these places. The ancient Babylonian cities followed their own traditional life, religion and institutions. Some families, like the Ahûtu-clan in Uruk, seem to have adopted a thin veneer of hellenism, possibly because they were involved in the government of the city and therefore chose Greek names and perhaps learnt the Greek language in order to be able to communicate with the central government. On the other hand they did not try to adapt their institutions to Greek customs. No doubt local people gradually adopted some Greek manners, but as long as the temple existed it determined the city life of the indigenous people. Possibly an increasing number of Babylonians became *politai* and were therefore allowed to attend the games in the gymnasium. In that case the list of winners in a Greek inscription (Schmidt 1941, 816–19) might contain Babylonians with Greek names (but cf. Sherwin-White 1982).

Old traditions were only very slowly abandoned. The cuneiform texts, so far known, continue to AD 75. In Uruk, even after the destruction of the Reš-sanctuary in the Parthian period, the dedicator of a piece of land to the god Gareus, mentioned in an inscription in Greek of 422 SE = AD 110 (*Nouveau Choix d'inscriptions grecques*, 168 no.33), bore a Greek name (Artemidorus son of Diogenes), as well as a Babylonian one, Minnanaios, son of Touphaios. The name Min-Nanaia is attested in a cuneiform tablet (Doty 1977, 87 = YBC 11633:4).

Thus the conclusion must be that Babylonian cities were only superficially hellenised and did not acquire Greek civic institutions, although they had representatives of the central government. The Greeks, as far as present evidence goes, seem to have had their own separate communities.

CHAPTER FOUR

# The Arab-Persian Gulf under the Seleucids*

## Jean-François Salles

The attempt to write a history of the Arab-Persian Gulf in the Seleucid period seems, at first sight, an almost impossible task: nothing suggests that the region was under the direct control of the Seleucid kings, nor is there any clear evidence that it formed part of their area of influence. Apart from stories concerning Alexander's *Anabasis* and Nearchus' return voyage from India by sea, there are only two texts that explicitly refer to the Gulf (or Erythrean Sea) during the Seleucid period.[1] Even these only make mention of brief incursions into the Gulf and give no support to the notion that the area was either conquered or subject to any form of effective domination. Yet the area was not an uncharted desert. Scattered references in classical authors[2] provide occasional information on some of the Gulf sites. These concern almost exclusively those located on the Arabian side – apart from Nearchus'

* This paper has been made possible thanks to a generous grant from the British Academy, which allowed me to participate in the Seleucid Seminar held at the Institute of Classical Studies, the University of London, Autumn 1984, and to complete some research in the United Kingdom. I would like to express my deepest thanks to Mr P. H. Brown, Secretary of the British Academy, to Averi! Cameron, Amélie Kuhrt and Susan Sherwin-White who organised my visit, to M. Crawford (Cambridge, now London), G. W. Forrest (Oxford), P. Parr (London) and many other colleagues for their kind and friendly welcome. The English version of this paper has been prepared by Huguette Salles and revised by Amélie Kuhrt and Susan Sherwin-White.
1. Polyb. 13.9.2–5: 'The Gerrhaeans begged the king not to abolish the gifts the gods had bestowed on them, perpetual peace and freedom. The king, when the letter had been interpreted to him, said that he granted their request . . . When their freedom had been established, the Gerrhaeans passed a decree honouring Antiochus with the gift of five hundred talents of silver, a thousand talents of frankincense, and two hundred talents of the so-called "stacte". He then sailed to the island of Tylus and left for Seleucia. The spices were from the Persian Gulf.' Pliny, *NH* 6.32.152: 'A cape in their territory points towards Carmania. A remarkable event is said to have occurred there: the governor of Mesene appointed by King Antiochus, Numenius, here won a battle against the Persians with his fleet and after the tide had gone out a second battle with his cavalry, and set up a couple of trophies, to Jupiter and to Neptune, on the same spot.'
2. For the United Arab Emirates see Pliny *NH* 6.32.149; for Tylus/Bahrain, Calvet 1984b; for Eastern Arabia, Pliny *NH* 6.32.159; for Icarus/Failaka, Calvet 1984a.

journey, the Persian side of the Gulf is virtually *terra incognita* both in the ancient sources and in terms of archaeological exploration. Both older and some more recent finds help to compensate for the sparsity of textual evidence for the Arabian side.

The term 'hellenistic' is used by Gulf archaeologists to define a very long time-span, until the advent of Islam; it has, therefore, been necessary to select what might be assigned to the Seleucid period from an extensive and varied body of material. It is important to remember that most of the finds come from surface surveys, sometimes from small soundings, and only rarely from regular excavations. This archaeological evidence shows a relatively extensive settlement pattern on a number of sites, albeit not comparable in size to Babylon or Susa. Furthermore, intense economic activity is attested by objects imported from, among other places, Mesopotamia and the Eastern Mediterranean. By exercising due caution one can also make use of written and archaeological sources from earlier and later periods. It should thus be possible to draw some inferences about the Seleucid Gulf from what is known about it in the Neo-Assyrian, Neo-Babylonian and Achaemenid periods on the one hand (Lombard 1985) and from what the Greek and Latin authors of the Roman Empire say about it on the other. It is, however, important to note that the latter, like all their predecessors save Polybius, derive their information from the same late fourth-, third- and second-century sources: i.e. Nearchus, Androsthenes of Thasos, Aristobulus, Agatharchides.

It thus seems best first to describe briefly the results of recent archaeological research in the Gulf, amplifying them wherever possible with the ancient written evidence. It will then be necessary to consider what interests the Seleucids might have been pursuing in the Gulf which determined their policy. Finally, it will be possible to obtain a better understanding of the probable character of the so-called 'Hellenistic' settlements in the Gulf.

## 1. The archaeological finds
(al-Wohaibi 1980; Boucharlat and Salles 1981; 1984; see Fig. 1)

In spite of some shared physical features in the region extending from the Shatt al-Arab to the straits of Hormuz (see Fig. 1), the Arab side of the Gulf does not constitute a homogeneous entity. As a result, over the millennia human settlement has tended to be restricted to certain prime areas: the Omani mountains, the island of Bahrain, the oases and coastal sites. Around the end of the first millennium BC, only two areas appear to have been entirely uninhabited: the region which extends between Abu Dhabi and the Qatar peninsula (*sabkha* Matti), and the north-eastern coast of Arabia from Jubayl to Kuwait.

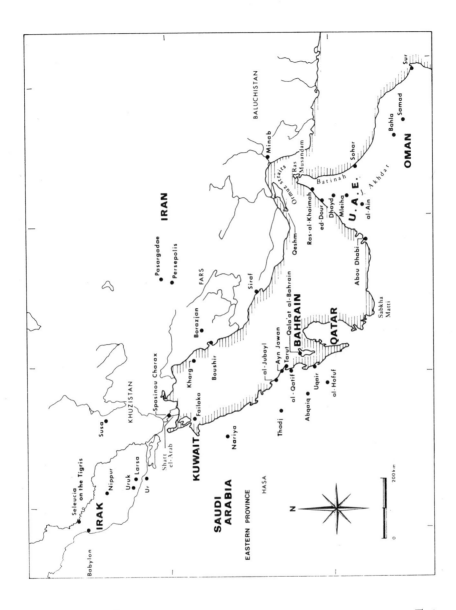

Fig. 1. Archaeological
sites in the Gulf area

1.i. *The Omani peninsula* (Boucharlat 1984; Salles 1978/9). This is probably the area most favourable to human settlement. East of Jebel Akhdar, a mountain range, the narrow coastal plain (the Batinah) offers a number of sheltered spots for harbours as well as being suitable for agricultural exploitation thanks to rainfall. It controls the main sea-routes of the Indian Ocean to the Indian sub-continent[3] and South Arabia.[4] At the western foot of the mountain range are rich oases, well-watered by the rains trapped in the mountains: Dhayd, Mleihah/al-Madam, Buraimi/al-Ain, Bat and others. In the south are a number of transverse valleys rich in archaeological remains, such as Wadi Bahla and Wadi Samad; the reason for this being the copper deposits which provided one of the main sources of wealth in the region during the third millennium BC and in the Islamic period (Weisgerber 1980; 1981; Cleuziou 1978/9). The Gulf coast, which is separated from the mountain range by a stretch of sand dunes, is arid and inhospitable, except in the north where the mountains adjoin the sea near Ras al-Khaimah. Despite this, human settlement appears to be very ancient here (Boucharlat et al. 1984).[5]

Rather surprisingly, the Omani peninsula does not appear to have been much inhabited in the Seleucid period, whereas it was an important centre in the third and second millennium BC and again played an active part at the beginning of the Islamic period.

The hellenistic settlement pattern may be summed up as follows:
—sparse remains in the Batinah where a few surface sherds may date from the third or second century BC; no trace of an important site has been found (Humphries 1974);[6]
—in the valleys of the interior such as Wadi Samad (Vogt 1984) and in some of the oases situated at the foot of the mountain range (al-Ain?, Mleihah) (Boucharlat *et al.* 1984; Madhloom 1974; Salles 1978/9) traces of a local culture have been found;
—along the Gulf coast there are a few sites, the most important of which is ed-Dour, about fifty kilometres from Dubai (al-Qaisy 1975; Salles 1978/9; 1980; 1984b). This was, by comparison with other local sites, a large settlement. It is now situated in the sand dunes but was

3. A Harappan trading post dated to the beginning of the second millennium BC has been discovered on the Omani coast at Ras al-Junayz (Tosi 1986; 1983, 19). People whose original homeland was India appear quite early among the coastal population of Oman (Williamson 1973).

4. During the Early Islamic period and possibly earlier, several tribes in Oman were in fact native in South Arabia.

5. New information was given by W. Yacine al-Takriti at the Seminar for Arabian Studies, Cambridge 1984; surveys south-west of Abu Dhabi have not been published; there are no hellenistic remains on the coast, except in the north from Dubai to Ras al-Khaimah.

6. It is not possible to identify Suhar with the Ommana of the *Periplus* (para. 36) or of Pliny (*NH* 32.149), nor with the Kommana of Ptolemy (*Geog.* 6.8.7); cf. Salles 1980; Kervran 1984, 285–98.

originally a port. As yet, it has hardly been investigated; an Iraqi mission cleared a small fort (25 × 30 m) with round towers at the corners. Other architectural remains are still visible indicating that the site must have been an important one. Material from surface surveys and the Iraqi sounding gives it an approximate time-span of five centuries, between *c.* 250 BC and AD 250.

More precise dates have been obtained from other archaeological finds. These include coins dating to the second half of the second century BC (al-Qaisy 1975; Salles 1978/9; 1980), and stamped Rhodian amphorae handles from the end of the third and beginning of the second century BC. The more usual items, such as terracotta figurines, pottery, steatite and stone vessels show precise parallels with those from City V at Qala'at al-Bahrain, the dating of which (third/second century BC) will be discussed in detail below.

Apart from the naval and land battle near Ras Musandam referred to by Pliny (see n.1), this region of the Gulf is never mentioned in the Seleucid period. It does not appear in the stories about Alexander's explorers, showing that they can hardly have touched this part of the coast (see further below section 2.i). The information of Pliny, which is fuller, is not always intelligible (*NH* 6.32.149): 'According to Juba the voyage beyond on that side has not been explored, because of the rocks – Juba omits to mention Batrasavave, the town of the Omani, and the town of Omana which previous writers have made out to be a famous port of Carmania, and also Homna and Attana, towns said by our traders to be now (*nunc*) the most frequented ports of the Persian Gulf'.

There are strong arguments for dating Pliny's description of the economic activities of these Gulf ports to an earlier period in spite of his use of 'now' (*nunc*). Thus Pliny's correction of Juba obviously refers to older sources. Further, in Pliny's time and later, the Roman trade with India via Alexandria did not make use of the Gulf ports, preferring the direct sea-route.[7] Yet during the first and second centuries AD, some sites such as ed-Dour, Qala'at al-Bahrain and Gerrha/Thaj still played a role in the commercial activities characteristic of the Gulf though they did not participate in the major Rome–India trade. The importance of these places, noted by Pliny and also attested by archaeological finds, cannot have been solely the result of the specific trading patterns developed in the first and second centuries AD; a more plausible explanation would be to regard them as continuing the

7. There is no room to give the extensive bibliography concerning the direct monsoon route to India; see most recently Casson 1980, 31–5; Raschke 1978. This is an appropriate place to emphasise the profound ignorance of the Gulf displayed by the *Periplus* author, who was perhaps a trader of the first century BC or AD and may never have entered the waters of the Gulf himself.

activities of an earlier, more prosperous period.[8] This brief survey of the Omani peninsula would not be complete without reference to Hormuz, on the Persian coast, facing Ras Musandam. There is little information concerning the political and military history of Carmania or its organisation in either the Seleucid period or later, although it certainly remained part of the Seleucid realm. It was here that Antiochus III made his winter quarters on returning from his Indian expedition and he does not appear to have had to capture it first (Schmitt 1964, 67ff; Will 1982, 64–5). On the basis of some very slight evidence Tarn (1951, 481–5) thought that there was a Seleucid settlement on the Persian side of the Straits of Hormuz, which had perhaps been founded by Alexander (or Nearchus) and functioned as a military outpost to protect the straits. This is a plausible hypothesis (see below sections 2.iv and 3.i), but so far no archaeological evidence has come to light to confirm or deny it.[9]

1.ii *Bahrain* (Salles 1984a, 151–63; Bibby 1972). This well-watered island has been occupied by man at least since the fourth millennium BC; it reached one of the high points in its history at the end of the third and the beginning of the second millennium BC with the 'Dilmun' civilisation. Its northern plain is intensively cultivated with palmgroves and gardens and produces much food.[10] In Larsen's study (1983, 55–8; 196) on the evolution of land-use in the island in antiquity, he estimated the area under cultivation during the Achaemenid and Seleucid periods to have been about 65 square kilometres, suggesting a population of between 8,000 and 19,000. The island, known as Tylus in classical antiquity, was an important calling point for shipping in the Gulf. In addition to its agricultural resources and strategic position, the pearl-fishing industry provided extra profits (Isidore of Charax, ed. Schoff, 10–11). The knowledge of the island revealed by ancient writers is vague (see n.10), and the references to it by Polybius are too scanty to help illuminate its history in the Seleucid period.

Archaeological sites are numerous, but very unevenly distributed. So far only one settlement has been found, Qala'at al-Bahrain, while all other remains of hellenistic date are either cemeteries or single tombs. It was originally thought possible that a settlement pattern for the hellenistic period might be arrived at by studying the distribution of the cemeteries and other ancient remains (Salles 1984a;

---

8. A handful of Eastern Sigillata Ware sherds has been collected at ed-Dour, but this need not in any way indicate continuous trade; any number of interpretations are possible (Morel 1983; below section 1.v). A more detailed study of trade and inshore navigation is in preparation (Salles in press).

9. For criticism of Tarn's view see Le Rider 1965, 378 n.5.

10. See Theophrastus' description quoted in Calvet (1984b, 344) and ibid. for other references in classical authors. A detailed study of the Christian sources is contained in Beaucamp, Robin 1983, 171–96; cf. Bowersock 1986.

1986). However, further excavations have shown this hypothesis to be untenable. It now seems more likely that the existing disparity between settlement pattern and cemeteries may be due to the particular role played by the island within the specific socio-economic structure of the Gulf area. This question will be explored further below (section 3.ii).

The Danish excavations at Qala'at al-Bahrain have revealed in City V a short-lived, but homogeneous, hellenistic level. Unfortunately, there is no precise information available on the architecture, town plan or types of building – only a city-gate and several houses have received a cursory mention. The material evidence, which is abundant and varied, is firmly dated to the third and second centuries BC as a result of comparison with the material from Failaka, Eastern Arabia, Babylonia and Susiana.

Particularly worthy of note are the following:
– a hoard of silver coins, probably buried between 245 and 215 BC (Mørkholm 1972; Robin 1974; Potts 1985). It contains two types of coins. Series I shows Zeus on the reverse seated on a throne, holding a sceptre in his left hand and an eagle in his outstretched right hand. The Greek legend reads *Alexandrou*, while some South Arabian letters (among them *shin*) perhaps rendered the name of the divinity Shamash. The mint, probably located at Gerrha (see below), issued this series between 280–210 BC. Although the legend and weight are consistent with the Attic standard, there is nothing to indicate that the series was produced by a royal Seleucid mint. Series II of the hoard consists of silver Arabian imitation tetradrachms, bearing the names of local rulers, probably of a Hagar kingdom in eastern Arabia whose capital may have been Gerrha (Robin 1974);
—sherds of black-glazed Attic pottery, possibly produced in the Levant, datable to the second half of the third century BC;
—a small number of inscriptions and fragmentary inscriptions. Among these is an Aramaic inscription on a (?)funerary jar which mentions the Babylonian god Nabu and may be dated to the fourth or third century BC.[11] An *ostrakon* with Greek letters contains only the end of a name: '. . .raioi'. It is possible that this represents the name of the Agraean tribe, although it would be premature to restore it thus (Bibby 1957). Very recently a funerary stele has been discovered bearing a Greek inscription. This is as yet unpublished. It was found, reused, in a first-century AD tomb and must therefore predate it. A man called Abidistaras – possibly a hellenised Semitic name i.e. 'Ishtar's servant' – who seems to have been a *gubernêtês* occurs in the text. Unfortunately the precise date remains uncertain;[12]

11. A study of this inscription is to appear in a forthcoming issue of *Syria*; see also André-Leicknam in press.
12. To be published by Jean Marcillet-Jaubert.

—several fragments of terracotta figurines in the Orientalising Greek style, very similar to the figurines produced in the Seleucid period at Babylon, Uruk, Seleucia and Susa.

The Danish excavators labelled as City V everything which post-dated the Neo-Babylonian/Achaemenid period (City IV) and preceded the Islamic settlement of the thirteenth century AD (City VI). However, the known stratigraphy of the site makes it possible to state definitely that the older hellenistic material was associated with the archaeological levels called City V (third to second century BC), while the later Parthian or Partho-Sassanian material came from fill and lacks any internal stratigraphy. On the basis of the finds from Qala'at al-Bahrain and the cemeteries on the island, it is possible to suggest a more precise chronology for the 'hellenistic' period, dividing it into four phases:[13]

*Tylus Va*, c. 300–100 BC: this is well-attested in City V at Qala'at al-Bahrain, but less well represented in the cemeteries; the material shows Seleucid influence.

*Tylus Vb1*, c. 100 BC–AD 100: absent from the stratified levels at Qala'at al-Bahrain, but strongly attested in the cemeteries; the material shows Parthian influence (Early and Middle Parthian periods).

*Tylus Vb2*, c. 100–AD 250: same as above (Late Parthian).

*Tylus Vc*, c. AD 250 – Islamic Conquest: scarcely attested in the cemeteries and entirely absent on the site: the material shows Sassanian influence.

The present archaeological evidence does not prove that there was a Seleucid presence in the island. Nevertheless it will be seen below that there was very probably a Seleucid settlement there (see below section 3.ii).

1.iii *The Eastern Arabian province: the Hasa.* Virtually no evidence of the Seleucid period is available for the Qatar peninsula. A few sherds datable to the third to second century BC have been found in partly destroyed tombs, but the cemetery at Ras Abaruk shows signs of having been reused (de Cardi 1978). The Danes excavated a site at Ras Uwainat Ali which has provided some hellenistic objects (Bibby 1965; 1966), but on visiting the site in February 1985 it was found to have been completely destroyed. Some late hellenistic sherds were collected at Joghbi (Umm el Ma' II), but the site itself appears to date to the Early Islamic period, contemporary with Murwab (de Cardi 1978; Hardy-Guilbert 1984).

13. The actual chronology is slightly different from that presented in Salles, 1984a, 157; this will be fully explained and justified in Boucharlat, Salles in press. More recent studies have been done by Boucharlat 1986 and Kervran 1986.

Because the long coastal stretch provided conditions suitable for ancient shipping which did not need deep-water harbours, the oases of the interior of Eastern Arabia, such as Thaj and al-Hofuf, were not isolated from the Gulf and were involved in the commerce and politics of the area. There is a further possibility that hydrographic conditions were more favourable then than they are today and that this led to the development of many more oases in the region (Bibby 1973; Potts et al. 1978; Zarins et al. 1979; 1980; Potts 1984a). The Arab kingdoms of Hasa (Robin 1974), known as Hagar in antiquity, acted as middlemen in the caravan and sea-borne trade. Though in close contact with the neighbouring great powers from the Neo-Assyrian kings down to Antiochus III, they tried always to maintain their independence and interests (see below section 2.iii). Ancient writers preserved an echo of this in the legendary wealth traditionally associated with the city of Gerrha (Strabo 16.3.3; Agatharchides § 102).

Potts (1984a, 119) has characterised the archaeological phase corresponding to the Seleucid period as follows: '*Middle Hasaean* refers to the period in which Thaj and the historically attested Gerrha flourished. Sherds of Greek black glazed pottery from Thaj may belong to the third century BC. Two coins from Thaj, one bearing the name of King Abyata', and the other Abi'el, can be dated roughly to *c.* 200–190 BC and 130 BC, respectively, on the basis of the presence of coins struck by the same kings in datable contexts at Gordion, Mektepini, Susa and Qala'at al-Bahrain. A painted Nabataean sherd found at Thaj belongs to Parr's early painted style and can be dated to *c.* 75–0 BC ... We may roughly date this period to *c.* 300–0 BC.' The phase thus defined by Potts is contemporaneous with the Seleucid and Early Parthian periods in Mesopotamia and Susiana and with Tylus Va plus Tylus Vb1 in Bahrain; in the present state of archaeological investigation there appears to be no gap during the first century BC in Eastern Arabia comparable to that in Bahrain and, even more clearly attested, in Failaka.

From the distribution of finds from surface surveys, older and more recent soundings, and chance finds by non-professionals in the course of building programmes undertaken as part of modern urban developments, three main areas of settlement may be defined (Potts 1984a, 95, map 4):

—*Thaj oasis*: Potts now identifies this with ancient Gerrha (Potts 1984b), although it is possible that another 'Gerrha-on-Sea' was located on the coast. Thaj oasis is, in fact, the only site which corresponds to the descriptions in ancient writers, in particular their mention of fortifications. The importance of the site in antiquity is amply illustrated by the extent of the remains (Potts 1984b; Potts et al. 1978). This is to be explained by its strategic location: it formed the terminus of caravan-routes from the Eastern Mediterranean, as

well as the routes from South Arabia through al-Hofuf; furthermore
it was a natural stopping-place for caravans travelling along the Gulf.
It forms the natural hinterland to all the coastal sites as well as
Bahrain (Potts 1983a; Salles in press). Considering the promising
soundings already undertaken, full excavation of the site would
greatly enhance knowledge of this part of Arabia;

—*al-Hofuf oasis*: this was one of the main oases of the Islamic period; it
was probably settled in the hellenistic period, but so far archaeological
remains are sparse. It forms another of the termini of caravan-routes
from South Arabia;

—*the coast* from al-Uqair to north of Jubayl: the apparent density
of material gives a somewhat distorted picture and should not be
overemphasised as most comes from surface finds only. It is uncertain
whether the coast was settled fairly extensively in the hellenistic
period. The implications of the distribution of sites on the coast will
be discussed below (section 3.i).


1.iv *Failaka* (Hannestad 1984a; Salles 1984c, 11–15). A Seleucid presence is most strongly attested on Failaka, the island lying off Kuwait.
A small hellenistic site is located in the south-western part of the
island, close to remains of the second millennium BC. No evidence of
other contemporary settlements has been found elsewhere in the
island, nor a cemetery. The Danish excavations (1958–1963) on the
island uncovered the following remains (Salles 1984c, 11–15; Hannestad 1984a):

—a square fortress (58 m²) flanked by square towers on the corners
and protected (later) by a deep moat (Albrectsen 1958; Jeppesen 1963);

—two sanctuaries inside the fortress. One is a typically Greek temple
*in antis*. The bases of the columns show Achaemenid influence while
the capitals are Ionic in style; the pediment is decorated with acroteria
(Jeppesen 1960);

—houses built inside the fortress at a later date; the chronology of the
building phases of these and any plan are at present unclear;

—a building located outside the fortress, situated on the beach to the
west; the excavators called it variously the 'Terracotta Workshop' or
the 'Emporion' (Roussel 1958).

Since 1983 the French excavations have brought to light two new
hellenistic sanctuaries (Calvet, Caubet, Salles 1984; 1985):

—B6 is located on the beach to the east of the fortress and has been
partly destroyed by erosion from the sea. It was dedicated to Artemis
and is datable to the first half of the second century BC (Caubet, Salles
1984);

—the other is located further inland at Tell Khazneh. Continuous
looting has almost completely destroyed the architectural remains; it

is however clear that the hellenistic sanctuary was built over an earlier Neo-Babylonian or Achaemenid one.[14]

As a result of these finds, it is now possible to provide a preliminary historical sketch:

—a local sanctuary existed at Tell Khazneh before the arrival of the Greeks (Calvet 1984a);

—the first Greek settlement, between *c*. 300–250 BC, is represented by the fortress including possibly two sanctuaries; this is termed Failaka Ia. Towards the end of the third century BC the settlement became so important that a new sanctuary was built outside the fortress as well as another structure, the function of which is unclear (= 'Terracotta Workshop'). Throughout this period the Tell Khazneh sanctuary continued in use;

—around 150 BC, perhaps because of unsettled politico-military conditions, the Artemis sanctuary on the beach was abandoned and the fortress surrounded with a moat (although the date of the latter is uncertain). The interior of the fortress was also reorganised, with houses densely packed inside it; this phase is termed Failaka Ib;

—around 100 BC, though the dating remains uncertain, the sites were abandoned, including the fortress and Tell Khazneh;

—during the first century AD the fortress was partially reoccupied, representing the phase termed Failaka II.

A number of Greek inscriptions allow further insight into the character and history of the site, particularly with regard to religious activities. The inscriptions discovered by the Danes have recently been studied in detail (Roueché, Sherwin-White 1985). Two very fragmentary Greek inscriptions found by the French mission have added some information on cults (Caubet, Salles 1984, 137–8 nn.41; 41 *bis*). An Aramaic inscription on stone, dated to around the fourth century BC and still awaiting translation, suggests that the island may have played a role in the Achaemenid period.

Two coin hoards were found inside the fortress, as well as a number of individual coins; more have been found in the sanctuary of Artemis (Mørkholm 1960; 1979; Callot 1984). Among them, a large number are coins of the Gerrha mint, but an equally large number are Seleucid coins dating from Seleucus I to Antiochus IV, issued by the royal mints at Susa or Seleucia-Tigris. One coin is from the kingdom of Characene.

In various parts of the site large numbers of terracotta figurines have been excavated (Mathiesen 1982), which illuminate aspects of the cults on Failaka. They also provide information on the diverse

14. The oldest Greek inscription found so far was discovered on this site: this is the Sotelês dedication (Roueché, Sherwin-White 1985); a preliminary report on the 1984 excavations can be found in Calvet, Caubet, Salles 1985.

artistic influences found on the island; thus figurines of Orientalising Greek style and hellenistic Tanagra style, as well as purely Mesopotamian products, are represented. The same mixture of stylistic influences can be discerned in other types of cult objects, especially the miniature altars or incense-burners.

The pottery includes a few sherds of Attic ware, some Rhodian amphorae handles and a number of imported wares, particularly from Susa (Hannestad 1983; 1984b). But the predominant ware is a green glazed one closely resembling that found at Seleucia-Tigris, Susa, Uruk and other Mesopotamian sites (see Colledge, below p. 146). The locally produced ware has strong affinities with the pottery of Eastern Arabia.

1.v. All these archaeological discoveries must be treated with the utmost caution in order to avoid jumping to false conclusions. It is important to remember that the archaeology of this period has only begun to be studied in recent years, and that, at present, it relies on a very small number of scientifically excavated sites, such as Qala'at al-Bahrain and Failaka. Much of the information has come from limited soundings (Thaj, Tarut, Ayn Jawan, ed-Dour *inter alia*) and from surface finds. New discoveries are made each year and these may invalidate the strictly provisional conclusions presented here.

Many generalisations are thus bound to be inaccurate: a small number of Rhodian amphorae handles need not be evidence for a thriving wine trade in the Gulf nor do a few Attic sherds necessarily indicate close contacts with the Greek cities e.g. of Asia Minor, Syria and the Greek islands. Bearing in mind this *caveat*, it may be possible to advance further. While it is certainly true that elsewhere Rhodian amphorae handles may be a 'direct reflection of transactions concerning goods for consumption' (Garlan 1983, 37; 40), Garlan's warning against over-interpreting isolated finds in remote spots which could be regarded merely as reused vessels (Mleihah? Thaj?), should be remembered. However, the occurrence of such quantitatively small finds must have *some* significance. Although they definitely do not attest regular trade such as took place in Egypt and other parts of the hellenistic world, they must mean that there was, at some point, a limited demand for foods for consumption, in this instance, wine. The demand might have been 'culturally' determined i.e. reflecting a change in the drinking habits of Arab tribes who may for a short period have switched from their traditional date-wine to Mediterranean wines; or it could reflect the socio-cultural situation, i.e. the presence of a small, non-indigenous community who wished to preserve their own food habits in an environment unable to supply them.[15] If the latter is the case, one would have to infer the presence of Greeks in the Gulf – or at least hellenised people – who were consumers rather than traders. Thus the amphorae handles would reflect a socio-cultural, rather than an economic process. One could similarly regard the black-glazed Attic sherds as reflecting the taste of a conservative clientèle rather than implying a regular commercial exchange (cf. e.g. Morel 1983).

It would, however, be wrong to dismiss totally an economic interpretation in favour of a purely socio-cultural one. After all, the distribution of coins in the area must point in the opposite direction. Virtually nothing is known of the economic systems in operation among the tribes living along the Gulf during the hellenistic period, though it is reasonable to assume that the caravan trade formed a major part. It is clear that a monetary system was absent before *c.* 300 BC and vanished again after *c.* AD 100, as neither local nor foreign coins datable outside these termini have yet been found. Thus the Arab tribes can only have practised a monetary economy for a limited period before their later integration into the monetary systems connected with Islam (Lowick 1974). The monetary economy in which they were involved (*c.* 300 BC-AD 100) exerted such strong external pressure that they not only minted silver coins for international trading purposes,[16] but also produced small bronze coins for local use (see Fig. 2c). Tribes using a new currency to conduct internal exchanges appear to run entirely counter to their local traditions, and the small volume of this exchange cannot possibly have been devised simply for economic activities between tribes.[17] What seems rather more plausible is that they may have needed coinage for conducting exchanges with non-indigenous communities accustomed to a money economy and unfamiliar with the local barter system. Commercial activities of this type, which were both geographically and quantitatively limited (i.e. small quantities of staple necessities in local markets), did not demand the issue of coins of high denominations.[18] This interpretation of the coin evidence would lend support to the hypothesis outlined above, namely that there were Greeks present in the area who were consumers rather than traders; although the silver coinage of Gerrha does attest the importance of the caravan-trade for some of the Arab tribes.

The arguments presented may in themselves seem slight, but they

15. The same problem of interpretation arises in relation to the stamped amphorae handles found in Mesopotamia: 9 in Seleucia-Tigris, 6 in Babylon, 3 in Susa and 3 in Uruk (Börker 1974).
16. Gerrhaean coins have been found in Phrygia (Mørkholm 1960, 206).
17. This statement is not based on historical evidence, but on analogies with traditional exchange patterns revealed by anthropological research.
18. This small coinage may have been cast in engraved moulds and not struck; Potts 1985 has an example of a terracotta 'coin'.

do suggest a new interpretation of the archaeological material; it is inadvisable to apply an economic analysis too narrowly defined.[19]

## 2. Seleucid policies in the Gulf

2.i. The involvement of the Greeks in the Gulf began with the explorations carried out at Alexander's orders: Nearchus' return from India along the Persian coast of the Gulf, and the expeditions of Archias, Androsthenes of Thasos and Hieron of Soli to the Arabian coast. For the purposes of this chapter I shall not discuss the difficult problem of Alexander's last plans, in particular the one which involved a conquest of Arabia (Schachermeyr 1966; Hornblower 1981, 87–97) and which was rapidly dropped by Perdiccas after the king's death; nor will I consider the details of the initial Greek explorations (Schiwek 1962; Roueché, Sherwin-White 1985). One should, however, note the cautious, rather half-hearted, nature of the Arabian expeditions: it seems to have been sufficient to locate the islands. Any real exploration of the landmass did not take place, except for a possible visit by Androsthenes to Gerrha if the account by Strabo 16.3.3 reflects an historical event. Not one of the expeditions passed beyond Ras Musandam and the Straits of Hormuz, so that any notion that a circumnavigation of Arabia to the Red Sea ever took place is untenable. The limited achievement of the explorers of the Arabian side of the Gulf stands in contrast to the aims which Nearchus assigned to his own mission on the Persian coast; the information gathering may have been too scanty for a plan of conquest and/or colonisation of the Arabian peninsula to be a viable hypothesis.

It is obvious, on the other hand, that the practical-minded Macedonian conqueror, who thought that this region could 'become as prosperous as Phoenicia' (Arrian *Anab.* 7.19.5), must have had strong economic motives (Briant 1977, 86–90; Pedech 1984, 187). The Greeks neither discovered nor created the Gulf trade route – they simply explored it 'for themselves' (as Strabo says about Androsthenes) and in order to exploit, or try to exploit, a very profitable trade which was actually being operated by other peoples.

A close study of the archaeological material and written documents indicates that commercial activity was developing anew in the Gulf during the first centuries of the first millennium BC. This activity led to a renewal of vigour and prosperity in the ancient region of Dilmun, i.e. Bahrain, the Eastern Arabian coast and possibly also Failaka, of which (together with Makkan and Meluhha) Esarhaddon, for example, claimed to be king in the seventh century BC (Larsen 1983, 52–5). Trade between Mesopotamia and South Iran or India flourished under

19. This qualifies some earlier statements, particularly Salles in press.

the Neo-Assyrian and Neo-Babylonian dynasties and continued very actively in the Achaemenid empire (Larsen 1983, 55; Schiwek 1962). The episode of Nabonidus' stay at Teima (North-West Arabia) and the interest shown by Neo-Babylonian and Achaemenid rulers in Arabian affairs cannot have lacked an economic motive. The trade with Meso-potamia in South Arabian frankincense and Indian goods through ports located on the south Arabian coast began in the eighth to seventh centuries BC (Van Beek 1958; Groom 1981). Traces of this activity can be found in the Gulf: coastal sites in the northern part of the United Arab Emirates which have been surveyed but not yet excavated, the impressive City IV at Qala'at al-Bahrain of Neo-Babylonian and Achaemenid date, scattered finds in Eastern Arabia[20] and some slight traces on Failaka.[21] The period is as yet poorly known, especially during the fifth and fourth centuries BC, but recent archaeological discoveries suggest a fairly dense population and intense commerce and agriculture. The hellenistic City V at Qala'at al-Bahrain clearly succeeded, without a break, the flourishing City IV, whose wealth is attested by its monumental architecture. It is equally plain that the apparently sudden appearance in ancient sources of the prosperous and powerful city of Gerrha around 300 BC cannot be a purely literary creation. It obviously had a long earlier history during which its economic power developed but it was only at this time that it became known to Greek explorers. Although the references are scattered through Mesopotamian and Classical texts and the sites insufficiently studied, the prosperity of the Gulf in the Neo-Assyrian, Neo-Baby-lonian and Achaemenid periods is plain.

As heir to the Achaemenid empire and thus to its trade routes, Alexander wished to utilise both its existing wealth and its potential profits. Looked at in this light, the preliminary exploration which he set afoot appears to have been intended to provide charts to aid sailors (mapping the coast-line, islands, ports-of-call, watering-points such as Tylus and Icarus) rather than to establish the basis for a conquest of the peninsula.

2.ii. Such economic and trading interests seem to have determined the policies of the Seleucid monarchs in the Gulf, far more than either the memories of Alexander's glorious eastern campaigns or any genuine plans to colonise. Nevertheless, Tarn (1929, 11) identified a deliberate policy of colonisation by drawing on the Seleucid foun-dations of Larisa, Chalcis, and Arethusa on the Arabian side (see

20. This is the Early Hasaean period of Potts (1984a, 119). One should also remember that according to an old tradition this area is supposed to have been settled by the Chaldaeans.
21. Among these are two inscriptions mentioning Nebuchadnezzar II (Glassner 1984, 49–50).

below section 3.i), Seleucia-on-the-Erythrean Sea (Seleucia-on-the-Arabian Gulf), and Antioch-Persis on the Persian side. Rostovtzeff (1951, 455–64), too, emphasised several times the importance given by the Seleucids to the maintenance of sea-routes with India and the Arabian peninsula.

The choice of Seleucia-Tigris as the Mesopotamian capital by Seleucus I has been much discussed.[22] Will, following Rostovtzeff, has pointed to 'the probable interest which Seleucus must have had in exploiting his Mesopotamian province' (1982, 270). Such an interest will almost certainly not have been limited to the local resources and the strategic location of the province at the centre of the empire, but also included its role as the terminus of the Indian trade routes which Alexander wanted to conquer. The city was located at the cross-roads of important overland routes leading east to the Upper Satrapies and west to the Eastern Mediterranean (Antioch), and was also a redistribution centre for merchandise imported through the Gulf.

Goods from Arabia and India appear very early in the Seleucid period: Seleucus' letter of 288/7 BC detailing his offerings to the Apollo temple in Didyma (Welles 1934, no.5) lists products whose origin is fairly certain. Frankincense is traditionally assumed to come from South Arabia, although the possibility of importation from India should also be considered (see below section 2.iii). Sources for cinnamon are East Africa with which the Seleucids had no connection, and the island of Ceylon; it is generally agreed that the *cinnamofera regio* should be located here. *Costus speciosus* (Vedic *kushta*) is a spice used in perfume and pharmaceutic recipes and a product typical of India (Schoff 1974, 168–9). These latter goods, then, came from the Indian subcontinent rather than from South Arabia. They were carried in the time of Seleucus I by sea-borne traders whose identity is unknown; they were more probably Indians or Arabs (the Gerrhaeans? see below) than Greeks. The evidence of merchandise clearly shows as early as the third century that the Indian and/or Arabian trade was operated for the direct benefit of the Seleucids.

A further aspect of the policies of the early Seleucid rulers should be mentioned although it is an *argumentum e silentio*. The military campaigns of Seleucus I and his successors were mainly directed against either the Upper Satrapies (Bactria, Iran etc.) or Indian satrapies. Will has stressed the peacefulness of the satrapies of Babylonia and Susiana (1982, 270), apart from the possible secession of Persis which might have had no effect on the commercial traffic in the Gulf. It is not always clear what interest the rulers had in these far north-eastern regions, whether they were primarily political and

22. For a conspectus see Sherwin-White 1983b, 269–70.

military or whether economic factors also played a determining part.[23] What is significant is the docility and loyalty of the Mesopotamian provinces. It is here that the Greek presence is well attested (Sherwin-White 1982), that the hellenisation of local élites was taking place (Sherwin-White 1983a) and that Seleucid kings can be seen as patrons of indigenous cults (see Sherwin-White, above, pp. 27–9); in fact, the separate communities seem to have lived together in exemplary fashion. Perhaps one should see the apparent loyalty and harmonious symbiosis as the result of a royal policy of '*Enrichissez-vous*'. The archaeology of the Gulf sites shows clearly that there was no interruption from the reign of Seleucus I through the whole of the third century BC in the commercial activities conducted by sea (cf. e.g. numismatic finds and imported objects). It may well have been the economic success of the Gulf trade which led the Lagids, from Ptolemy II on, to try to conquer part of the South Arabian trade (Tarn 1929; Préaux 1939, 355).

2.iii. It is certainly in Antiochus III's reign that these policies emerge most clearly. The eastern expedition of Antiochus III has been interpreted in various ways; thus, Rostovtzeff and Tarn believed that the aim was to establish, re-establish or re-inforce commercial relations between the Seleucid world and India and that the friendly treaty with Sophagasenus might have included economic and commercial clauses in addition to the agreement to supply war-elephants, as may have been the case with the earlier treaty concluded by *c*. 303 between Seleucus I and Chandragupta (Tarn 1951, 100–1; Rostovtzeff 1951, 459). Will (1982, 62–4) remarks that Antiochus III 'was satisfied with appropriating as much as he could in the course of his expedition', i.e. large amounts of money and valuable Arabian products in the way he was later to do at Gerrha. It is impossible to guess at the true intentions of the king or the concrete results of his expedition; all that is certain is that Antiochus III brought back considerable amounts of precious metal, exotic goods and money.

Le Rider (1965, 303–6) attributes genuine commercial objectives to Antiochus III, namely, '. . . to establish or consolidate commercial links with the Kabul valley', 'increase the volume of trade along the southern route (i.e. Carmania and Persis)', and 'display an active interest in the sea-route' by which he means the Gulf. Le Rider's hypothesis is that Indian products imported via the Gulf, or at least a proportion of these goods, were conveyed to Susa where caravans from Seleucia-Tigris would come to buy them. The argument is based on the marked increase of coins from the Seleucia mint found in Susa

---

23. At the time of the *Periplus*, it seems that the convoys sailing through the Gulf consisted primarily of vessels heavily loaded with raw materials; a large part of the trade may have followed a land-route running parallel to it (Salles in press).

from Antiochus III's reign on and particularly after his *anabasis* (see Fig. 2d). Will does not directly dispute Le Rider's conclusions, but emphasises the slightness of his hypothesis, based, as it is, exclusively on variations in currency circulation within a limited geographical area (1982, 62; 354). While the hypothesis may be appropriate for the reign of Antiochus III it is not so for Antiochus IV's reign. It must also be remembered that Seleucia-Tigris was a royal capital and thus almost certainly contained the most important mint. Further, the presence of bronze coins from Seleucia-Tigris in Susa need not necessarily imply the actual presence of traders from Seleucia in Susa; if the large quantity of currency, consisting mainly of coins of small denominations, is taken to indicate an intensification of trade between the two towns it is still not known whether the movement was from Seleucia towards Susa or vice versa (Salles in press). Finally, the numerous coin hoards which punctuate the route from Failaka to Seleucia and further on to the north-west should not be forgotten (Callot 1984, 164–7).

It would, however, be a mistake to underestimate the perceptible increase in currency circulation under Antiochus III and his successors, which is particularly attested at Susa. It can also be matched in the Gulf (see Figs. 2a & b). There can be little doubt that such growth must be due to an increased volume of trade in the Gulf. A precise inventory of archaeological finds securely dated to the reigns of Antiochus III, Seleucus III and Antiochus IV from Gulf sites shows this to have been a period of intense activity. One of the consequences of Antiochus the Great's expedition was, undoubtedly, an increased import of Indian products via the Gulf. Then, encouraged by the success of his treaty with Sophagasenus and the commercial perspectives it opened up, Antiochus III, after staying for a while in Antioch-Persis,[24] tried to secure the Arabian trade for his own benefit. It is at this point that the Gerrha episode took place.

The town of Gerrha is described by Strabo and mentioned several times by classical authors; its wealth was legendary and derived from the caravan-trade along which South Arabian products were brought from Marib to the east coast of Arabia, and another which brought goods from their own city to Petra, via Teima and Dumat/al-Jauf (Rostovtzeff 1951, 457–8; Potts 1983a). Strabo, following Aristobulus, further states that the Gerrhaeans traded using the sea and river

24. Antiochus III's stay in Antioch-Persis was more than simply a brief visit (Will 1982, 67). Antioch-Persis has generally been identified with Bushire, but a recent proposal identifies it with Taoke, which is commonly taken to be the modern Borazjan, about twenty kilometres inland from Bushire (Bivar cited by Roueché, Sherwin-White 1985, 9 n.18). But *if* Antiochus III really did embark at Antioch-Persis to sail to Gerrha, it indicates that it was a coastal city, or at least a city connected with the sea by a navigable water-way (the Hilleh river if Antioch= Borazjan?).

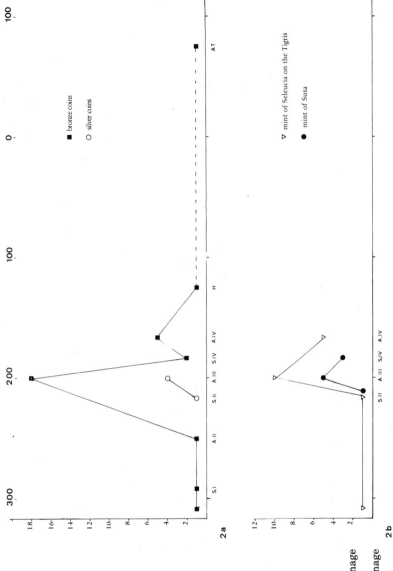

Fig. 2a. Seleucid coinage
in the Gulf area
Fig. 2b. Seleucid coinage
in Failaka

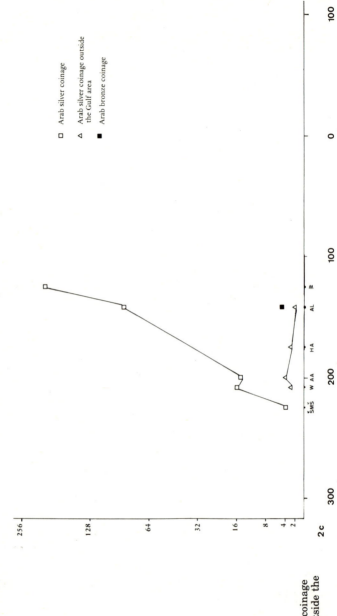

Fig. 2c. Arab coinage
inside and outside the
Gulf area

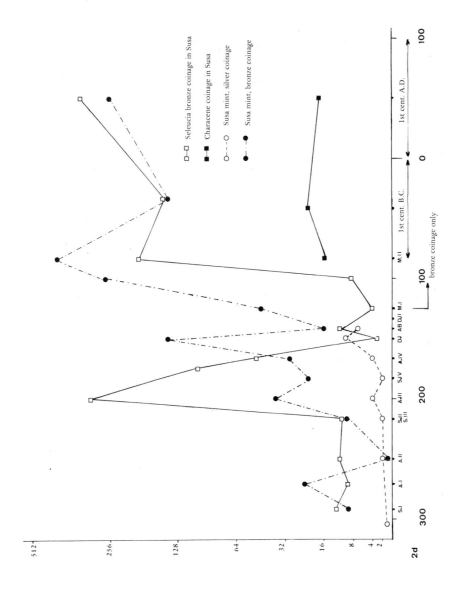

Fig. 2d. Monetary
findings in Susa

route, which ran from the north of the Gulf along the Euphrates as far as Thapsacus.[25] In this context one should note that the common-ware pottery from Failaka has very close connections with Eastern Arabia. The Gerrhaeans conveyed South Arabian frankincense as well as products from further east which arrived in South Arabian ports (van Beek 1958). A surprising feature of this trade network is the length of the incense route, Marib-Gerrha-Petra, which crossed the desert twice instead of using the direct route from Marib to Petra. Tarn (1929) argued that this was the result of Ptolemaic competition over Arabia; but it may be preferable to advance a simpler hypothesis according to which some of the Gerrhaean incense may have come from India, which produced a different, but also much sought after, species (*Boswellia serrata*) (Salles in press).

According to Tarn (1951, 443ff), the Gerrhaeans were privileged allies of the Seleucids: their administrative organisation, and the division of the region into provinces are to be seen as exact copies of Seleucid satrapal organisation, if one accepts the designation 'Chattenia' as reflecting administrative terminology, as Tarn does. Irrespective of this speculative interpretation, Antiochus III's visit could be regarded as a renewal of friendly relations; in fact, the caravans of the city worked both for the Seleucids and for the Ptolemies. We have already noted that they probably provided Seleucus I's offerings to the Milesians; in addition, Gerrhaean frankincense is mentioned as present in Ptolemaic ports of Syria as early as 261 BC (Préaux 1939, 362) and Agatharchides states that 'the Gerrhaeans have enriched the Syria of the Ptolemies' (*GGM* §102). Antiochus III's expedition to Gerrha, which may not have been an event of the magnitude supposed by Rostovtzeff (1951, 458), must then be seen as an attempt to impose a Seleucid alliance on the Gerrhaeans and also to draw them away from the Ptolemaic trade. The high price paid by the Gerrhaeans for preserving their freedom suggests that the Seleucid intervention was effective in imposing a change of policy[26] at a time when the direct route through the Red Sea opened by the Ptolemies was perhaps beginning to harm Gerrhaean trade (Préaux 1939, 361–5).

2.iv. At this stage in the analysis one might pause and consider the means the Seleucids had at their disposal for imposing their policies on, and ensuring respect for them in, the Gulf. Several modern

25. Strabo, 16.3.3: 'Aristobulus says on the contrary that the Gerrhaeans import most of their cargoes on rafts to Babylonia, and thence sail up the Euphrates with them (to Thapsacus), and then convey them by land to all parts of the country.'
26. Compare the idea of a compulsory gift ('don contraignant') as defined by Briant (1976, 192–3). The 'spontaneous' donor remains free – thus, for example, the Gerrhaeans do not pay tribute – but his gift ratifies the duty he is obliged to perform, so that he is, in fact, surrendering a part of his freedom. According to Briant this would be a kind of regulated war situation.

historians have maintained that there must have been a Seleucid fleet operating in the waters of the Gulf (Rostovtzeff 1951, 458; Schmitt 1964, 49; Walbank 1967, 422; Tarn, Griffith 1952, 240). This suggestion rests on two arguments:

—Antiochus III's need of a fleet for his expedition to Gerrha. Even if his stay in Antioch-Persis was quite long, the king had neither the time nor the necessary raw materials to have a new fleet built; there must, therefore, have been one ready.

—Numenius' expedition, mentioned by Pliny, the date of which remains unclear, implies the presence of a fleet.[27]

Two arguments may be added to strengthen this very reasonable hypothesis. The province of the Erythrean Sea was created before Antiochus III's expedition, and even preceded Molon's revolt (Polyb. 5.46.7). It cannot have been created by the young king in 224 BC and must thus date from an earlier reign even if the exact date is uncertain. Nothing prevents it dating from the first Seleucids.[28]

The geographical limits of this province, which certainly included territory probably from both the neighbouring provinces of Susiana and Babylonia, are unknown, and its creation cannot be explained by the natural resources of the region which are poor *pace* Strabo's description (16.1). The capital of the province is not mentioned, but it is likely to have been Alexandria, refounded as Antioch-Charax by Antiochus IV. The town does not seem to have had any important commercial role before the second half of the second century BC. Exactly when the province became a genuinely distinct administrative entity is also unclear; it was first termed 'the districts of the Erythraean Sea' and later known as Mesene and as Characene.[29] The creation of such a province can only have been justified by the precise function it was intended to fulfil; this is likely to have been to regulate and guard the southern approaches through the Gulf. The fact that the governor of this province, Numenius, was in charge of a fleet and task-force seems to confirm the maritime and commercial function of the Erythrean Sea province, which was to police and ensure the security of the Gulf.

Other arguments are archaeological and nautical. We have seen that the sites which have yielded material of the Seleucid period are not large international trading-places (apart from Gerrha, none of

27. Initially, Will dated the expedition to Antiochus III's Anabasis (1962, 72ff); later he admitted that it was impossible to decide between the reigns of Antiochus III and Antiochus IV. The same doubts are expressed by Le Rider 1965, 303; in favour of Antiochus III, Schmitt 1964, 49, Walbank 1967, 422; in favour of Antiochus IV, Altheim 1948, 45.

28. A list of *stratêgoi* is given in Bengtson 1952, 409; Pythiades 222/1, Tychon 220, Numenius under Antiochus III.

29. Mesene province is first mentioned in Strabo 2.1.31 (Weissbach *RE* xv col. 1082); for Characene, see Nodelman 1960.

them possesses a hinterland) and that their existence cannot be justified by their economic activity alone. Another factor is that the distances in Gulf sea-faring are long, the journeys often difficult and lacking reliable supply-points.

The presence of a permanent flotilla in the Gulf waters implies the establishment and maintenance of entrepôts for shelter and re-supplying. It is unnecessary to postulate a single central base for this; indeed, it was preferable for the Seleucids to have a number of sites, scattered along both sides of the Gulf, where ships patrolling the Erythrean Sea could call, or even stay for longer periods; in other words, sites either fortified or with natural defences. It was also essential that sailors should be able to find supplies for their voyages there and put in for extended stays when necessary. Therefore, these sites were not simply stopping-points, but fully equipped bases controlled by the Seleucids and with a military presence. It is essential, then, to suggest new approaches for understanding the distribution of sites in the Gulf in the light of the hypothesis outlined (see below section 3).

2.v. In the course of the second century BC written documents are rarer, and the archaeological evidence somewhat confused. It is impossible to grasp the full import of Antiochus IV's eastern projects, and statements concerning his Persian policies must remain hypo-thetical, even if the Numenius episode is assigned to his reign, as his presence in Susiana and Babylonia in 164 BC does not reveal his actual aims (Altheim ap. Will 1982, 354). Information about his successors is still more tenuous and is generally limited to reporting their conflicts with the Parthians. Antiochus VII appears to have been the last Seleucid king involved in Babylonia (thus presumably also with the Erythrean sea province?) before being defeated there by Phraates in 129 BC.

In Susa commercial activity (= coin finds) slows down from Anti-ochus IV's reign (Le Rider 1965, 309; 347ff); it diminishes under Deme-trius I, Alexander Balas and Demetrius II (see Fig. 2d). Le Rider argues that one should deduce from this a parallel decline in maritime trade in the Gulf, and, indeed, no Seleucid coins later than Antiochus IV have been found on Failaka (Mørkholm 1979; Callot 1984). A coin of Hyspaosines was found, but it is uncertain whether it should be dated to the beginning or end of his reign and only seems to confirm the end of commercial activity on the island. We have also pointed out that the buildings outside the fortress were abandoned after the middle of the second century BC, and the pottery finds and terracotta figurines indicate that Failaka Period I must have come to an end some time before 100 BC (Hannestad 1983, 78; Mathiesen 1982, 73). The Hagarite coins of Thaj in Arabia, struck in the name of Abi'el and dating to c. 140/130 BC, appear to be the latest evidence of its

flourishing trade, which is also reflected in the dedication of a
Gerrhaean merchant on Delos (Robin 1974). The amphorae stamps,
which are the latest precisely datable finds, date to the middle of the
second century BC, while the common-ware pottery is not assignable
to a clearly defined period. In Qala'at al-Bahrain, the precise chronology of City V is still unknown, particularly with regard to the end
of the period; but there is no imported material which can be dated
with any certainty to the first century BC, while the classification of
local pottery remains uncertain for the present. On Failaka, as well
as at Qala'at al-Bahrain, the abandonment of the sites towards the
end of the second century between 150 and 100 BC appears likely,
despite the fact that in Qala'at al-Bahrain, the unstratified material
overlaps with the following period (Parthian), not attested strati-
graphically but well represented in fills and in the tombs of the hellenistic cemeteries. Finally, the economic revival of Mithridates II's
reign (c. 100 BC), noted by Le Rider, is not attested anywhere within
the Gulf, which developed a new regional role only from the second
half of the first century AD onwards. The fact that the history of the
Gulf in the second half of the second century BC is almost entirely
unknown appears to be connected with the decline of Seleucid power.
The disappearance of Seleucid rule in Babylonia and consequently the
loss of the province of the Erythrean Sea and of the Gulf resulted in
increasing interruption of maritime traffic and eventually the abandonment of coastal and island sites. This general trend, of course,
probably developed fairly slowly in the period between the reigns of
Antiochus IV and Antiochus VII Sidetes (by c. 130 BC). Conversely,
the conquest of Babylonia and Susiana by the Arsacids and the independence of Characene under Hyspaosines and his successors seem to
have had no tangible effect on the history of the Gulf, at least on the
sites of Seleucid character which still survived in the middle of the
second century BC and were temporarily deserted after c. 100 BC. If
future archaeological finds confirm this impression, they will show,
by contrast, that the history of the Gulf during the third and the
second century BC was exclusively Seleucid.

### 3. The Seleucid settlements in the Gulf (see Fig. 3)

3.i. It would be premature to suggest interpretations of the sites in
the eastern area of the Gulf (the Straits of Hormuz, the United Arab
Emirates and Oman) which as yet remain unexcavated. It is essential
that the construction of the small fort at ed-Dour be dated more
precisely, and that a systematic survey of the islands (Kishm, Hormuz)
and the Persian coast of the straits be undertaken. The name of a
small Islamic fortress located north of Ras al-Khaimah, 'The Queen
of Sheba's Castle', might be derived from a very ancient tradition. In

fact, only a methodical exploration of the sites can cast light on the possible Seleucid control of this area.

Archaeology can provide only sparse information concerning the eastern province of Arabia because of recent urban development, in particular along the coast. Several modern historians, however, think a Seleucid presence in Eastern Arabia is indicated by Pliny's mention of three towns: Larisa, Chalcis and Arethusa, which scholars tend to agree must have been founded by Seleucus I.[30] The Pliny passage is rather imprecise and the allocation of these towns to eastern Arabia is closely related to the precise location of the *gentes Agraei* who appear in the same context (Robin 1974; Potts 1984a, 112). The existence of a town called Chalcis in the area of the Saudi Arabian town Nariya has no archaeological basis, and the whole north-eastern part of the eastern province appears to be empty of remains. To locate Larisa on the latitude of the bay of Kuwait seems curious as no hellenistic archaeological evidence has ever been found in this region. This lack of material is true both of the hinterland of Kuwait, which is a complete desert, and the Wadi Batin, which is the natural passage between Iraq and Arabia because the bay itself is entirely without water and oases, except for Jahra. Communication between Arabia and Mesopotamia seems to have been almost totally maritime, with the land-route (Potts 1984a, 97–8) providing no evidence of use in antiquity.[31] It is thus, perhaps, unnecessary to seek a Seleucid foundation in the mainland of Kuwait. The location of Arethusa, west of the Euphrates, between Nasiriyah and Basra, *may* be reflected in the foundation of an unnamed city 'near the lakes, in the direction of Arabia' by Alexander himself;[32] archaeological investigation has not yet confirmed such an hypothesis.

Two facts, however, remain inescapable; one is the tradition, current in antiquity, that there was a Greek settlement in eastern Arabia; the other is the density of finds of Hellenistic date on the coast of this region (Potts 1984a, map 4, 85). It seems unlikely that Greeks would have settled in the inland oases, such as Thaj, Abqaiq and al-Hofuf, given their purely Arabian character. Apart from a few imports, the archaeological material is mainly local (Hasaean inscriptions,

---

30. Pliny 6.32.159: 'Here were also the Greek towns of Arethusa, Larisa and Chalcis, but they have been destroyed in various wars' (Loeb, 1947). These towns are located in Eastern Arabia by Peters 1972, 224–5; Cohen 1978, 18 n.75 and map; Potts 1984a, 105. They all echo Tarn 1951, 66: '... the Seleucids took such trouble to colonise the inner Persian Gulf in spite of the heat ... on the Arabian side, Arethusa, Larisa, Chalcis, Artemita ...'.
31. The importance of the main land-route appears to be the result primarily of the Mecca pilgrimages from Iraq to Saudi Arabia.
32. Arrian *Anab.* 7.21.7: '... he sailed to the Pallacopas and down, by it, to the lakes in the direction of Arabia. There he saw a good site and built a city there and fortified it and settled there some of the Greek mercenaries ...' (Loeb, 1958).

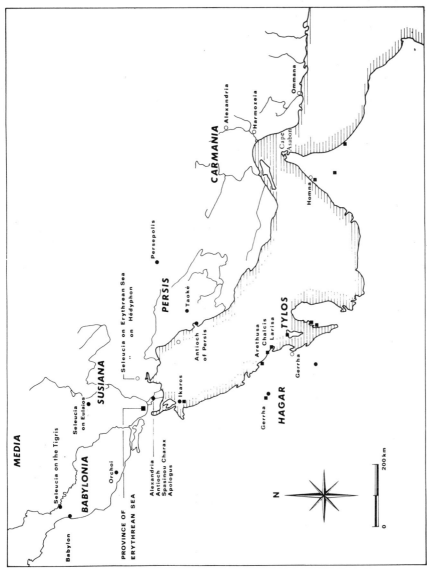

Fig. 3. Tentative map
of the Gulf area under
the Seleucid
monarchy

Hagarite coins) and Antiochus III's visit to Gerrha clearly shows that the city was not inhabited by Greek people.[33] If, by contrast, one accepts the idea discussed above of a Seleucid fleet operating in the Gulf and in some of its ports of call, it appears feasible that there might have been Greek 'establishments' on the coast (garrisons? villages? forts? ports?); and one might then, conjecturally, locate the towns of Larisa, Chalcis and Arethusa here. One would then have to visualise the situation as consisting of an autonomous Arabian mainland fronted by a more or less hellenised coast. Unfortunately, it seems likely that this suggestion will remain unverifiable.[34]

3.ii. The problem of Bahrain seems easier to deal with and there is reason to hope that the continuing archaeological explorations will cast new light on still unanswered questions. Foreign influence on the island is certainly present. The coin hoard at Qala'at al-Bahrain, the Attic black-glazed pottery sherds, a few isolated finds, such as terracotta figurines in the Greek Orientalising style and Greek graffiti, and, finally, some funerary evidence (Salles 1986), suggest contacts with the hellenised world and possibly even the presence of foreigners on the island. The excavations at Qala'at al-Bahrain, limited though they are, allow one to assume a very large settlement.

When one compares the material coming from Qala'at al-Bahrain with that from Failaka where explorations of the hellenistic remains have been intensive, one is struck by the similarities of the two places. Besides the marked similarity of the pottery (the same glazed pottery, the same imports from Eastern Arabia), the similarity of major categories of the material must be stressed: coin hoards including coins from Gerrha, Greek figurines of Orientalising style, which are, for example, absent at Thaj, incense burners, bronze objects. Both sites share the same differences and the same unique features. Their chronology appears to be identical (the question of the date of the foundation of Failaka – first half of the third century BC? – will be discussed below), as the coin hoard at Qala'at al-Bahrain was buried between 245 and 215 BC (Mørkholm 1972, 201), which makes it possible to place the foundation of City V in the preceding decades and thus roughly contemporary with the foundation of Failaka. Even though the later history of the capital of Tylus/Bahrain diverges from that of Icarus/Failaka and resembles the development of Eastern Arabia in

33. See, for example, the reference to the translation of the letter from the Gerrhaeans.
34. It would be interesting to know what sort of remains underlie the Islamic fort at Tarut, off Qatif, and to what period the Cyclopean architecture belongs of which the Danish excavators just caught a glimpse (Bibby 1973, 29–30). Other sites on this small island have yielded hellenistic remains.

the same period,[35] during the third and second centuries BC the history of the two sites seems to exhibit a similar pattern.

Recent excavations have clearly shown that the thirteenth-century Islamic fort at Qala'at al-Bahrain followed the plan and foundations of an older fortress (Kervran 1986). The exact date of this earlier building is still uncertain (Boucharlat 1986), but most of the material from the ancient levels of the Islamic fortress can be dated to the third and second centuries BC. Similarities with the Failaka fortress are its size and the presence of a moat. One possible objection to the comparison is that the watch-towers of the Qala'at al-Bahrain fort are round whereas hellenistic tradition in this area seems normally to have used square ones, such as are found on Failaka. This question needs careful research, but one should not reject *a priori* the existence of a Seleucid fortress at Qala'at al-Bahrain/Tylus.

The presence of a fort might help to explain Antiochus III's visit to Tylus. How, after all, could the king have imposed his will on the Gerrhaeans for any length of time if he had merely embarked on a naval adventure with no follow-up? If the Gerrhaeans were afraid of anything it might well have been the island of Bahrain, which was adjacent to their territory and formed a natural outlet for their maritime trade. Antiochus III's visit to Tylus where he is not said by Polybius to have received either tribute or gifts, might then be interpreted either as an inspection of a Greek post (a garrison? a port of call for the Seleucid fleet? a surveillance-point for the neighbouring mainland?) or as a stop in order to found one.

The presence of a Seleucid fortified site on Tylus would help to clarify the problem of the historical geography of the island during the hellenistic period, i.e. the multiplicity of cemeteries and the lack of settlement sites apart from Qala'at al-Bahrain. The following approach is both preliminary and new and will be developed more fully elsewhere.

The economy of the island, on the evidence of historical and archaeological sources, is based primarily on dates and pearl-fishing together with a variety of food-crops. The first two products do not need major financial investment and were operated as small freeholds during the medieval and modern periods; that is, individuals owned the boats used for pearl-fishing or were owners of small and medium-sized palmgroves. This parcelling out of the economy was, however, integrated into the tribal system, which created associations and/or relations of dependency. At the top of the hierarchy was a tribal aristocracy which organised the trading and marketing; it played a decisive role in

35. Note the close similarities between the end of Potts' Middle Hasaean and Salles' Tylus Vb, as illustrated in Lombard and Salles 1984.

directing the export of valuable commodities such as pearls and dates, and also occasionally attempted to exercise a monopoly over the land.[36]

There is little reason to believe that the socio-economic structure was substantially different in the hellenistic period. Because of its commercial interests the leading aristocracy was urban; and the function of the Qala'at al-Bahrain site, apart from its military character, was that of a central market for the Bahraini economy (cultivated land is never further than 25 kilometres from the town) and an export-centre for the island's valuable products.[37] The 'working class', engaged in date-cultivation and pearl-fishing, whatever its precise status may have been, was scattered through small dispersed settlements, villages or hamlets located all over the northern plain in gardens and plantations, or in coastal settlements, all of which were built of light materials (such as the *barastis* made of palm-leaves) which leave no archaeological traces.[38] Only the tombs and cemeteries attest the scattered character of the settlement pattern. The political development of the island is thus only visible in the city, inasmuch as it is the place where any power, be it economic or military, local or foreign, was located. The installation of Neo-Assyrian, Neo-Babylonian or Achaemenid rule would not entail any change in economic organisation or the settlement pattern (cf. Briant 1982d, 181; 182; 1982c, esp. 412–15); only the town would reflect such changes, including the possible establishment of Greek domination.

This would explain why a Seleucid presence would only be visible inside the site of Qala'at al-Bahrain, while the rest of the island remained entirely untouched by any process of colonisation. There may have been a fair-sized Seleucid garrison, isolated from the world and the inhabitants of the island, but allied with the local aristocracy for whom the Greek military presence was a protection. This hypoth-

36. See, for example, the steadily increasing control of landed estates on the island by the al-Khalifa family since 1783. The analysis here developed is based on Khouri 1980, chs 2–4.

37. If this sedentary aristocracy was not urban it has left no remains of any kind of 'palatial' settlement outside the capital. There are some traces of 'high-ranking persons' in a small number of important tombs scattered over the northern plain (Salles 1986); these may, however, indicate their place of origin rather than residence.

38. The northern plain of the island has been intensively cultivated for millennia by a population which is fairly large when compared to the small size of the island. The result is that all archaeological remains have been obliterated, save temples and cemeteries, i.e. no secular building remains have been preserved. Small villages and hamlets are the traditional settlement types on the island; according to the *Gazetteer of Arabia* 1979, s.v. Bahrain, there were only ten villages with houses constructed of durable materials at the beginning of this century, and 73 villages of huts only, with an average of 36 huts per village. The density of population on the arable land (estimated surface area: 85 km$^2$, Larsen 1983, 11) was 1.165 per km$^2$ (compared with 2.941 in 1971). On the construction of *barastis*, see Bibby 1972, 102–3 and pl. 9.

esis, still subject to confirmation and study, differs in several points from that proposed by Larsen (1983, 203). It is, however, very similar to the pattern which has been suggested for the thirteenth century AD and one might profitably compare with this the Portuguese occupation of the island (Kervran 1986).[39]

3.iii. In dealing with Failaka the first problem to be considered is the date of the foundation of the hellenistic site. The Sotelês dedication dates to the end of the fourth/beginning of the third century BC on palaeographic grounds; this means that it is more or less contemporary with the expeditions undertaken at Alexander's behest (Roueché, Sherwin-White 1985). It must be remembered, however, that the inscription is not necessarily related to the foundation of the site; it was found at Tell Khazneh, a few hundred metres from the hellenistic fortress, on the site of a pre-hellenistic local sanctuary, later rebuilt by Greek settlers, and there is no evidence of any settlement around the building (Calvet, Caubet, Salles 1985). It is perfectly possible that Greek explorers simply offered a sacrifice to their gods after a difficult sea-voyage quite unconnected with any plans of conquest or colonisation. Indeed the wording of the inscription appears to reflect a thanksgiving of precisely this type (there are references to Poseidon and *Soteira*), and although it was naturally offered to Greek gods it was set up in the sanctuary of a local divinity.[40] It is, therefore, impossible to associate the Sotelês dedication with the *foundation* of the site F5 (= the fortress) though it could attest the installation of a garrison-force. One should not exclude the possibility of a small Greek presence as early as the beginning of the third century BC.

Unfortunately the archaeological finds offer no solution to this problem. Some pottery and terracotta figurines may be related to earlier periods such as the Neo-Babylonian and Achaemenid ones, but their evolution is unknown and their dating uncertain as they lack well-dated stratigraphical contexts. Chronological indications provided by inscriptions refer to later dates: the long letter from Anaxarchus to Ikadion is dated to 239 BC by Jeppesen (1960, 196) and 203 by Roueché and Sherwin-White (1985). The painted altar inscription from the Artemis sanctuary (Salles 1984c, 137) and a still unpublished inscribed sherd from Tell Khazneh date to around the middle or second

39. In the thirteenth century the Islamic fort was the main, if not the only, centre for the storage, processing and distribution of dates (Rougeulle 1982, 67–77). The absence of Portuguese remains on the island, both physical and socio-cultural, has frequently been remarked; the explanation lies in the fact that the Portuguese lived enclosed in the fortress and had no real contact with the population of the island.
40. For references to pre-hellenistic cults on Failaka, Calvet 1984a; Roueché, Sherwin-White 1985; on the possible antecedents of the cult of Greek Artemis on Failaka, Salles 1984c, 181–2. It is not clear whether the divinity worshipped in Tell Khazneh was male or female.

half of the second century BC. The complex stratigraphy of the latter site is too disturbed to trace its development. Finally, despite the evidence of some isolated finds dating to the pre-hellenistic periods inside the fortress and in the beach-sanctuary, the construction of these buildings cannot be dated before the hellenistic period.

The numismatic finds do not come from precisely dated archaeological levels, apart from the hoards, and their potential significance is thus limited. The excavations in F5 (= the fortress) have yielded a coin of Alexander (mint unknown), struck between 336 and 300 BC (Mørkholm 1979, 227), another of Seleucus I, 310–300 BC (Mørkholm 1960, 207) and one of Seleucus II from the Susa mint (Mørkholm 1979, 221), all earlier than the numerous coins of Antiochus III. Unfortunately there are not enough of them to date conclusively the original foundation of the site. However, many other features such as the Sotelês dedication, the numismatic finds, early pottery and figurines all point to a foundation (of what type is unclear) as early as the first half of the third century BC. We should probably connect the foundation of this site with the creation of the province of 'the districts of the Erythrean Sea'.[41]

The second problem requiring consideration is the exact nature and status of the Greek settlement of Icarus/Failaka. If one accepts Cohen's analysis (1978), the site of Failaka would match perfectly the development he postulates as typical of a Seleucid colony: an active garrison of soldiers (ibid. 5) which begins by fortifying the place (ibid. 23) and to which eventually lands are allotted (ibid. 5; 29). The presence of a colony on Failaka would be justified by the need to defend frontiers and protect trade routes (ibid. 7; 25). As in the case of many other colonies in the Seleucid Empire, the colony was established near a temple or associated with a 'temple-state' (ibid. 21; 66). The colonists tried to preserve the Greek ideal far from their cities of origin by holding games or forming associations (ibid. 36; 76). Cohen, in fact, refers explicitly to this concept of a military colony in dealing with Failaka (ibid. 42–4; 68–9). Cohen's analysis has been severely criticised (Sherwin-White 1980) and his conclusions cannot be accepted without discussion.

In the present state of research, it is obvious that the settlement never became a *polis*, and equally obvious that it was part of the *chôra basilikê* – compare the land-allotments referred to in Anaxarchus' letter. Roueché and Sherwin-White (1985) note that Anaxarchus' letter is addressed to *oiketai*, i.e. to all free inhabitants of the island, Greek and non-Greek, *not* to the *katoikoi*, the 'military' settlers of a typical Seleucid colony. Further, the inhabitants are never described

41. *Contra* Jeppesen 1960, who suggests a connection of the site with the Susiana; cf. also Roueché, Sherwin-White 1985.

by a city-ethnic which would enable them to be identified as members of a *polis*.[42] 'There is, therefore, no evidence for any administrative organisation on Ikaros other than that of the cult (or cults) on the island' (Roueché, Sherwin-White 1985, 31). The Seleucid settlement would then be a garrison (*phrourion*), situated near a local sanctuary, which was maintained and tended by inhabitants native to the island whom the king wanted to protect against Greek encroachments.

The question of the precise status of Icarus remains to be solved; it is to be hoped that new discoveries will help with this. The function of the site seems easier to understand even if some points remain unclear. It was in all likelihood a port of call and place of supplies for a Seleucid fleet, held by a garrison living in a small fort. One should remember the role of the island as a port of call for long-distance trade because of its abundant supplies of fresh water. It should not be seen as an *emporion* or an international market – it very probably functioned as a local market (compare the pottery imported from Eastern Arabia) with a limited range. The instructions issued to Ikadion seem to have been intended to restrict trading-activities, protect the island's sparse resources and safeguard the import of products necessary for the survival of its inhabitants.

What is striking is the prominence of religion. There are two sanctuaries inside the fortress, another along the shore and a fourth at Tell Khazneh; in other words, four separate cult-places all in use at the same time in a small island. The religious aspect of the island was of great antiquity and particularly prominent during the Dilmun period, i.e. at the beginning of the second millennium BC. It is the only feature of the island remarked upon by ancient writers when they mention it before the arrival of the Greeks. Further, all the Greek inscriptions from the site deal with religious life, above all Anaxarchus' letter – which refers to the 'removal' of the Artemis sanctuary, which cannot, unfortunately, be identified in the archaeology of the site, and the concession of new rights or the renewal of ancient prerogatives, perhaps only to the temple-staff.[43]

42. As Anaxarchus' letter is addressed to all the inhabitants of the island, the omission of any 'Icarian' ethnic is appropriate. It is conceivable that such an ethnic never existed, see the dedication of an altar by *hoi ex Ikarou* (Roueché, Sherwin-White 1985). Nothing is known of the ethnic origin of the Greeks who settled on the island, except for the mention of *Sotelês Athenai[ou]*, the precise import of which is uncertain (ethnic? filiation?).

43. Temple A was definitely built at the same time as fortress F5, in the course of the first half of the third century BC and not later than 250 BC (see above). Temple A is thus earlier than sanctuary B6 and if the 'removal' of the sanctuary mentioned in Anaxarchus' letter refers to sanctuary B6 on the beach it must have been *from* the fortress. On the other hand it is possible that the pre-Greek cults of Tell Khazneh were moved into the fortress at the time it was built; but there is no evidence of a female divinity at Tell Khazneh which was in use down to the end of the second century BC.

The purpose could then have been to maintain good relations with the local religious aristocracy, to please the temple-staff (and priests?) at a time when a hellenisation of the cult is indisputable: certainly by the end of the third century BC the old local sanctuary at Tell Khazneh appears to be entirely Greek.

The reasons for the religious importance of the island have still to be clarified, but research into earlier periods, such as the Dilmun and Kassite periods, as well as further hellenistic finds, might help to elucidate them. We also need to know more about the secular life of a small Greek garrison like this one which formed an outpost on the fringes of the Seleucid empire.

## Conclusion

During the second half of the first millennium BC, the history of the Gulf is best attested in the Seleucid period both by written sources and by archaeological finds. The Achaemenid period remains obscure, probably because of insufficient study of the sparse information available. The greatest confusion prevails in texts of the Roman period and in the precise chronology of the archaeological material of the Partho-Sassanian period.[44] The interest shown by the Greeks in this area reflected not so much a simple enthusiasm for discovering new lands as a deliberate policy of the Seleucid kings.

The venture was not one of conquest and 'colonisation'. The natural conditions of the region did not favour the direct exploitation of local resources which are limited and mainly useful to the inhabitants of the desert and its fringes; i.e. the restricted ecological base of the Arab societies in the region, which results in their prime economic activities being the caravan-trade and pastoralism, makes them resistant to any attempts at centralised control (Briant 1982e, 179; 236–7). The aims of royal policies, such as Antiochus' personal visit to Tylus, appear to have been entirely commercial. The intention was to protect and possibly control the sea-route and the long-distance trade with Mesopotamia and the Eastern Mediterranean. The Greeks were not responsible for creating this commercial axis but inherited it from the

---

44. The Gulf is not completely absent from written sources. The island of Tylus still occurs in Ptolemy and other geographers (Calvet 1984b, 342). The attractive suggestion has been made that it also appears in a bilingual inscription from Palmyra dating to AD 131, in the distorted form Thilouan (Seyrig 1946, 197, l.4). If correct, Thilouan would then be a satrapy of Characene, which is perfectly plausible if one bears in mind the control exercised over the Gulf by the kingdom of Characene at this period (Salles in press; Teixidor 1984). It is almost certainly Bahrain/Tylus which is meant by the reference to Thalun in a letter of the Nestorian archbishop Iso'yab III (AD 649–659) (Beaucamp and Robin 1983, 178).

Achaemenids who in turn were probably the heirs of their predecessors.[45] The means adopted by the Seleucids to realise this policy appear to have been mainly military: the creation and maintenance of a (possibly) permanent fleet in the Gulf, supported by fortified garrisons located on, probably, both sides of the route.[46] Failaka, so far, is the only one of these which is beginning to throw some light on this strategy, but it is not unreasonable to hope that the hellenistic site at Qala'at al-Bahrain will supply similar evidence in the future.

What is remarkable about Seleucid policy is its awareness of, and respect for, local conditions, such as traditional political relationships, local economic interests and indigenous cults. There is no sign of a profound Greek influence on the Arab material cultures which, of course, outlasted the Seleucid period, despite traces of some foreign influence. Furthermore no *major* cultural exchange between Arabs and Greeks is observable in this region of the hellenistic world. Certainly no phenomenon similar to the developments in Bactria and Gandhara can be seen. The Greeks, settled in a small number of isolated spots on the fringes of the desert, did not leave a deep imprint on the populations with whom they came into contact. It would seem excessive to claim any kind of hellenisation of the Gulf. One should not, however, underestimate the gradual influx of Greco-Roman civilisation with an admixture of Iranian elements, which became visible later in the spread of Christian communities in the Gulf.

45. Written sources for the Achaemenid period are rather less clear than assumed by Briant (1982e, 165). The completion of Necho's canal by Darius I was not meant to link the Mediterranean to the Gulf via the Red Sea; a forty-day journey from Cilicia to Susa is impossible if one bears in mind the difficulties in navigating the Arabian peninsula. Necho's canal was intended to establish a link between the eastern Mediterranean and the Indian merchandise arriving in South Arabian ports. The Ptolemaic kings followed the same policy later (see section 2.ii). Further, it seems an exaggerated assumption that Alexander's conquest of Arabia would have resulted in a 'fundamental reorganisation of the commercial routes' (Briant 1982e, 177); given the present state of research, the sea-route from Alexandria to Susa including a circumnavigation of Arabia could never have functioned as a viable trade route. It seems more likely that Alexander wanted to gain control of the two major arteries along which the Far Eastern and South Arabian trade moved: (a) the direct route from Susa to India through the Gulf; (b) the route from India to South Arabia which linked up at that point with the caravan trade moving between South Arabia and the Mediterranean, resulting in an inevitable and considerable rise in the prices of Far Eastern and Arabian commodities. Route (a) appears to have been in operation, with occasional interruptions, from the Achaemenid to the Sassanian period; route (b), an entirely independent network, only became a wholly maritime route from the first century BC onwards, thus fulfilling Darius I's and Alexander's dreams.
46. If this proposed scheme is plausible, the task of identifying more garrison-sites on both the Arab and Persian sides of the Gulf devolves on the archaeologists. The present number found is not enough to have ensured protection and supplies for a fleet operating over the entire length and breadth of the Gulf.

# CHAPTER FIVE

# The Problem of Hellenistic Syria*

## *Fergus Millar*

And it came to pass after the victory of Alexander the son of Philip, the Macedonian, who came out from the land of Kittim and smote Darius, king of the Persians and Medes . . . and started many wars and conquered many fortified places and slew the kings of the earth . . . And his sons ruled, each in his own place, and after his death they all assumed diadems, and his sons (ruled) after him for many years and multiplied evils in the land (1 Maccabees 1.1–9).

The first book of Maccabees in its opening paragraph reflects an important aspect of the impact of hellenistic rule in Syria, the prevalence of conflict, war and instability. It does also, however, illustrate something quite different, the possibility of a communal historical consciousness and a national culture which might provide a framework within which a community in the Syrian region could have absorbed and reacted to the fact of Greek conquest. That this was true of the Jewish community of Jerusalem is beyond all question (Millar 1978). 1 Maccabees, written originally in Hebrew, directly continues the tradition of Old Testament historiography. It has indeed also been argued that Chronicles and the books of Ezra and Nehemiah were also written in the hellenistic period (Eissfeldt 1965, 529f). If that is dubious, the book of Ecclesiasticus (*Ben Sira*) was certainly written around 200 BC or soon after, and Daniel, in its final form, in the 160s (Schürer 1986, 198f; 245f).

The culture of Judaea and Jerusalem thus exhibits both a profound continuity with the pre-Greek past and an equally undeniable absorption of Greek elements (Hengel 1974). As is well known, the first attested use of the word *hellenismos* comes in 2 Maccabees (4.13), and refers to the enrolment of the Jerusalemites as 'Antiochians', the setting-up of a gymnasium and the wearing of Greek clothes.

* The work on which this survey of the problem of Hellenistic Syria is based was carried out at the Institute for Advanced Study at Princeton, during an enjoyable and profitable visit from January to April 1984. Successive versions were presented at seminars held at the Institute and, in Autumn 1984, at the Institute of Classical Studies, London. The paper has benefited from assistance, advice and criticism from the editors and from a number of friends and colleagues, notably G. W. Bowersock, Pierre Briant, P. M. Fraser, J. F. Gilliam, Chr. Habicht and Javier Teixidor. It will readily be accepted that the remaining imperfections are due to the author.

We can therefore use Maccabees to pose at least one of the many questions which can in principle be asked about hellenistic Syria. By 'hellenistic' in this sense I mean simply the period from Alexander to the mid-first century BC. By 'Syria' I mean anywhere west of the Euphrates and south of the Amanus Mountains – essentially therefore the area west of the Euphrates where Semitic languages were used: Aramaic in its various dialects, Phoenician, Hebrew, and earlier forms of Arabic. This begs a question about Asia Minor (and especially Cilicia), from which Aramaic documents are known, and a far more important one about northern Mesopotamia and about Babylonia. Should we not, that is, see the various Aramaic-speaking areas of the Fertile Crescent as representing a single culture, or at any rate closely connected cultures, and therefore not attempt to study the one area without the others?

The first question is one of cultural identity. Can we observe else-where in Syria, i.e. outside Judaea, either the continued survival of a non-Greek culture, or the fusion (*Verschmelzung*) in Droysen's sense of Greek and non-Greek cultures? As I have argued elsewhere, there is perhaps just enough evidence to show that this was the case in the Phoenician cities of the coast (Millar 1983). But elsewhere, with the exception of Judaea, we meet a problem which haunts one and all of the questions we would like to ask. If we are going to ask about the nature or limits of hellenisation, there is a prior question: the hellenisation of what? Whether we think of northern Syria, the Orontes valley, or Damascus, or present-day Jordan, we find that almost nothing is known, from either literary or documentary or archaeological evidence, about what these places were like in the Achaemenid period (the archaeological evidence is largely confined to individual domestic or decorative objects and weaponry (Moorey 1975; 1980); only the evidence from the Judaean area has been systemati-cally assembled by Stern 1982). Our best evidence for the personal life, nomenclature and religious observances of non-Jewish Aramaic speakers in the Achaemenid period comes in fact from the private letters in Aramaic from Egypt (Milik 1967). The not very numerous monumental inscriptions in Aramaic from Syria (Donner, Röllig 1964–68, nos. 201–27; Abou Assaf, Bordreuil, Millard 1982) are no later than the seventh century BC. The only known cuneiform archive from Syria, found near Aleppo and dating to the Neo-Babylonian and early Achaemenid periods (Fales 1973), will serve to remind us of how much we do not know. The only cuneiform tablet of the Achaemenid period so far discovered in Jordan (Dalley 1984) is, however, more revealing. Written in Harran in the first year of a king named Darius, it records a sale by two people with Aramaic names to a person whose father has the Edomite/Idumaean name of Qusu-yada'. It was found at Tell Tawilan near Petra, and thus clearly reflects the type of movement and interchange round the Fertile Crescent hinted at above. It is also significant that the same Idumaean name reappears on an Aramaic/Greek bilingual *ostrakon* of the third century BC (below p. 118). By contrast, formal inscriptions in Aramaic are rare (though note that of *Tobiah* from 'Araq el-Emir, Mazar 1957). Otherwise, it is only in Teima in north-west Arabia, on the southern borders of what would later be the Nabataean kingdom, that we can find Aramaic inscriptions, west of the Euphrates and south of the Amanus, in the Achaemenid period itself (Donner, Röllig 1964-1968 nos. 228–30; Winnett, Reed 1970; see Bawden et al. 1980; new texts in Livingstone et al. 1983). Aramaic *ostraka* of the Persian period are, however, known from a number of sites in Israel, e.g. Beer-Sheva (Naveh 1973), and from Arad (Naveh 1981). It can reasonably be expected that archaeological investigation in areas outside present-day Israel would produce more; and Aramaic material of the Persian period has, for instance, been discovered at Tell el Mazar in Jordan (Yassine 1983).

For the moment our evidence on Achaemenid Syria is very limited (see e.g. Rainey 1969), and what we know of its social and economic history is still largely dependent on passing allusions in classical sources, for instance Xenophon's account of his march across north Syria from Myriandrus, a Phoenician trading-post, through an area of villages, and one satrapal palace and associated *paradeisos*, to the city of Thapsacus on the Euphrates (*Anab.* 1.4.6–11). There were apparently no cities on the route which they took between the coast and the Euphrates at that moment. Did they deliberately avoid Aleppo, or had it declined as a city? Of the inland cities of the Syrian region which may still have been inhabited in the Persian period only Damascus is really certain. It was there that Parmenio captured the treasures of Darius (Q.C. 3.12.27; Arrian *Anab.* 2.11.9–10); and Strabo 16.2.20 (756) says that it was the chief city of Syria in the Persian period. Berossus also reports (*FGrHist.* 680 F 11) that Artaxerxes II (405/404–359/358 BC) set up images of Artemis Anaitis in various places, including Ecbatana, Babylon, Susa, Sardis and Damascus.

Our ignorance of Achaemenid Syria is a major problem also for any assessment of the economic consequences of the Macedonian conquest. From a 'Marxist' standpoint, for instance, the late Heinz Kreissig (1978) argued that the Seleucid empire continued to be based on the 'Asiatic mode of production', meaning the labour of peasants who were not slaves and owned their own means of production, but were dependent on those to whom they paid their surplus. Pierre Briant (1982b, 248), from a similar standpoint, once equated the 'Asiatic mode of production' with the 'royal economy' briefly sketched in the Aristotelian *Oeconomica* II. But if we look for specific and provable instances of dependent villages in Syria in the Achaemenid period, we will find precisely, and only, those in north Syria which Xenophon states had been granted to Parysatis (*Anab.* 1.4.9). We need not dispute Briant's generalisation that the village was a predominant social formation throughout the Near and Middle East through both the Achaemenid and the hellenistic periods. But we do *not* know what was the typical set of existing economic relationships, into which the Macedonian conquest obtruded.

The fact of military conquest is indeed about all that is clear from the early hellenistic period. Beyond that we would want to ask, for instance, some of the following questions: (1) What new Greek cities were founded, when and where? (2) Were they accompanied by Greek or Macedonian settlement in the surrounding territories? (3) What substantial changes, if any, accompanied the acquisition of Greek *names* by existing cities? (4) Was there significant immigration and settlement by Greek speakers outside the context of city foundations? (5) Are we to think of a degree of social and cultural fusion between Greek settlers and the existing population, or rather, as Briant (1982b) has argued, of the Greeks forming separate enclaves? (6) Did the period see the introduction into Syria of what 'Marxists' define as the 'ancient mode of production', i.e. one based on a monetary economy, private property and the exploitation of slave labour? Any temptation to make sweeping generalisations in this topic should be tempered by the important evidence of the papyri from the Wadi Dâliyeh, north of Jericho (Cross 1969; see Lapp 1974). Though full publication of these documents is still awaited after nearly a quarter of a century, preliminary descriptions show that they date to the fourth century, before Alexander's conquest (one is firmly dated to 335 BC); they may well, as Cross suggests, have been deposited in the cave where they were found in the aftermath of the Samaritan rising of *c.* 332 BC. The papyrus of 335 BC records the sale of a slave for 35 pieces of silver. There were also a number of coins, imported and local (especially Tyrian), which also remain unpublished.

These documents are also potentially relevant to a final question, (7) What changes were brought about, outside the area of Greek settlement, in the culture of the inhabitants, e.g. in literacy? What combination of literacy was there in Semitic languages (Hebrew, Aramaic, Phoenician, and later Nabataean), in Greek, in both or in neither?

The only substantial area where it is beyond question that new city foundations transformed the map of the region is Syria, with Seleucus I's foundation of Antioch, Apamea, Seleucia and Laodicea, a process brilliantly described by Seyrig (1970b). Near Antioch there was said to have been briefly a city 'Antigoneia', founded by Antigonus Monophthalmus, and settled by Athenians (so Malalas, apparently following a chronographer named Pausanias, *FGrHist.* 854 F 10). At Laodicea there was similarly said to have been a village called 'Mazabda', and at Apamea one called 'Pharnace' (ibid. F 10, 9–10).

Excavations on this site have revealed one object from the Persian period, a fragment of an Attic pyxis (Balty 1977). What is significant is that it is *only*, so far as I have discovered to date, in the area of these cities that we find smaller settlements with Greek or Macedonian names. For instance, Diodotus Tryphon, who seized the Seleucid throne in the 140s, came from a *phrourion* called 'Cassiana' which, like others with the names 'Larissa', 'Megara', 'Apollonia' and so forth, belonged to Apamea, where Tryphon was educated (Strabo 16.2.10 (752)). Even so, there were also villages in the territory of Apamea with non-Greek names, like the *kômê Kaprozabadaiôn* which an inscription reveals (*IG* XIV 2558; photo in Balty 1971, 17; see *BE* 1960, 95). The word 'Kapro' reflects Kfar, meaning 'village', in Aramaic, as in Hebrew (see *BE* 1958, no.295). Some 30 miles east of Antioch, there was a village with the name 'Maroneia', which may be Greek; but, at any rate in the fourth century AD, a person from there would speak Syriac (Jerome, *V. Malchi* 2). Similarly, 20 kilometres north of Laodicea there was a place called 'Heraclea Thalasse' (*IGLS* IV, 1252, of 108/7 BC; cf. Pliny, *NH* 5.79). If there was any area where Greek settlement may have produced significant direct effects on property-relations and 'modes of production', it will have been in the territories surrounding the new cities of the north Syrian tetrapolis.

Elsewhere concrete evidence for new city foundations of the earlier hellenistic period is remarkably sparse. There were none along the Phoenician coast or in Idumaea or Judaea. Late sources record that a Macedonian settlement was established by Alexander or Perdiccas on the site of Samaria (Schürer 1979, 160). In this case there is substantial archaeological evidence which can be brought into relation with this settlement. The round towers added to the existing wall of the acropolis are dated to the late fourth century; an outer circuit of walls, with square towers, perhaps belongs to the second century BC (Crowfoot 1942, 24–31). It seems certain that this small fortified town on a hill-top is that of the Macedonian settlers and their descendants, to be distinguished from the Samaritans proper, who in the later fourth century had established their own temple on Mount Gerizim (Schürer 1979, 161; see further below p. 124).

The cults followed by the settlers are illustrated (if no more than that) by a finely-cut inscription of the third century BC from Samaria with a dedication by Hegesander, Xenarchis and their children to Sarapis and Isis (Crowfoot et al. 1957, 37, no. 13; illustrated in Avi-Yonah 1972, 37). But in many places we cannot be *certain* what social changes are implied by the appearance of cities with Macedonian place-names, like Beroea, Cyrrhus or Gindarus in the north-east, or Pella or Dium in Jordan (for toponyms in Syria see the illuminating survey by Frézouls 1978). Excavations at Pella have now revealed some evidence of the earlier hellenistic period (Smith 1982). But

Cyrrhus, for example, makes no appearance at all in our sources until 6,000 'Cyrrhestian' soldiers are recorded as mutinying against Antiochus III in 220 (Polyb. 5.50.7–8; 57.4; see Frézouls 1954/5; 1977). It is reasonable to believe that it was a Macedonian settlement of the early period, like Dura-Europus on the Euphrates. But again, very little is known of the social character of hellenistic Dura except the vital item that some at least of the land there was classified as *klêroi* (*P. Dura* 15, second century BC). As a physical structure it was, like Samaria, a fortified site of moderate extent (the three longer sides measuring just under 1,000 metres each), sited on a plateau above the Euphrates, and equipped with walls. Internally, it was set out in regular blocks on the well-known Hippodamian plan, with a central agora. It is uncertain which, if any, temples can be attributed to the initial hellenistic phase. No evidence for a theatre or other public buildings of this period has been found (Perkins 1973, 10–16). It is natural to presume that we should envisage both Samaria and Dura as Macedonian military settlements, placed for strategic purposes in alien landscapes, and with modest pretensions to being the bearers of a wider Greek culture. In the case of many other foundations there is still less evidence. Beroea (Aleppo) is recorded as a foundation of Seleucus I (Appian, *Syr.* 57). Once again we have nothing to show whether the ancient city of Aleppo still existed at the moment of the settlement; but the street plan to this day reflects the rectangular axes which may well be those of the colony (Sauvaget 1941, 40).

The same problems persist if we look at places which subsequently gained hellenistic dynastic names: Philadelphia (Amman) and Ptolemais (Acco) from Ptolemy Philadelphus (near here Strabo 16.2.27 (758), notes three place-names which may reflect Ptolemaic rule: 'Sykaminôn polis', 'Boukolôn polis' and 'Krokodeilôn polis'). Epiphaneia (Hama) presumably gained its name from Antiochus IV Epiphanes. This was of course another ancient city, which, as Josephus records, the *epichôrioi* still called 'Hama' (*Ant.* 1.138). But, paradoxically, excavations on the site have seemed to suggest that it was unoccupied between its destruction by Sargon II in 720 and the beginning of Greek settlement in the second century BC (so Fugman 1958, 269). On the other hand, Sargon is recorded to have settled 6,300 Assyrians there, and there continue to be occasional mentions of Hama as a place in documents of the intervening period (ibid., 264); the archaeological evidence should not be interpreted on the *assumption* that the site was desolate after 720 (see now esp. Francis, Vickers 1985), and imported hellenistic pottery appears there before the reign of Antiochus IV (Christensen, Johansen 1971, 1). The evidence for continuity of settlement is therefore ambivalent; and while the evidence for the hellenistic city remains unpublished, it is impossible to say whether it would suggest the implantation of an organised settlement at a specific moment. But if Epiphaneia did receive an actual settlement of Greeks, there was certainly no such settlement in Jerusalem in the 170s, when the population briefly acquired the title 'Antiocheis'. The settlement on the Akra in Jerusalem in the 160s was another matter.

The provable extent of organised Macedonian or Greek settlement is thus limited to one area, north Syria. Other towns which acquired Greek names may well also have received settlements, but some certainly did not. If we consider the entire non-desert area west of the Euphrates, Greek colonial settlement must be regarded as a relatively limited phenomenon, largely restricted in time also, to the reign of Seleucus I. Whatever created the conditions for a large-scale transformation, fusion or conflict, if anything did, it was not, except in north Syria, a massive process of colonisation.

Was there none the less extensive private immigration, either for settlement on the land or for other purposes, such as trading in slaves? Here again we have to say that we do not know. We can easily illustrate, for instance, the presence in Syria of Ptolemaic soldiers from various parts of the Greek world; the inscription from Ras Ibn Hani on the coast 8 kilometres north of Laodicea (Rey-Coquais 1978) which records some of these is the earliest Greek public inscription from north Syria, dating to about the second half of the third century. Excavations on this site have shown that a fortified Greek town, whose name remains unknown, was established there in the same period, probably by the Ptolemies (Leriche 1982). Greeks also entered the service of local dynasts: a papyrus from the Zenon archive shows us soldiers from Cnidus, Caunus, Macedon, Miletus, Athens and Aspendus serving in 159 under Tobias in Ammonitis (*PCZ* 59003 = *CPJ* I, 1). In the second century we come across a Macedonian settled at Abae in Arabia and married to an Arabian wife (D.S. 32.10.2), or a *politeuma* of Caunians settled in Sidon (*OGIS* 592). No doubt we could accumulate further illustrations; but it would hardly be significant, since it would be more than surprising if there had been *no* Greek private settlement in this region. But it does have to be emphasised that there is no positive evidence to suggest that there was private immigration on a scale which would by itself have brought profound changes in culture, social relations or the economy.

If we go back to the major cities of the Syrian tetrapolis, there is certainly adequate evidence to illustrate their character as Greek cities in the hellenistic period. It should be stressed that in the absence of large-scale documentary evidence we still depend quite significantly on passing items of narrative material, like the papyrus report (the Gurob papyrus), from the Ptolemaic side, of Ptolemy III's invasion of Syria in the 240s. It records the priests, *archontes* and the other citizens of Seleucia, with the *hêgemones* (officers of the Seleucid garrison) and soldiers, coming down to greet the invading forces. A similar scene is said to have followed at Antioch, with a ceremonial greeting before the city by 'satraps and other *hêgemones*, and soldiers and *synarchiai* and all the *neaniskoi* from the gymnasium', and the rest of the population, bearing cult images (*FGrHist.* 160; Austin 1981 no. 220). Seleucia does not reappear in our evidence until we come to Polybius Book 5, and the narrative of its recapture by Antiochus III in 219; it turns out to be a place of modest size, with some 6,000 'free men' (which may mean citizens only, or all non-slave male inhabitants); perhaps therefore some 30,000 persons in all (5.61.1). These cities produce nothing like the vast harvest of monumental Greek inscriptions which characterise (say) Delphi, Delos or some of the Greek cities of western Asia Minor in this period. It is true that at both Antioch, Seleucia and Laodicea subsequent occupation greatly limits the possibilities of excavation; for the scanty evidence on early hellenistic Laodicea see Stucky 1983, 173f. But it should still not be assumed that the social conditions which elsewhere led to the large production of public inscriptions necessarily applied in Syria in the same way. Public inscriptions from Seleucia in Pieria do reveal, for instance, the vote of a statue for the Seleucid *epistatês* of the city in 186 BC (Welles 1934 no. 45 = *IGLS* III.1, 1184); or a letter of Antiochus VIII or IX, of 109 BC, confirming the freedom of the city (*OGIS* 257 = Welles 1934 nos. 71/2). There is no substantial corpus of the public inscriptions of Seleucia; excavation of the relevant public buildings, when identified, might of course reveal them. From Laodicea the only known public decision recorded on stone from the hellenistic period is the *gnômê* (proposal) of Asclepiades and the *archontes*, approved by the *peliganes* (the councillors, a Macedonian word) in 174 BC (*IGLS* IV, 1261), concerning the sanctuary of Isis and Sarapis. From Antioch and Apamea there are no public decrees at all surviving from the hellenistic period; though one inscription from Antioch shows *theôroi* (sacred delegates) honouring an *agonothêtês* from Seleucia in 198/7 BC (Kraeling 1964; *BE* 1965, 436); and one from Daphne shows Antiochus III appointing a priest there (Welles 1934 no. 44). Passing literary references indicate at least the existence of gymnasia at Laodicea (Appian *Syr.* 46) and at Daphne near Antioch (Polyb. 30.26.1), and e.g. of a hippodrome near Seleucia (Polyb. 5.47.1). Poseidonius' remarks on the luxury of life in Syria (*Ath.* 210e–f = 527e–f) imply that gymnasia were common. None of these cities, however, has revealed any trace of a *theatre* that can be firmly dated to this period. It is surely, I think, a revealing fact that there is no certain archaeological evidence for a theatre of the hellenistic period anywhere in the Syrian region. Given the relative indestructability of theatres built against hillsides, as hellenistic theatres normally were (e.g. those of Priene or Delos), this is one case where negative evidence may be suggestive (so Frézouls 1959; but see Colledge, below p. 151).

Outside the places which we know to have been royal foundations, or to have acquired Greek names, we do have some evidence, from various periods, of the spread of a recognisably Greek way of life. A site called Ayin Dara, north-east of Aleppo, for instance, shows traces of occupation in the Persian period and then a substantial urban area with walls from the hellenistic period, with pottery and coins of the second and first centuries BC (Seirafi, Kirichian 1965). This site, whose Greek name, if it had one, is unknown, is a reminder of just how much of the evidence of hellenistic Syria may simply be lost. For contrast we have Tel Anafa in northern Galilee, whose heated bath house of the later second century BC is the earliest known from the Near East (Herbert 1981); and the well-known site of Marisa in Idumaea, a small urban settlement of six acres, built in the third or early second centuries BC, and enclosed by a fortification wall. Greek was in use there, as shown by some execration texts in Greek, and the inscriptions on the well-known painted tombs. But the house-types are non-Greek and at least some of the inhabitants identified themselves in Greek as 'Sidonians in Marisa' (*OGIS* 593; Horowitz 1980). The mixed culture of this area in the third century BC is now vividly illustrated by a group of ostraca from Khirbet el-Kôm, four in Aramaic, one in Greek and one Greek-Aramaic bilingual; the latter records the borrowing of 32 *zuzn* by Niceratus from one Qus-yada'/Kosides (cf. above p. 112), described (in both texts) by the Greek word *kapêlos*, 'trader' (Geraty 1975). This text, probably of 277 BC, thus reveals the *kapêlos* as a loan-word in a dialect of Aramaic. These ostraca are closely paralleled by an Aramaic ostracon of the third century from Jerusalem, also containing what seem to be two Greek loan-words (Cross 1981).

The ostracon is given the date 277 on the supposition that the 'sixth year' referred to in it is that of Ptolemy Philadelphus. Most of the evidence which illustrates Greek economic activity in Syria comes from the Ptolemaic phase of control. All we have is fragments, occasionally illuminating. Some cities, as we saw, gained dynastic names, Akko becoming 'Ptolemais', and Rabbat-Amman 'Philadelphia'. Scythopolis and Philoteria in Galilee must also have gained their Greek names in the Ptolemaic period. Our main evidence comes from the Zenon papyri, discussed by Tcherikover (1937). These papyri of course owe their survival to the particular conditions of Egypt, and thus cast a side-light on Syria somewhat comparable to that shed by the Aramaic documents from Egypt of the Achaemenid period (above p. 111). But while the relevant climatic and soil conditions, allowing the survival of perishable writing materials, very rarely apply in the

Near East, they are not wholly unknown, as the documents from Qumran and the Wadi Dâliyeh show.

The first thing that the Zenon papyri clearly illustrate is the slave trade. Among the immigrant Greek *klêrouchoi* serving at Birtha in Ammanitis under Tobias, mentioned earlier (*PCZ* 59003 = *CPJ* I, 1), one sells a slave-girl named Sphragis, apparently from Babylon or Sidon, to another, who then sells her to Zenon. In Marisa Zenon also bought some slaves (*sômata*), two of whom escaped and had to be searched for (59015). One Menecles appears as having transported some slaves (*sômata*) and other merchandise (*phorta*) from Gaza to Tyre, and as intending to tranship them without paying the export tax or having an export-permit (*exagogê tôn sômatôn*) (59093). Tobias also sends to Apollonius a group of four slaves as a gift, two described as circumcised and two not (59076 = *CPJ* I, 5). There is no obvious reason in the text for regarding either of the circumcised men as Jewish; if they were not, then this is evidence for the continuation of the custom of circumcision among the Syrians generally in the hellenistic period.

Much more informative for the continuity of a non-Greek culture is a papyrus letter of 156 BC from Egypt (*PZenon* no. 121; see Vaggi 1937) mentioning a slave who was 'by race a Syrian from Bambyce' who was 'tattooed on the right wrist with two barbarian letters'. The letters can only have been Aramaic ones; Bambyce is Hierapolis, an important centre of a non-Greek culture, on which see further below. Lucian, *On the Syrian Goddess*, written in the second century AD, which is about the goddess Astarte of Hierapolis, records (59) that the Syrian adherents of the cult were tattooed on the neck or wrist – 'and thence all *Assyrioi* bear tattoos'.

To come back to the economic impact of Greek rule, slavery and the slave trade was clearly a feature of it; but whether this was a *novelty* remains unclear. The most striking reflection of slavery in hellenistic Syria remains the well-known edict of Ptolemy II Philadelphus dating to April 260, which surely can be taken to illustrate a causal connection between foreign domination and slavery (Lenger 1980 no. 22; Austin 1981 no. 275): 'If any of those in Syria or Phoenicia have bought a *sôma laikon eleutheron* ('free native')', or have acquired one in any other way, they are required to prove that they were slaves at the time of acquisition. Those bought at royal auctions, however, are legally owned even if they claim to be free. Moreover soldiers or others who are settled (*katoikountôn*) who are living with *gunaikes laikai* ('native wives') need not declare them as slaves. In the future it will be forbidden to acquire possession of *sômata laika eleuthera* except those sold up by the superintendent of the revenues of Syria and Phoenicia. Whatever the legal definitions involved, the order clearly reflects a notion of the particular liability of the free 'native' population of south Syria to slavery; in particular it is significant that the document has to make clear that the 'native' wives of Ptolemaic soldiers and settlers do *not* have to be categorised as slaves. Strikingly, in this case, the king is taking steps to limit the circumstances under which individuals found themselves regarded as slaves.

As was hinted earlier, any notions of what social, economic, cultural or social status is implied by the expression *sômata laika eleuthera* must remain hypothetical. Even if we disregard acute regional variations (see below) it is no use pretending that we have any idea of the typical forms of property-relations in the Syrian area either before or after Alexander's conquest. We can of course see *examples* of various different things, for instance the exploitation of private landed property in the Ptolemaic period in Palestine, perfectly exemplified in a papyrus from the Zenon archive (*P. Lond.* 1948) of 257 BC. An agent, Glaucias, is writing to Apollonius about his enormous vineyard at Bethaneth, which was somewhere in Galilee:

> On arrival at Bethaneth I took Melas with me and inspected the plants and everything else. The estate seems to me to be satisfactorily cultivated, and he said the vines numbered 80,000. He has also constructed a well, and satisfactory living quarters. He gave me a taste of the wine, and I was unable to distinguish whether it was Chian or local. So your affairs are prospering and fortune is favouring you all along the line.

This does on the face of it seem to be an example of the deliberate increase of productive capacity of a sort which, for Ptolemaic Egypt generally, Alan Samuel (1983) has recently sought to deny. There is, however, no indication of how the estate was worked, whether by slave labour, free hired labour or dependent villagers. The question of dependent, but non-slave, agricultural labour in the hellenistic world has attracted an enormous amount of attention. But the evidence comes almost entirely from Seleucid land-grants or sales in Asia Minor; moreover the real social and economic relations alluded to in these inscriptions remain extremely obscure (Welles 1934 nos. 10–13; 18–20; 62; cf. Briant 1982f). It is also from Asia Minor, and entirely from Strabo's *Geography*, that we have almost all the available descriptions of large communities of *hierodouloi* attached to temples (Welwei 1979; Debord 1982, 76f). Comparable evidence is hardly available from Syria. There are I think, just three items. First the mutilated inscription from Hephzibah near Scythopolis (Bethshean) first published by Landau 1966 and re-edited by Fischer 1979 (cf. Bertrand 1982). The dossier contains petitions to Antiochus III from Ptolemaeus, described as *stratêgos* and *archiereus*, and the king's replies, concerning properties owned by Ptolemaeus. The context is immediately after the Seleucid conquest in 200. All that is clear is that the dossier speaks of *kômai* 'of' Ptolemaeus, and that as owner he is concerned to protect the people (*laoi*) in his villages from official exactions and the quartering of troops (*epistathmeia*). One phrase may imply that some *kômai* had been inherited by him, and others added by the king's command. We can accept that the document embodies the notion of owning villages and (in some sense) of owning or being responsible for the people who inhabit them.

Further north, from the hills inland from Aradus, we have the famous inscription of the temple of Baetocaece (*IGLS* VII, 4028; Austin 1981 no. 178). In response to a report about the *energeia* of the god Zeus of Baetocaece, King Antiochus – which one is uncertain (Seyrig 1951; Rigsby 1980; Baroni 1984) – announces his decision to grant to the god the village of Baetocaece, which a certain Demetrius formerly 'had' (*eschen*), so that its revenue (*prosodos*) may be spent on the sacrifice, and any other steps taken for the improvement of the shrine by the priest appointed by the god. There is to be a monthly tax-free fair, the sanctuary is to be *asulon*, and the village is on no account to be subject to billetting.

It is clear that the cult of Zeus of Baetocaece already existed. The village had, up to the moment of the king's grant of it to the temple, been in private possession. This may mean no more than that there had previously been a (revocable) grant of it to a private person by an earlier king; that is to say that the village belonged in the category of *chôra basilikê*, royal land (so most recently Baroni 1984). No such legal prescription is actually stated in the document, and it is clear from the king's decision that some representation had been made to him about the 'power' (*energeia*) of the god. It is, therefore, equally possible that he is approving the transfer to the sanctuary of land which had previously been in full private ownership. Exactly what is meant for the status of the inhabitants is uncertain. In inscribing this document in the 250s AD, and also a little earlier, in the 220s (*IGLS* VII 4031), they describe themselves as *katochoi* of the god.

The city of Aradus is not involved in this initial transaction, though it was later, under Augustus. Are we then dealing with royal land (*chôra basilikê*) either in the sense of an individual royal property, or in the wider sense, commonly imagined in modern books, that *all* the land outside city territories was 'royal', i.e. in some sense owned and exploited by the king, and at his disposition? In my view this notion goes far beyond what our evidence shows. As what is said below will illustrate, it is very questionable whether this concept has any reflection in the real-life social and economic relations which our sources attest. There were many non-city areas where no direct control was, or could be, exercised by any king.

Where we do find land in royal possession, and then being assigned for cult purposes, is in the remarkable documents from Commagene in which Antiochus I (*c.* 69/38 BC) proclaims his institution of a cult for various gods, for his deceased father, Mithridates Callinicus, and for himself (Waldmann 1973; Wagner and Petzl 1976). Among the other provisions he states that he has dedicated a group of *mousikoi* who are to learn the arts necessary for performing at the cult-festivals, and to be succeeded in the same skills by their sons, daughters and all their descendants. They are described as *hierodouloi*, and are to maintain this hereditary role for ever. It is not clear, however, whether these are or are not the same as the inhabitants of the *kômai* which, in the Nemrud Dagh text, he says he had dedicated to the gods, or (in the text from Arsamea-Nymphaius) of the land *ek basilikês ktêseôs* ('from that in royal possession') which he has dedicated with its revenues, to be looked after by the priests. But at least we confront here an unambiguous reference to specific royal properties, and also, once again, a category of non-free persons (*hierodouloi*) which does not descend from a remote past, but is being created in the first century BC.

Not far away, and at about the same time, Cicero fought his miserable little campaign against the 'free Cilicians' of the Amanus, whose town, Pindenissum, was high up, well-fortified and inhabited by people who had never yielded obedience to the (Seleucid) kings (*fam.* 15.4.10). It took him a siege of 56 days to capture it. The mountainous or marginal areas of the Syrian region were covered with fortified villages, whose inhabitants, as far as we can see, were integrated in no system of property-relations imposed from outside, and did not belong in any functional sense to any state. Internally, of course, they had their own systems of social stratification. We see this best in one vivid report which relates to two village communities in Moab in about 160 BC. A people called the 'sons of Jamri' were celebrating the wedding of the daughter of one of the notables (*megistanes*) of Canaan, conducting the bride in a great procession laden with possessions. From the opposite direction the bridegroom with his friends and brothers was on his way to meet the bride, accompanied by musicians playing tambourines, and an armed escort. At that point the scene stops; for Jonathan and Simon Maccabaeus with their followers leap up from ambush, slaughter as many as they can, put the rest to flight and take all their possessions (1 Macc. 9.37–42).

The two books of Maccabees, especially the first, give us the best – and more or less contemporary – picture which we have of social formations and settlement patterns in the southern part of the Syrian region in the second century; they would deserve further investigation, directed to the hints which they provide as to non-Jewish social structures in this period. The Maccabean wars stretched from the cities of the Philistine coast, like Azotus with its temple of the Philistine god, Dagon ('Bethdagon', 1 Macc. 10.83–4), to the fortified villages (*ochuromata*) of Idumaea (2 Macc. 10.15) or Transjordan (1 Macc.

5.6–9). In 1 Macc. 5.26–7 a whole string of places across the Jordan, all of which have retained analogous Arabic names until modern times – 'Bosora', 'Bosor', 'Alema', 'Chaspho', 'Maked', 'Karnaim' – are described as large, fortified *poleis*. These too will have been fortified villages; it is worth noting that the author of 1 Macc. has no notion that *polis* ought to be restricted to self-governing cities formally recognised as such; he uses it for instance of Modein (2.15), the village from which the Maccabees came (but see van der Spek, above p. 58). Similarly, Polybius uses the word *polis* of Atabyrion, a settlement on Mount Tabor (5.70.7).

The narratives of Maccabees also illustrate the very close geographical conjunction between different social/economic groupings which characterised this area, since the operations bring the Jewish forces into repeated contact not only with cities and with fortified villages, but with groups described as 'Arabs', following a nomadic, or at any rate non-sedentary, way of life. Even on the coastal strip near Jaffa, Judas Maccabaeus is attacked by not less than 5,000 Arabs with 500 horsemen, described as *nomades*. When defeated, they offer cattle as a pledge of friendship, and retire to their tents (*skênai*; 2 Macc. 12.10–12). The social pattern of an intermingling and mutual dependence, balanced by recurrent hostilities, between various gradations of settled, pastoral and truly nomadic communities using camels, is of course well-known, and nowhere better described than by Donner (1981), on the early Islamic conquests. It is worth noting that Diodorus, concluding his account of the Nabataeans, gives a succinct account of the social relations involved (19.94.10): 'There are also other tribes of Arabs, of whom some even cultivate the soil, intermingled with the tax-paying peoples, and (who) share the customs of the Syrians, except that they dwell in tents'.

I return below to the question of the movement of Arab peoples into Syria and their settlement there, a subject discussed in an interesting way by Dussaud 1955; see also Briant 1982e, ch.3 (an important study) and Shahîd 1984. For the moment note Diodorus' contrast between Arabs living in tents, and those settled populations who can be made to pay taxes. In many parts of the Syrian region, in the mountains and on the fringes of the desert above all, the Seleucid (or Ptolemaic) state either never had, or only occasionally had, any effective presence as the Achaemenids before them who, however, maintained a contractual relationship with them (Briant 1982e, 170ff).

Most of what I have been saying so far has been designed to suggest how limited, variable and erratic the Greek presence in the different parts of the Syrian region was in the hellenistic period, at any rate so far as our present evidence shows. I now wish to look at the other side, and ask what if anything we know of the non-Greek culture of the area, or of essentially non-Greek communities within it. The

Phoenician cities of the coast preserved their historical identity and culture, while evolving, by steps which we cannot really trace, into Greek cities (Millar, 1983). A similar evolution seems to have taken place in the ancient Philistine cities further south, Azotus, Ascalon and Gaza (Rappaport 1970; Schürer 1979, 98–110). As with many other places in the Near East, their non-Greek, or not wholly Greek, identity is expressed most clearly in dedications made on Delos. Perhaps the most striking example is the well-known dedication by a man from Ascalon: 'To Zeus Ourios and Astarte Palestinê, Aphrodite Ourania, the listening gods, Damon son of Demetrios, of Askalon, having been saved from pirates, (offers his) prayer. It is not permitted to introduce (here) a goat, pig or cow' (*ID* no.2305; Bruneau 1970, 346–7). The notion that these, or any other existing communities, could be *made* into Greek cities purely by the issue of some sort of charter or the granting of a Greek constitution, without either a settlement or building operations, still seems to me to need further examination. It is more in accordance with the evidence to see these coastal cities as places which had been in close contact with the Greek world before Alexander, and where, after the conquest, a continued process of hellenisation took place gradually against a background of cultural continuity (see Colledge, below p. 137). But we should not think of the non-Greek elements as being static features of a world in which cultural change came only from the Greek side. For instance, some 9 kilometres from Acco/Ptolemais a Greek inscription of probably the second century BC shows a man with a Greek name dedicating an altar to Hadad and Atargatis, 'the listening gods' (Avi-Yonah 1959). Rather than being an example of the continuity of local non-Greek cults, this inscription is the earliest attestation of these deities on the Phoenician coast.

A much greater problem is presented by those inland cities or communities which are not known to have received any formal Greek colony or settlement. With Jerusalem and Judaea the essential features of cultural and religious contact and conflict are well-known: a significant level of hellenisation, met by a conscious and violent reaction and reassertion of 'national' tradition. The Samaritans too retained and reasserted their 'Israelite' identity. This fact is perfectly illustrated by two dedications of the middle and late second century from Delos in Greek (Bruneau 1982) put up by 'The Israelites on Delos who pay their tithes to holy Argarizein (Mount Gerizim)'.

By contrast, if we think for instance of Damascus, virtually nothing is known of its character as a city or community at the moment of the Macedonian conquest except the bare fact of its existence. Nor has any significant evidence about it through the hellenistic period survived, beyond some coins of the second and first centuries BC with the legend *Damaskênon*, and passing mentions of it as an object of successive dynastic conflicts (Schürer 1979, 127–30). The occasional documents of persons from Damascus abroad in the hellenistic world are not very informative, though they do illustrate the adoption of Greek nomenclature. It is not surprising that Semitic names might also be retained, for instance 'Martha, Damascênê', on a late second-century inscription from Delos (*ID* nos. 2286–7).

No real insight into the internal life of Damascus can be attained until the middle of the first century, when we come to Nicolaus' account of his father Antipater, who was presumably born around the beginning of the century, and was a skilled orator (in Greek, as is clearly implied), who filled all the offices (*archai*) in the city and represented it before the various dynasts who ruled in the surrounding area (*FGrHist.* 90 F 131). In the chaotic conditions of fluctuating empires and local tyrannies which marked the history of Syria in the middle of the century (see esp. Rey-Coquais 1978) this will have been an essential function. The education and culture to which Nicolaus laid claim (*FGrHist.* 90 F 132) was wholly Greek, and nothing in the extensive fragments of his works suggests any influence from a different historical or cultural tradition. In this he offers an obvious and striking contrast to Josephus, who was to make so much use of him as a source (see esp. Rajak 1983).

A combination of different cultural traditions is certainly expressed in the monuments and inscriptions of one local dynasty which emerged in north Syria in the second century, the royal house of Commagene (for the dynasty see Sullivan 1977; Wagner 1983). But if what we are interested in is a local 'mixed' culture, Commagene is not a true exception, for everything that we can observe there is, first, a royal invention; and secondly, though the kings consciously draw on two traditions, they do so in relation to Greek and *Persian* elements, not Syrian or Aramaic ones: Greek gods and Ahuramazda; royal descent from Persia and Macedon; Persian dress to be worn at festivals (Waldmann 1973). It was natural, in creating a new royal ideology, to look to the two major monarchies of the Achaemenids and the Seleucids. But there is still a contrast, for instance, with the contemporary coinage of the Hasmoneans in Judaea, which incorporates both Greek, Hebrew and Aramaic elements (Schürer 1973, 602f).

So far as I can find, a real continuity is traceable in just one place outside Phoenicia and Judaea, namely Bambyce, also called in Aramaic/Syriac Manbog, and soon to be called in Greek Hierapolis, some miles west of the Euphrates. This is the place from which came the slave in Egypt with his wrist tattooed in 'barbarian letters' (above p. 119). It may be worth putting together what we know of this place, somewhat increased since Goossens' book of 1943. The location of Bambyce, not far from the Euphrates and northern Mesopotamia, may well be significant. Since we know even less of the culture of northern

Mesopotamia in the hellenistic period than we do of the various areas of Syria itself, we can only speculate about how far the two areas shared a common cultural history. But it is at least clear that a remarkable variety of non-Greek influences steadily gained ascendancy, from the first century BC onwards, in the Macedonian colony of Dura-Europos; that Syriac script is first attested, in the very early first century AD, on the Euphrates (Pirenne 1963; Drijvers 1972); and that another Macedonian colony, not far across the Euphrates, Edessa, was to be the focus of Syriac culture (Segal 1970; Drijvers 1977). For the wider cultural contacts around the Fertile Crescent, it is suggestive that Lucian's account of the 'Syrian Goddess' of Hierapolis/ Bambyce records (10) that offerings came there not only from various regions west of the Euphrates but also from Babylonia.

At the time of Alexander's conquest Bambyce was producing coins with Aramaic legends, with the names of ' 'Abdhadad' (meaning 'servant of (the god) Hadad'), or ' 'Abyaty', or (still in Aramaic letters) ' 'Alksandr (Alexandros)'. One has a longer legend ' 'Abdhadad, priest of Manbog, who(?) resembles Hadaran his lord'. (In general see Seyrig 1971b, who recalls the image in Ecclesiasticus 50, of the high priest Simon as he emerged before the people from within the Temple; but, as Seyrig recognises, the reading and interpretation are not certain). The reverse of this same coin shows a priest, presumably 'Abdhadad himself, standing before an altar wearing a long tunic and tall conical hat. Other coins represent Atargatis of Bambyce, the 'Syrian goddess', and one of these has, in Greek, the letters SE, presumably 'Seleukos'. According to Lucian the temple which stood there in his time had been rebuilt by Stratonice, the wife of Seleucus I (*dea Syr.* 17).

In the next century inscriptions of 128/7 BC onwards record men from this place, described as a *polis* with the name Hierapolis (e.g. *ID* no.2226), acting as priests of Hadad and Atargatis at Delos, where a whole range of Syrian cults are represented explicitly in a way which is hardly attested in the hellenistic period in Syria itself (Bruneau 1970, 466f). Probably a little earlier, an inscription from Larisa in Thessaly reveals a man called Antipater, a 'Hierapolitan of Seleucis', described as 'a Chaldaean astronomer', evidently resident over a long period in Thessaly. The description of him as a 'Chaldaean', later repeated by Vitruvius (Bowersock 1983a), would naturally suggest either that Hierapolitans were felt to be in some way associated with Babylonia, or that his astronomical learning was acquired there, or both.

In the first century BC the wealth of the temple was evidently well-known, and in 54 BC Crassus removed treasures from it (Plutarch, *Crassus* 17). Under the Roman empire one of the few inscriptions from the site (*IGLS* I nos.232–52) shows that the place had a *boulê* and *dêmos* in the normal way (no.233). But the most striking of all the evidence is the relief, in two halves found 50 years apart and joining perfectly, showing a priest in a long tunic, and conical hat surmounted by a crescent (Stucky 1976). A Greek inscription records that this is a statue of Alexander, 'the incomparable high priest', put up by his friend Achaeus, who offered libations and prayed to the gods to preserve his *patris* (homeland) in *eunomia* (good order). The statue dates to the second century AD, the time when Lucian describes – the cult of the goddess and lists the vestments of the various priests – the others in white robes and pointed hats, the high priest in purple robes and a tiara (which is visible in the relief, round the bottom of his tall hat). In this case there is enough evidence to show a non-Greek cult which was already in existence before the hellenistic period, and continued in a closely similar form into the Roman empire. Very early on in the hellenistic period it seems to have gained royal patronage; in the next century its cult is on show in Delos; under the Roman empire it is a curiosity and tourist attraction, and a suitable subject for Lucian's parody of Herodotus.

Outside Phoenicia and Judaea there is nowhere else in Seleucid Syria of which we can say the same. Those few non-Greek, or mixed Greek and non-Greek, cultures which our evidence at present does allow us to observe either came from outside the area of Seleucid control or are creations of the very late hellenistic and the Roman period, or both. By contrast with the dearth of Aramaic inscriptions of the Achaemenid, hellenistic and Roman periods from Syria, inscriptions in the various pre-Islamic Arabic scripts are known in large numbers and cover a considerable range in space and time (Roschinski 1980; Teixidor 1981). First, Thamudic inscriptions begin in north-west Arabia around 400 BC and continue until the third or fourth century AD. The sub-category of them known as 'Safaitic', from the volcanic region called the Safa, south-east of Damascus, was in use from the second century AD to just before the rise of Islam; scattered examples have been found as far away as Dura-Europus and Hama. Secondly the Nabataeans, whom our classical sources regard as Arabs, could already write in 'Syrian letters' when Antigonus made his unsuccessful campaign against them in 312 BC (D.S. 19.96.1). Nabataean inscriptions, of which some 4,000 are known, begin in the first half of the second century BC, and continue until the fourth century AD (Starcky 1966; Bowersock 1983b). The northward spread of the inscriptions mirrors the spread of Nabataean control, which for a period in the first century BC, and possibly again in the first century AD, included Damascus. Thirdly, as regards the parallel case of the Palmyrenes, there is evidence of continuous occupation from the third millennium onwards on the tell where the temple of Bēl stood, and a mud-brick temple may have been constructed there in the early hellenistic period. But a tomb of the mid-second century BC seems to be the earliest

datable hellenistic structure on the site (Seyrig 1970a; Colledge 1976;
Fellmann 1970; see Will 1983). In the middle of the first century BC
we find both the earliest Palmyrene inscriptions, and the earliest
evidence of monumental building (Drijvers 1977). Both of these cases,
Nabataea and Palmyra, are unquestionably to be regarded as the
sedentarisation of Arab peoples, and the construction of new urban
centres exhibiting highly distinctive local varieties of Greek architecture. Fourthly, a settled population of mixed Greek and non-Greek
culture, with buildings and inscriptions, also emerges in the same
period in the Hauran (Djebel Druze), south-east of Damascus. The
earliest known monument there is the temple of Balshamen at Si'a,
dated by a bilingual Greek/Nabataean inscription to 33–1 BC (Dentzer
1981).

It would be absurd to pretend that we can in any way *explain* these
closely parallel developments. All I wish to underline is that we can
see the visible manifestations of a number of mixed cultures emerging
first outside the areas of Seleucid, or Roman, control, and then
spreading inwards. Or so it seems; at Baalbek/Heliopolis, a place
which we would naturally think of as distinctively Syrian, there is no
certain archaeological evidence from before the early Roman imperial
period. Von Gerkan did however argue (1937) that under the major
temple of the mid-first century AD there were the foundations of a late
hellenistic temple of different design. Emesa, further north up the
Orontes valley, was also of course, at least by the second and third
centuries, the site of the conspicuously non-Greek cult of Elagabal,
whose cult object was an aniconic black stone. The place is not known
to have existed until the first century BC, when there appeared the
local dynasty of Sampsigeramus and his son Iamblichus (Sullivan
1977), the 'tribal leaders' (*phylarchoi*) of the *ethnos* of the Emiseni, as
Strabo calls them (16.2.10 (753)), saying that they ruled nearby
Arethusa (a settlement of Seleucus I, Appian, *Syr.* 57). These dynasts
too were characterised by contemporaries as 'Arabs' (Cicero *fam.* 15,
1, 2: 'Iamblichus, phylarchus Arabum'), and the first part of Sampsigeramus' name is based on the Semitic word *shemesh*, the sun. On
Seyrig's view (1971a), the sun-cult in Syria is typically of Arab origin.
But, just to confuse our conception of the background, the main cult
of Emesa in this period does not itself seem to have been a sun-cult.
What seems to be the earliest documentary attestation of the name
'Elagabal' as a divine name offers a new etymology for the word,
namely 'god mountain'. This is an inscription in Palmyrene lettering
of the first century AD, found some 80 kilometres south-east of Emesa
and 100 kilometres south-west of Palmyra, and naming, along with
the Arab deity Arṣu, another deity called ' 'Ilh' gbl', that is 'Elaha
Gabal' – 'god mountain' – represented as an eagle with outstretched
wings standing on a rock (Starky 1975/6). Then, to add a further

confusing element, when we come to Herodian's famous description of the cult of Elagabal (5.3.2–6), he characterises it as 'Phoenician'; just as Heliodorus, the author of the novel *Aethiopica*, calls himself 'a Phoenician from Emesa' (10.41.3).

However we ought to characterise the cultural background out of which the Emesa of Roman imperial times emerged, Seyrig elsewhere (1959) saw its brief prosperity as a city as having been closely linked to the caravan trade of Palmyra. That raises questions which cannot be dealt with here. All I wish to emphasise is that there is nothing to show that Emesa or its cult even existed in the hellenistic period proper. One hypothesis is to see its emergence as a product of the movement of 'Arabs' inwards from the desert fringes, followed by their settlement and creation of a new cult, or at any rate one which was new to that site.

If we move somewhat further north, to Seleucus' foundation at Apamea, here in the Roman empire there was a cult of a non-Greek deity, whom Dio (79.8.5) describes as 'Jupiter called Belos, who is worshipped in Apamea in Syria' and who gave oracular responses. The god Bēl, worshipped also in Palmyra (Teixidor, 1977, 135–40) is first attested in Babylonia. How and when the cult had come to be set up in a Greek city, or to be associated with a cult already there, we do not know (Balty 1977, 129, n.184C; Balty 1981). But in the entire range of our evidence there is probably no more concentrated example of cultural fusion than the brief inscription from Apamea which Rey-Coquais published a decade ago (Rey-Coquais 1973, 67), a Greek dedication by a Roman citizen: 'On the order of the greatest holy god Bēl, Aurelius Belius Philippus, priest and *diadochos* of the Epicureans in Apamea.'

The enigma of hellenistic Syria – of the wider Syrian region in the hellenistic period – remains. None the less, I am tempted to speculate that the positive impact of hellenistic rule was relatively slight. If we think of it in terms of the foundation of wholly new cities, these were not numerous, except in north Syria, and only a few of them are known to have closely resembled what we think of as a fully-fledged Greek city. If we think of an economic or social impact, there were many areas where the Seleucid empire certainly never exercised any direct or effective control (but see above Introduction; Sherwin-White; Salles). What the Seleucid state did was to raise taxes where it could, and to enrol troops either (perhaps) by direct levies among Macedonian *klêrouchoi*, or, more probably, via the Greek cities, like Cyrrhus, via local dynasts like the Hasmoneans, who from time to time supplied contingents, or were supposed to (1 Macc. 10.36; 11.44), or from Arab dynasts like Zabdibelus, who led 10,000 Arabs at the battle of Raphia in 217 (Polybius 5.79.8). The Seleucid state, like most ancient states, was primarily a system for extracting taxes and forming armies. Much of Syria was disputed territory between the Seleucid and Ptolemaic kingdoms throughout the third century BC. Antiochus IV's final invasion of Egypt in 168 had as an immediate consequence the desecration of the temple in Jerusalem (or so it seemed to one contemporary, Daniel 11.30–1), and the imposition of a Seleucid garrison. A mere six years later, with the escape of Demetrius I from Rome, there began a series of civil wars over the succession to the Seleucid throne which did not end until the occupation of Syria first by Tigranes of Armenia and then by the Romans.

The nature of the Seleucid state, as seen by its subjects, is suggested by the importance of the right of *asylia* as granted to cities (Bickerman 1938, 155), just as it is by Ptolemaeus' concern, immediately after the conquest of southern Syria, to have his villages protected from billetting by the Seleucid army (above pp. 120–1). Some decades later, after the death of Antiochus VII Sidetes while on campaign against the Parthians in 129, his *stratêgos* Athenaeus, when in flight, was refused entry or supplies by the villages which had been 'wronged in connection with the *epistathmeiai*' (D.S. 34/5.17.2).

It is worth suggesting the hypothesis that the remarkable absence of tangible evidence from Syria in the hellenistic period may not be an accident which further discovery would correct, but the reflection of a real absence of development and building activity in an area dominated by war and political instability. Given this absence of evidence, we cannot expect to know much about the culture of Syria in this period, or whether there was, except along the coast, any significant evolution towards the mixed culture which came to be so vividly expressed in the Roman period. The hints which we gain of such a culture are hardly worth mentioning: for instance the fact that Meleager of Gadara, whose epigrams are entirely Greek in spirit, at least knew what words were used as expressions of greeting both in Aramaic and in Phoenician (*Anth. Pal.* 7.419; Gow and Page 1965, 217, no.iv). But there is nothing in the quite extensive corpus of his poetry to show that he had deeply absorbed any non-Greek culture in his native city, although no formal Greek or Macedonian settlement is attested there (Schürer 1979, 132–6). On the contrary, he self-consciously represented his native city as 'Attic Gadara situated among the *Assyrioi*', and says of himself 'If (I am) a Syrian, what is the wonder? My friend, we inhabit a single homeland, the world' (*Anth. Pal.* 7.417; Gow and Page 1965, 216, no.ii). For evidence of non-Greek culture on the part of the inhabitants of inland Syrian cities in the hellenistic period, one can add a passing allusion to the fact that Antonius could find in Antioch in the 30s BC a leading citizen who knew Aramaic, or perhaps Parthian (Plutarch *Ant.* 41).

One of the major problems in the understanding of hellenistic Syria is thus the relative scarcity of direct and contemporary evidence for any non-Greek culture, or cultures, in the region, either in the Achaemenid or the hellenistic period itself. That might not matter, if we were confident that the evidence available for the Roman imperial period could be used to show cultural continuity, rather than the importation of new elements, from the desert, from Babylonia or from Mesopotamia. The question of chronology may be crucial, and certainly cannot be ignored. To give one central example, in his famous book of 1937, *Der Gott der Makkabäer*, Bickerman argues that we should envisage the pagan cult imposed in 167 BC on the temple in Jerusalem not as Greek but as Syrian. In particular he explains the emphasis which Jewish sources place specifically on the desecration of the altar by the 'abomination of desolation', by the parallel of Arab worship of the altar as a cult object in itself. To reinforce this, he uses the example of an inscription from Jebel Sheikh Barakat near Beroea (Aleppo) with a dedication to Zeus Madbachos, 'Zeus of the Altar'. But there is an acute problem of chronology here: the temple from which this inscription comes did not exist in the second century BC. It was constructed by persons with Greek names between the 50s and the 120s AD; the earliest inscriptions recording its dedication to Zeus Madbachos and Selamanes, 'the ancestral gods', probably date to the 50s AD (*IGLS* II, nos. 465–75, see Callot and Marcillet-Jaubert 1984).

The ancestors of these people may indeed have worshipped these same deities through the hellenistic period. The god Shulman/Selamanes is in fact attested in Syria long before that. But nobody, so far as we know, put up a temple for these gods on this site, or composed a dedicatory inscription for them until the first century AD. The problem therefore remains. Whatever the society, economy and culture of the Syrian region was like in the hellenistic period, the 'hellenistic' Syria, with a distinctive mixed culture, which our evidence allows us to encounter is that which evolved under the Roman empire (see esp. Teixidor 1977, for the popular religion attested in the inscriptions of this period).

That is, however, in the first instance, a fact about our evidence. It is not presented here as a definite conclusion about the 'real' world of the Syrian region in the hellenistic period, but as a strategic device whose purpose is precisely to bring into sharper relief significant new items of evidence as they appear. First, to insist on the sparseness of evidence for the culture and social structure of the region in the Achaemenid period, with the possible exception of Judaea, and to a lesser extent Phoenicia, is to prevent the unconscious projection of general notions about 'oriental' or 'Near Eastern' civilisation on to this area. Secondly, to emphasise the limits of the empirical data which we can actually use to give substance to the notion of 'hellenisation' or 'hellenism' in this particular time and place is both to call these concepts into question and to insist on testing them, so far as possible, area by area and period by period. Thirdly, the notion of a 'fusion' of cultures is doubly open to question if we have very little direct evidence for the nature of either of the cultures concerned, let alone for the manner in which they may have interacted, or occupied separate spheres. 'Hellenisation' might, as is often supposed, have extended very little outside the towns or the upper classes. Yet as regards towns, or urban centres, there is enough evidence to suggest that it was possible to absorb Greek culture without losing local traditions; and that Hierapolitans, Phoenicians and Samaritans when abroad positively emphasised their non-Greek identity.

Nor, by contrast, is it certain that country areas remote from the centres of Greek or Macedonian settlement remained immune to Greek presence or influence. This paper concludes with what seems to be (so far) the only formal bilingual inscription, in Greek and Aramaic, dating to the hellenistic period, and discovered west of the Euphrates. This is a dedication from Tel Dan, first published in a brief archaeological report (Biran 1977) and discussed by Horsley (1981, no.67) in one of his valuable surveys of new material relevant to early Christianity. The site seems to have been a high place of the Israelite period (tenth-ninth centuries BC), on which further construction, possibly including an altar, subsequently took place in the hellenistic period. The inscription, carved on a limestone slab, seems to date to the late third or early second century BC (*BE* 1977, no.542). The Greek text, quite finely carved, presents no problems: 'To the god who is in Dan Zoilos (offers) his vow' (*thêoi/tôi en Danois/Zôilos euchên*). Immediately underneath it comes an Aramaic text, more amateurishly carved, of which just enough survives to show that the author, and hence the date, is the same. It reads either [BD]N NDR ZYLS L' [LH'] – 'In [Da]n, vows of ZYLS (Zoilos) to the god', or (more probably) [H]N NDR ZYLS L' [LH' DN] – '[This] (is the) vow (of) Zoilos to the [god in Dan].'

On either interpretation this modest document is of immense significance for the cultural and religious history of the Syrian region. First, it is one of the earliest formal Greek inscriptions from the whole area. Secondly, it is both the only formal Aramaic (as opposed to Phoenician) inscription and the only formal Greek-Semitic bilingual inscription (as opposed to ostraca) from the Syrian region in the hellenistic age. Thirdly, the archaeological evidence clearly suggests the continuation, or at least the resumption, of worship at an ancient cult-site. Fourthly, the site itself occupies an inland location, near the headwaters of the Jordan, separated from the coast by some 40 kilometres of hill-country, and some 50 kilometres away from the nearest Greek, or semi-Greek, cities, Damascus and Gadara. There is no way of knowing whether Zoilos was an immigrant Greek who had either acquired some knowledge of Aramaic, or at least knew the necessity of having his vow recorded also in Aramaic; or whether he was a person of Syrian origin who had learned Greek, and adopted the Greek custom of the dedicatory inscription, and paired it with an inscription of a less well-established type, in his native Aramaic. In either case a rustic cult-centre saw worship directed to its nameless deity, and recorded in a fine Greek inscription. Here at last we have a precise example, from the earlier hellenistic period, of the meeting of two identifiable cultures.

CHAPTER SIX

# Greek and non-Greek Interaction in the Art and Architecture of the Hellenistic East*

## Malcolm Colledge

Interaction between Greek material culture and the non-Greek architectures and arts of the east Mediterranean and western Asia had been going on for a very long time before the arrival of Alexander the Great. To understand properly the forms this interaction took in the hellenistic phase a preliminary glance at previous cultures and patterns of interchange will be necessary, to give the general context in which later developments took place. The hellenistic phase will then be divided for purposes of analysis into four periods, to see if any trends in cultural interactions emerge from this study.

### Greek influence in the Near East before Alexander

By the time of Alexander (334 BC), Western Asia had generated sophisticated cultures for millennia. In the later fourth and third millennia BC, a vigorous and influential civilisation crystallised in southern Mesopotamia, the area later called Babylonia. Throughout its long history, the culture showed a strong tendency to maintain elements developed early in its evolution. Architecture was normally of local materials: mud brick, some baked brick for important items, and wood and stone (usually limestone) where available; lintels and roofing might be of wooden beams, although both 'pitched-brick' and radial vaulting became common from the late third millennium BC. Evidence for town planning is virtually non-existent, except occasionally around important buildings. Religious architecture was characterised by chapel-filled sanctuaries, rectangular temples with a vestibule and entry through one long side (the 'broad room' type) and enormous superimposed platforms that towered to the sky (the ziggurats). Palaces and houses consisted of rectangular rooms arranged around internal courts. Some representational work was of a schematic

---

* Versions of this paper were given at the Seleucid Seminar held at the Institute of Classical Studies, London University, Autumn 1984, and as an inaugural lecture on 28 February 1985, at Westfield College, University of London.

character in linear styles that displayed a love of decorative detail, although at various periods very lively, almost naturalistic forms were preferred (Uruk, Agade, Neo-Assyrian). Other important cultural developments also took place elsewhere in western Asia in the late third and earlier second millennia BC, such as the Harappan civilisation in north-west India, lasting for approximately 500 years. From a similar period important elements were established in Anatolian cultures, such as the 'megaron' room type and the combination of wood and stone with mud-brick in architecture. Around 1300 BC Iranian tribes including the Medes and Persians moved slowly into western Iran, where they seem to have continued to follow a pastoral existence. Before the Persians emerged as a politically dominant element *c.* 550 BC, the Medes had come into contact with and probably developed the architectural forms in use in that area in the early first millennium BC, e.g. the column-filled chieftains' halls. But the curious, so-called 'fire-temple' at Nush-i Jan may have been a specifically Median building (Frankfort 1970; Burney 1977).

Throughout the second millennium BC and the following three centuries of the Geometric period down into Archaic times, the Greeks were constantly adopting and transforming cultural ideas from the east (Lawrence 1973; Robertson 1975). But from the start of the sixth century BC, that is, from the later stages of the Greek Archaic period (which ended around 480 BC), the pattern of these contacts changed. From the early first millennium BC numerous Greek towns, such as Smyrna, Ephesus and Miletus were established along the coast of west Asia Minor and inland, in an area much of which was called Ionia. They enjoyed several centuries of comparative independence, during which they developed their own material culture, with painted pottery, houses, temples, towns and eventually sculpture and coinage. As happened on the Greek mainland, they experimented from the later seventh century BC with building, especially within sanctuaries, in carefully dressed ashlar blocks of local stone or marble (Coulton 1977, 31–7). The appearance, therefore, from 600 BC of similarly dressed masonry at Sardis, the capital of the neighbouring, inland kingdom of Lydia, must surely mark a Greek cultural influence in the reverse direction; and *if* the find of early electrum coins at Ephesus means the Greeks invented coinage, then the early spread of coinage to Lydia would be another example. A later Lydian king, Croesus (*c.* 560–547/6? BC), subsequently conquered western Asia Minor, including some Greek cities (Hdt. 1.28); this very possibly strengthened Greek cultural influence in the Lydian kingdom (Stronach 1978, 40–2; for coins: Jenkins 1972, 27–30).

Further Lydian expansion, however, was checked by the Persian king Cyrus II, who perhaps in 547/6 BC incorporated Lydia into his newly established empire. Lacking a developed imperial background and base, Cyrus created a capital and palace complex at Pasargadae in west Iran (Fars), where he assembled craftsmen from various of his recently won territories to create an innovative Persian imperial architecture and art. Here the building forms were primarily Iranian, and the decorative art mainly Mesopotamian and particularly Assyrian in derivation. But nevertheless it is possible to recognise an input from Greek and Lydian west Anatolia. This is visible architecturally in the finely dressed stone blocks, column base forms, the taper in columns, the masonry techniques such as *anathyrôsis* and the setting of iron clamps in lead. Further examples include the use of three-step bases for a viewing platform and Cyrus' tomb, the colonnades in palaces S and P, and the occurrence of west Anatolian masons' marks; the rosettes on the pediment of Cyrus' tomb and the robe of the four-winged Guardian on a palace door-jamb relief are of Ionian Greek type. But overall this contribution was a minor one. Important developments took place under Darius I (522/1–486 BC), who created an architectural and artistic style in his palaces at Susa, Persepolis and perhaps elsewhere which radically developed that of his predecessors, became classic in its own right and provided a canon for all his successors to follow. His inscriptions boast of the many nationalities employed on his projects, including Ionians, whose presence at Persepolis is confirmed by a Greek sculptor's doodle on the foot of a relief figure of Darius himself. They introduced into Iran the stone-carving tool that had been invented in Greece around 560 BC – the claw chisel with its serrated cutting edge, used for limestone and marble and for both architectural and sculptural purposes. The fluting of column drums seems to have been a Greek idea, and drapery folds were strongly influenced by those of around 525 BC in Archaic Greek relief. Lydian and Ionian Greek coins also provided the inspiration for the first official Achaemenid coinage, introduced by Darius I (as Herodotus confirms, 4.166) by c. 500 BC (as indicated by a hoard of coins from Smyrna), perhaps to pay mercenaries. This coinage comprised gold darics and silver *sigloi*, with an incuse reverse and four very similar designs of a stereotyped royal figure with a bow on the obverse, the design of which remained unchanged throughout the existence of the empire (Colledge 1977, pl. 38a). But again, the Greek contribution is minor: the overall result of the commissions of Darius I, and of his son Xerxes and their successors, was to create a specific and recognisable Achaemenid Persian imperial style.[1]

Quite the converse, however, was true of a number of commissions, by governors (satraps), local dynasts and local aristocrats, on the

1. Cyrus: Stronach 1978; Greeks working at Pasargadae: Nylander 1970. Darius: Schmidt 1953–70; Tilia 1968; Farkas 1974; Shahbazi 1976; Root 1979; Cook 1983. Greek sculptors: Richter 1946; Farkas 1974; Roaf 1980. Coins: Jenkins 1972, 41 figs. 116–17, 121–2; Root 1979, 116–18.

western frontiers of the empire, particularly in Anatolia and especially during the last century of its existence. Here works were executed by artists either of clearly Greek training or from workshops in which formal eastern styles were combined with the newly developed naturalistic, Greek 'classical' style (*c.* 480–*c.* 330 BC). Despite the fundamental divergence of these two art forms, Greek work became increasingly popular in western Anatolia as well as Phoenicia as illustrated by surviving funerary art and architecture, coins and perhaps gems. Early examples of the first include the reliefs of the 'Harpy' tomb (*c.* 500–470 BC) at Xanthos, the decoration on the 'Painted House' at Gordium, and the heads on the Egyptian-style royal sarcophagi at Sidon. Between *c.* 430 and 330 BC, the quantity of such Greek-influenced works increased enormously in these regions (see also Kuhrt, above pp. 50–1). Independent gravestones with low-relief banqueting and hunting scenes in a 'Graeco-Persian' style spread over north-west Anatolia. Rock tombs, often with reliefs portraying the deceased, were cut in many places in western Anatolia. Sarcophagi were found in royal tombs at Sidon with fine Greek-style reliefs, such as the carved 'Satrap' and 'Lycian' sarcophagi of around 400 BC, and the imported Attic sarcophagus of the Mourning Women of *c.* 350 BC. Striking tomb monuments were erected in the south-western subject kingdoms of Lycia and Caria, in which a number of Near Eastern, local and Greek architectural elements were combined with Greek-style sculptures. There seems to have been a massive increase in building activity in Lycia around 400 BC, exemplified by the Heroon enclosure at Trysa with the fore-parts of winged bulls guarding the exterior and scenes from Greek legend within, and by remarkable tombs at the capital, Xanthos, of the local type on a high platform. Examples include the sarcophagus-type 'Payava' monument on a high base with audience, chariot and combat scenes, and the Nereid monument on a lofty base with reliefs around the top and above this an Ionic temple with reliefs of the ruler fighting and giving audience, servants bringing tribute, and statues of the Breezes (Nereids). At the Carian capital, Halicarnassus, the most famous Anatolian funerary monument was constructed: the gigantic Mausoleum begun for himself by the local dynast Mausolus in 353 BC, executed by expert Greek artists, combining the typically local high podium with an Ionic Greek temple and Egyptian pyramid, and decorated with rich reliefs and free-standing sculptures, among which the so-called statue of 'Mausolus' exemplifies a predilection for highly individualised features.

This strong Greek influence was not limited to such monumental works; it is particularly marked in a series of locally minted coins showing again individualised profile heads of satraps, such as Tissaphernes, the style of which developed from late-fifth-century formalism to greater naturalism in the fourth century. It eventually formed part of an amalgam of Greek, Persian and local designs, scripts and weights (Colledge 1977, pls. 38–9). Most interesting, perhaps, are a group of gems, carved intaglios in semi-precious stones, of the period which include a Greek-influenced 'Graeco-Persian' group which falls into three subdivisions: a 'Court' style imitating that of the Achaemenid court but including some Greek shapes and motifs, a 'Greek' style with Achaemenid shapes but either Persian or east Greek designs, and a 'Mixed' style embodying formal eastern styles and subjects from Greek art. This mixing of Greek and Persian has suggested Anatolia as their still unknown place of origin.[2]

From this evidence some idea of the patterns of interaction before Alexander may be gained. The eastern neighbours of the Greeks had developed their own specific styles from ancient times that gave each a strong cultural identity, which continued to flourish throughout this period. Until the end of the seventh century BC the Greeks borrowed from them, but from around 600 BC some rulers and aristocracies in the Near East and Anatolia came into contact with (east) Greek material cultures and borrowed from this source to help create a new style with which to impress contemporaries and subjects. Such borrowing was very limited in the imperial centres of Lydia and Persia, but in the case of the satraps, dynasts and élites of western Anatolia and the coastal regions of Syria and Phoenicia, Greek influence from the beginning of the fifth century onwards was at times enormous. The mixing of the different eastern and Greek styles took various forms (I shall henceforth refer to this as 'hybrid'). One was the creation of a work belonging to a category appropriate to one culture in the style of the other, as, for example, the Greek-style but iconographically Persian, audience relief on the Xanthos 'Harpy' tomb, or the Graeco-Persian gems of the 'Court' type. A second form was the juxtaposition of discrete elements from different cultures within a single monument, as in the Mausoleum where local, Egyptian and Greek ones were used in this way. Finally some items such as certain of the coins and the Graeco-Persian gems of the 'Mixed' style exhibit an actual blending of style and iconography. In these ways then, those Near Eastern élites who, as a result of their physical proximity, had become familiar with Greek culture commissioned work which embodied a proportion of Greekness, and thus helped to promote a variety of new styles for them.

2. Funerary art: Eichler 1950; Akurgal 1961; Lawrence 1972, 173–202; Shahbazi 1975; Childs 1978; Waywell 1978; Hornblower 1982. Gordium: Young 1956; 1962. Coins: Jenkins 1972, 126–42. Gems: Boardman 1970, 303–27.

### The hellenistic period

The analysis of interaction between Greek and the various non-Greek material cultures through this period is made difficult by the patchiness of surviving evidence; doubtless the frequent wars of the period, the often perishable materials used by craftsmen, and the accidents of discovery, have all contributed to this. Nevertheless it is worthwhile to try to establish to what extent the Greeks, who were now the new political masters of Western Asia, imposed their own developing and sophisticated material culture, how their subjects and neighbours reacted and how far these interactions varied from period to period. To do this architecture and art will be examined in four periods: the opening phase (the reigns of Alexander and Seleucus I), the third, second and first centuries BC.

*The opening phase of Alexander and Seleucus I (c. 330-281/280 BC)*

Through his conquest of the Persian empire (334–323 BC), Alexander had gained control of a huge territory with cultures already ancient and vastly different from the Greek. Some promotion of things Greek is discernible. In the realm of art, there are definite signs of Greek activity. Some importation is indicated by sherds of later fourth-century Athenian black-painted pottery. More significant are items made in various places in the east. Still overlooking the west Iranian city of Hamadan, stands a huge stone lion, weathered and damaged but nevertheless clearly of Greek workmanship. It is considered by many to be a memorial raised by Alexander to his Companion Hephaestion, who died at Ecbatana of alcoholic poisoning and whose main monument was to rise at Babylon (see below). Of more lasting significance, however, was Alexander's coinage. The study of this is as yet incomplete, but some aspects have become clearer. The important types, each issued in different denominations, were: a gold stater, with a helmeted head of Athena on the obverse and a standing winged personified Victory (Nike) on the reverse; a silver drachm and tetradrachm, with the head of the young Heracles in lion-skin headdress and a left-seated Zeus on a throne on the reverse; and a bronze unit, with an obverse similar to that of the silver, and on the reverse a bow in a case and a club. The coins were produced in mints dotted across the western half of the empire (only) (Hamilton 1973; Colledge 1977; Bellinger 1963; Thompson 1982). Yet Alexander also demonstrated his own awareness of the value of preserving those persons, practices and institutions of the former Achaemenid empire which could be of use, to the dismay of some of his own Macedonian followers. Arrian reports that he commanded the restoration at Babylon of two juxtaposed monuments of enormous significance, the shrine of the great god Marduk, consisting of the gigantic, lofty religious platform (ziggurat) called Etemenanki, and the associated temple, Esagila (see Kuhrt, Sherwin-White 1987). Babylonian documents refer to work being done. Thus, Alexander actively maintained a number of traditional buildings of symbolic value,[3] while objects in daily use (such as figurines and pottery) remained unaffected by the conquest.

Alexander himself promoted the idea of 'blending' Greek and Achaemenid elements. This was expressed late in his campaign, in 324, by his public prayer for 'harmony and partnership in rule between Macedonians and Persians'. A physical expression of this may have been the gigantic memorial he is said to have raised at Babylon for his deceased Companion Hephaestion, comprising a towering five-storey platform, probably evoking the Mesopotamian ziggurats, with both Greek and Persian weapons placed at the top; it suggests a building of Babylonian type decorated with Greek and Persian weaponry. Some of his coins also provide further instances of Achaemenid motifs. Thus his remarkable continuation of darics and double-darics (and probably *sigloi* also), but with slightly hellenised designs, provides examples of items appropriate to one culture being produced in the style of the other. Others show this even more clearly, for example the Persic-weight coins of Tarsus, and the light-weight 'lion staters' minted at Babylon by the satrap Mazaeus (Hamilton 1973, 133–4, 144, 146; Bellinger 1963, 61–76, esp. pl. 3, nos.1,3,4,6). Thus Alexander fostered architectural and artistic production of three kinds: Greek, some carefully selected eastern types and some of Greek with non-Greek styles of the same kind that had existed already in the Achaemenid empire.

Seleucus I was responsible for the foundation of cities, often given dynastic names and using the Hippodamian grid-plan of streets, most notably with his two new capitals of Seleucia-Tigris (founded *c.* 305–301 BC) and north Syrian Antioch-Orontes, perhaps established towards 300 BC; under his rule another north Syrian grid-plan town was founded, Dura-Europus on the Euphrates (*c.* 300 BC?), which boasted ashlar outer wall foundations (fig. 4). It may also have been Seleucus who laid out the settlement at the junction of the Kokcha and Oxus rivers in northern Afghanistan, the ancient name of which is as yet unknown. The site is therefore called by its modern name, Ai Khanum. It had many Greek architectural features from this period: the street plan, walls, acropolis, propylaea and chamber-like Heroon of Kineas, who was probably responsible for the installation of the earliest stage of Macedonian settlement there. Perhaps also of this period are early phases of forts established on the Arabian coast

---

3. In general: Hamilton 1973. Persepolis: Hamilton 1973, 88–9. Esagila: Arrian *Anab.* 3.16,4; 17,1–4; Strabo *Geog.* 16.1,5; Smith 1924, 117ff; Grayson 1975a, 116 n.6; and cf. the curious BM 36613 pub. Sachs 1977, 144–7; Downey (forthcoming) ch.3.

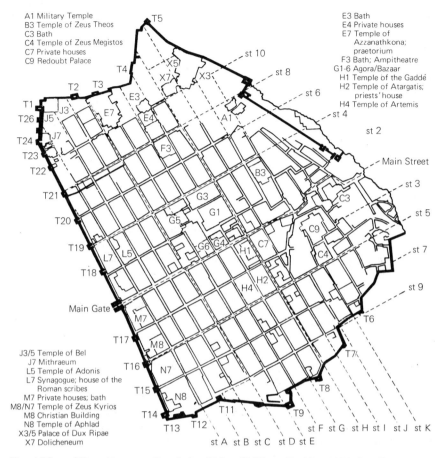

A1 Military Temple
B3 Temple of Zeus Theos
C3 Bath
C4 Temple of Zeus Megistos
C7 Private houses
C9 Redoubt Palace

E3 Bath
E4 Private houses
E7 Temple of
  Azzanathkona;
  praetorium
F3 Bath; Ampitheatre
G1-6 Agora/Bazaar
H1 Temple of the Gaddé
H2 Temple of Atargatis;
  priests' house
H4 Temple of Artemis

T5
st 10
st 8
st 6
st 4
st 2
Main Street
st 3
st 5
st 7
st 9

J3/5 Temple of Bel
J7 Mithraeum
L5 Temple of Adonis
L7 Synagogue; house of the
  Roman scribes
M7 Private houses; bath
M8/N7 Temple of Zeus Kyrios
M8 Christian Building
N8 Temple of Aphlad
X3/5 Palace of Dux Ripae
X7 Dolicheneum

Main Gate

st A st B st C st D st E st F st G st H st I st J st K

Fig. 4 Plan of Dura-Europus, founded c. 300 BC(?) [From Perkins 1973, fig. 2]

of the Gulf (see Salles, above pp. 85; 100ff) and the first phase of the Greek theatre built at Babylon (cf. Sherwin-White, above pp. 20–1; Van der Spek, above p. 65). Seleucus ordered a statue, which later became famous, from the sculptor Eutychides of Sicyon to personify the Good Fortune (Tyche) of one of his capitals, Antioch-Orontes, a piece now known only in Roman copies. Seleucus, like other hellenistic kings, commissioned portrait sculptures of himself; none has certainly survived although some scholars have identified a bronze head now in Naples as Seleucus on the basis of profile heads on his coins. A Greek palmette funerary stele, possibly Athenian, was imported into Sidon. Other work in Greek style, more important for our enquiry, was executed within the Seleucid realm. Greek pottery types and shapes now influenced local pottery production in the Seleucid empire (see Hannestad 1983). The plain limestone sarcophagus of Kineas, at Ai Khanum, has a gabled lid which is typically Greek. Seleucus, like some of the other Successors, introduced a significant innovation in his coinage by placing on the obverses his own right-facing profile head, so individualised as surely to be a realistic portrait, with his name included in the legend on the reverses[4] (Colledge 1977, pl. 38c).

Seleucus, like Alexander, continued the restoration of the great sanctuary of Marduk at Babylon, as Babylonian documents and historical texts inform us. At Persepolis, a curious building was constructed below the platform of the now ruined Achaemenid palace. This is the so-called 'Fratadara' temple, the plan of which follows a late Achaemenid architectural development, i.e. a 'Centralised Square Hall' with four columns forming a central square and surrounding corridors. On each of the two surviving door-jambs is carved a full-size figure in relief, representing on one side a prince (?) in Iranian dress holding a ritual bundle of rods ('barsom'), and on the other a princess (?). The occurrence at the Greek settlement at Ai Khanum of Mesopotamian temple architecture is very remarkable and deserves to be fully stressed. Here, in a sanctuary on the main north-south street inside the city stood an almost square temple, the earliest phase of which (phase V) belongs to the late fourth or early third century BC. It had thick walls, and a simple plan, with a vestibule (antecella) and hall (cella) each occupying the full width of the structure and entered through the middle of one long side; it stood on a raised podium which itself was set on a platform. This is an example of the ancient Mesopotamian 'broad room' temple type, current already in the later fourth millennium BC and to remain popular in western Asia from the third century BC for about five hundred years; from its later ornamentation it is known as the indented temple (*à redans*): see Fig. 5. But why here? Various suggestions have been made such as that it was the result of the influence of Mesopotamian colonists among the settlers, or that it may be an Iranian development which was adopted. The local production of figurines and pottery continued,[5] indicating perhaps the mixed character of the population of the city.

Apart from the Greek and Mesopotamian styles, a 'mixed' style is represented most notably in a grand administrative complex, doubt-

4. In general: Colledge 1977; Downey (forthcoming). Gulf: Salles (this volume); Antioch, early traces: Lassus 1972, 140–1; Tyche: Dohrn 1960. 'Seleucus I' head: de Franciscis 1963, 65 pl.IV; Richter 1965, III 269–70 figs. 1865–8. 'Athenian' stele in Sidon: Parlasca 1982, 6 pl. I.1. Coins: Richter 1965 loc. cit; Colledge 1977, 104 with references.
5. In general: Colledge 1977. Babylon: Downey (forthcoming) ch.3. Ai Khanum, 'indented' Temple phase V: Bernard 1971, fig. 19. Ai Khanum, 'Mesopotamian colonists': Pidaev 1974, 33–8 fig. 2; Bernard 1976a, 307 n.16. 'Iranian': suggestion of A. T. L. Kuhrt.

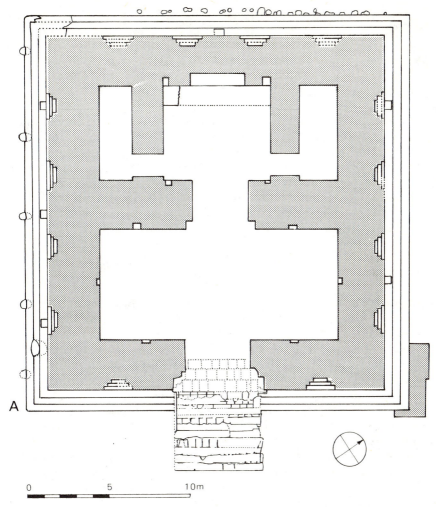

Fig. 5 Ai Khanum, plan of the indented temple, phase IV (c. 300 – 250 BC) [From Bernard 1971, fig. 17]

less the governor's palace. To the early period belong an imposing colonnaded court, corridors and rooms. The peristyle court, and much architectural decoration, are Greek in origin. But there are non-Greek features: the use of the court as a passageway, of flat roofing, of Persian-type limestone column bases, whose orthogonal planning and associated corridors recall Assyrian and Persian palace designs, and particularly the so-called Harem of Xerxes at Persepolis. This palace, at a provincial city, presumably echoes still grander examples in the cities, now lost. Its scale, and reminiscences of Persian predecessors, as the excavator pointed out, illuminate hellenistic royal ideology: its blending of Greek and Achaemenid imperial styles symbolised both the change wrought by conquest and the political traditions to which it was heir. This was further expressed by those of Seleucus' coins which continue Alexander's series of darics and double darics, and of lion staters, although by Antiochus I's reign this series was no longer produced.[6]

To sum up, the same kinds of artistic production continued under and were encouraged by Seleucus: selected Greek, Mesopotamian and Achaemenid elements and the development of the new style which combined Greek and a variety of local artistic traditions. The juxtaposition of Greek and Achaemenid elements is exemplified in the Ai Khanum palace, while an interchange of styles appears in the darics; and actual blending occurs in the Ai Khanum palace layout and the lion stater coins.

### The third and early second centuries BC

Antiochus I (281/0–261 BC) created a still partly extant and huge earthwork at Merv to defend the central Asian province of Margiane from the raids of nomads. Under him and his successors in the third century more Greek-style work was produced. At Dura-Europus in north-east Syria the 'Redoubt' and 'Citadel' palaces were of Greek type with colonnaded ('peristyle') court. The earliest sanctuary of Artemis, of the third or second century, consisted of a cut-stone court with a colonnade in the Doric order and an altar, possibly recalling a Greek parallel in the Delphinium at Miletus. At Seleucia-Tigris, a small building interpreted as a Heroon may have been first erected at this time. Work on the forts and staging-posts of the Persian Gulf continued, such as Qala'at al-Bahrain and the island of Failaka. Here by *c.* 250 BC the fortified enclosure had two partly ashlar temples of Greek type, one Doric, with a circular stone altar in front, and the other Ionic. The latter had two porch columns between projecting spur walls and thus *in antis* (but with bell-shaped Persian-style bases) and a rectangular stone altar before it. At Bactra (Balkh), perhaps the capital of the satrapy, a hellenistic level has been located at the Bala Hisar mound, which functioned as the acropolis. At Ai Khanum, an ashlar fountain was built by the Oxus river *c.* 250 BC and the lower city rampart was refurbished about then. Further evidence for extensive building activity includes limestone Corinthian column bases of *c.* 250–200 BC in the palace, a gymnasium perhaps dating to this period, and a Greek theatre, albeit with mud-brick seating, in use *c.* 225–150

6. Ai Khanum palace plan: Bernard 1973, 113–20; 1976a, 288–93; 1978, 444–61, fig. 18; 1980a, 435–57. Royal ideology: id. 1973, 117; 1978, 444–61. Coins: Bellinger 1963.

I. (Old) Nisa, Turkmenistan USSR: reconstruction of the interior of the 'Square Hall' as rebuilt in the mid-Parthian period (*c.* 150 BC — AD 100?) with 'quadrilobate' Doric columns

II. Khurha sanctuary, west Iran: view with Ionic columns with 'watchspring' capitals, perhaps second century BC

III. *above* West Iran(?):
bronze figurine of horseman in
cap, *c.* 300 — 150 BC(?) [British
Museum WA 117760;
ht. 17.5 cm.]

IV. *right* Laodicea (Nihavand),
west Iran: bronze figurine of the
goddess Fortuna/Isis [Teheran
Museum 2437; ht. 10 cm.]

V. Rome: marble portrait head probably of an eastern Greek king (Euthydemus I?), perhaps a later copy of a hellenistic original [Rome, Museo Torlonia, Villa Albani; nearly life-size]

VI. Ai Khanum, gymnasium: limestone bearded head from a cloaked 'herm', second century BC [Kabul; ht. *c.* 20 cm.]

VII. *left above* (Old) Nisa 'Treasury', Turkmenistan, USSR: marble figurine representing a goddess (? — the head does not belong), probably second century BC [Leningrad, Hermitage; ht. *c*. 18 cm.]

VIII. *left below* (Old) Nisa 'Square Hall', Turkmenistan, USSR: female (divine?) figure in clay and stucco on wooden frame from wall niche, *c*. 150 BC — AD 100 [Ashkhabad Museum; ht. 2.5 m.]

IX. *below* Ai Khanum 'indented' temple: limestone statue of a female figure beside a pillar, *c*. 200 — 150 BC(?) [ht. *c*. 1 m.]

X. *right* Bisitun: rock relief of Heracles reclining, inscribed and dated, June 148 BC [*in situ;* ht. 1.90 m., width 2.10 m.]

XI. *below* Bisitun; rock relief depicting a Parthian king (Mithridates II?) before four dignitaries (to the left), all in profile view, *c.* 123 — 110 BC? [*in situ;* ht. *c.* 4 m.]

XII. (Old) Nisa 'Treasury', Turkmenistan, USSR: three carved ivory drinking horns (rhytons) with figured decoration, perhaps second century BC [Leningrad, Hermitage; ht. *c.* 20 cm.]

XIII. Arsamea-Nymphaeus (Eski Kâhta), Commagene, south Turkey: limestone relief of king Antiochus I of Commagene shaking hands on equal terms with the god Heracles, c. 69 — c. 31 BC [in situ; ht. 2.26 m]

XIV. Shami shrine, west Iran:
bronze statue of a chieftain,
perhaps a Parthian vassal,
c. 50 BC — AD 150 [Teheran
Museum 2401; ht. 1.90 m.]

BC. Between about 250 and 150 BC the palace had a striking wall decoration, executed in brick and stone and doubtless imitated from examples in other centres, namely a blind arcade, anticipating those of the Parthian capital of Nisa and of republican and imperial Rome and thus establishing the clearly hellenistic origin of this feature.

A sensitive marble portrait head in Paris is considered by many, on the basis of coin profiles, to represent Antiochus III (but see Stewart 1979, 82–4); if correct, then he hired a Greek sculptor and material for this work. Some importation of Greek objects has been revealed by the finds at Ai Khanum, which included plaster casts of relief figures of Athena and other subjects for the making of Greek-style metal vases, the remains of a sandalled left foot and hands in marble from a 'acrolithic' statue (of Zeus?) in which the extremities would have been of marble and the main part of clay and stucco, and a silver religious relief (*oscillum*) from western Anatolia depicting Cybele.

Royal mints, now located across the region, minted coins on many of which the king's portrait in profile occupied the obverse; the reverse normally contained deities surrounded by a Greek legend giving the ruler's name. Graeco-Bactrians produced similar fine issues (Colledge 1977, pl. 39h). At Uruk and at Seleucia-Tigris, lumps of clay (*bullae*) used for sealing documents bore carved gem-impressions depicting divinities, royal heads and animals. Greek pottery types remained influential, mainly at Greek foundations such as Seleucia-Tigris and Ai Khanum, as did Greek figurines. In western Iran, bronze mirrors from Masjid-i Solaiman had elegant handles in the form of nude females. A limestone altar from Laodicea (Nihavand) was decorated with garlands in relief. It is also possible that the fragments of a limestone bowl or altar from Denavar, which had satyr and silenus heads, should be dated to this period. At Ai Khanum, the limestone river fountain of *c.* 250 boasted originally six heads as water-spout gargoyles of which a lion, dolphin and New Comedy mask survive. The gymnasium in its earliest phase (III) yielded traces of pebble mosaics. The indented temple vestibule was enlivened with three high-relief figures in clay and stucco, including a male head which was gilded.[7]

Work in accordance with the various local traditions continued throughout the third century. In Mesopotamia, houses and tombs of Babylonian types continued to be built. At Uruk, vigorous and creative use was made of old Babylonian religious architectural forms, as local documents and excavations testify. A towering platform (ziggurat)

7. For architectural and art items mentioned in the rest of this chapter see in general Colledge 1977 ch.3, with references and bibliography. Gulf: Salles (this volume). Ai Khanum rampart: Bernard 1970, 316–17; 1976a, 307; 1980a, 457–8. Theatre: id. 1976a, 314–22; 1978, 429–41. Gymnasium: id., 1976a, 301; 1978, 422–9. Fountain: id. 1976a, 307–13 (sculptures); 1978, 429 (date).

was built once again on a grander scale than before, as were the associated shrine of Anu and his consort Antum, called the Bit Reš, and Ishtar's apparently new temple complex, usually called Irigal (Colledge 1977, 74, fig. 35; for the problems of change see Doty 1977). Old forms, including 'broad room' temple types and glazed brick decoration, were adapted for these purposes, almost certainly under royal patronage. Textual evidence demonstrates that Seleucid rulers continued to exhibit their respect for the local temples at Borsippa, Ur and Babylon, especially Esagila, and there are traces of work on the enclosure wall of its ziggurat, Etemenanki (see Sherwin-White, above pp. 28–9; Kuhrt, above pp. 51–2).

The ancient Mesopotamian 'broad room' temple type was also used in the great temple 'of Athena' and the lesser 'of Heracles' on the religious platform at Masjid-i Solaiman, and in two mud-brick temples at Ai Khanum. One of these, as yet undated, was located outside the walls, and the other inside (a rebuilding in fact of the indented temple, now with a wall decoration of traditional Mesopotamian niched type (*à redans*) to match its plan). Iranian architectural forms continued to be used. At the Greek (or originally Achaemenid?) site of Shahr-i Qumis, possibly Hecatompylus, in north-east Iran the strange, square, possibly cult buildings (IV, VII and XIII) with their rectangular projections on each face, seem to evoke an antecedent in the 'Median fire-temple' at Nush-i Jan (*c.* 750–600 BC; Colledge 1977, 39, fig. 11), while a fortified residence on site VI with rooms and corridors opening on to a great court seems rather to have contemporary central Asian connections (Fig. 6B, cf. 6A). Their precise dating in the late third, or earlier second century BC remains uncertain. In west Iran, Achaemenid forms inspired some early Seleucid-period column bases at Istakhr (near Persepolis), probably an ashlar tower at Nurabad (seemingly a pale reflection of the 'Zendan' towers at Pasargadae and Persepolis), and the great open-air religious platform at Masjid-i Solaiman (with its 'broad-room' temples). A puzzling religious structure at Ai Khanum, as yet undated, may be related to this: an open-air sanctuary by the south-west corner of the acropolis with a stepped, flat-topped podium perhaps for ritual of Persian type.

Local art forms flourished as well. Figurine types included the traditional stiff, frontal nude goddess, found right across western Asia at such sites as Seleucia-Tigris, Failaka and Susa, as well as horseman figures in Mesopotamia and west Iran (Plate III). Old pottery forms continued, Mesopotamian and Persian. A now battered limestone male statue (if of this period) found at Susa was inspired by Achaemenid style, as were damaged rock reliefs perhaps of *c.* 200 BC at north Mesopotamian Qizqapan and west Iranian Dukkan-i Daûd and Deh-i Nau depicting profile male figures, and some rare fragments of linen textiles discovered in the indented temple of Ai Khanum, datable

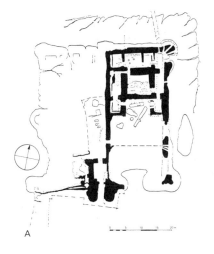

A

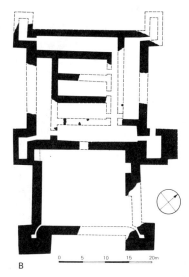

B

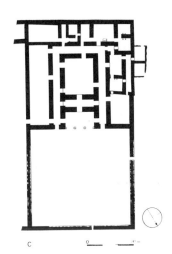

C

Fig. 6 Plans of dwellings which incorporated a central room, corridors and court: (A) Citadel of Babish Mulla, Chorasmia, USSR, fourth to second centuries BC [From S. P. Tolstov, *Po drevnim deltam Oksa i Iaksata*, Moscow 1962, fig. 89]; (B) Hecatompylus (Shahr-i Qumis), north-east Iran: fortified residence on site VI, late third to mid-first century BC [From J. Hansman, *JRAS* 1970, 143, fig. 1]; (C) Ai Khanum: house in the south ('Kokcha') quarter in stage II, mid-second century BC(?) [From Bernard 1970, fig. 9]

to the third or second centuries BC and showing friezes of walking animals.[8]

During the third century the production of works combining different artistic traditions was maintained. Certain architectural structures incorporate stylistically pure elements from more than one

8. Uruk, Seleucia-Tigris: see n. 4 above. Ai Khanum temple outside the walls: Bernard 1976a, 303–7. Pasargadae: Stronach 1978. Persepolis: Schmidt 1953–70. Ai Khanum platform: Bernard 1976a, 305–7.

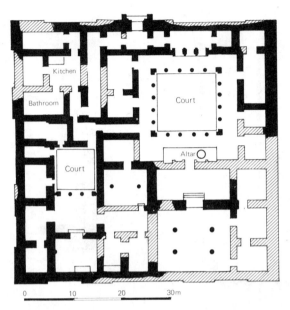

Fig. 7 Nippur, Babylonia: plan of the 'palace' c. 250 BC(?) [From A. U. Pope (ed.), *A Survey of Persian Art*, Oxford 1938, I, fig. 106]

culture, such as the great sanctuary at Masjid-i Solaiman which consisted of temples of Mesopotamian 'broad room' type set on a Persian platform. Other buildings juxtaposed traditional and Greek elements – the 'palace' at south Mesopotamian Nippur had a Mesopotamian plan but a Greek peristyle court featuring tapered Doric columns of baked brick (with the bricks arranged like the slices of a cake) (Fig. 7). On Failaka the two columns of the Ionic temple had Persian-type bell-shaped leaf ornamented bases. At Ai Khanum the rebuilt indented temple of 'broad room' type, in addition to its Babylonian decorative wall niches, was provided in the vestibule with high-relief figured decoration in Greek style, and set on a high three-step podium which might possibly recall the three-step stone platforms characteristic of Greek temples.

Other buildings showed a blending of styles. At the capital, Seleucia-Tigris, an administrative building incorporated two suites of seven rooms each with central columns and doors in the short sides reminiscent of Achaemenid 'centralised square' designs. On Failaka some architectural decoration of Greek derivation, including palmette temple roof ornaments (*acrôtêria*), was treated in a stylised fashion; the palace of Ai Khanum had an 'orientalised' Corinthian order (*c.* 250–200 BC) and palmette roof decoration used in a non-Greek way. The Parthians, too, made use of this 'blended' style, as

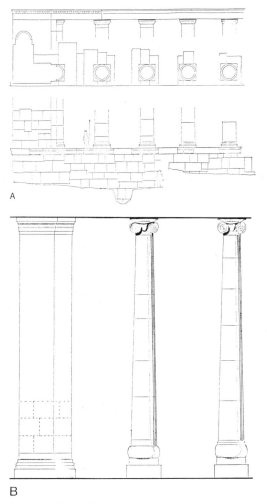

A

B

Fig. 8 Architectural orders of west Iranian sanctuaries, perhaps second century BC:
(A) Kangavar, Doric; (B) Khurha, Ionic [From E. Herzfeld, *Iran in the Ancient East*,
Oxford 1941, figs. 380, 383]

is exemplified by a temple-like mausoleum on the site of New
Nisa which had a frontal colonnade with thin columns on stepped Persian-type bases and unusual Ionic capitals of the variety
sometimes called 'watchspring' from the spiral character of the
volutes (cf. Fig. 8).

Artists, too, continued to show interest in developing these hybrid
designs. In many cases, this took the form of the use of Greek style
for non-Greek subject-matter. In Babylonia, marble figurines were
carved representing reclining and standing nude females – doubtless

divine – with attachments in plaster and, interestingly, eyes inlaid in the ancient Mesopotamian manner. A series of metal – mainly silver – plates and bowls with rich relief decoration, of unknown but possibly Bactrian origin, may have begun at this time. The plate ornaments include rosettes, heads or busts of deities, real or legendary animals, war-elephants with figures riding them and Dionysus. The bowls have rosettes again, floral ornament, animals, busts of deities, depictions of hunting, libation and banqueting, and even perhaps scenes from Greek drama. Coins offer further examples. Two groups were issued by Iranian kings, in Greek style and on the same reduced Attic Greek weight standard as the Seleucid coinage, but with local subject matter. In Persis, in south-west Iran, the local subject kings began issuing their own coinage, principally in silver, perhaps at some point between about 250 and 200 BC, although a second-century date is also possible. On the obverse was a bearded head in a floppy Persian hat or bashlik, facing right, as on Seleucid issues; on the reverse a popular design comprised a standing figure in Iranian dress worshipping at a fire altar, and any legends were in Aramaic (Colledge 1977, plate 38e, ee). The second group seems to have emanated from what became the Parthian territories of the south-eastern Caspian and north-eastern Iran. Some early Parthian coins, silver drachms, close in material and technique to those of Bactria, have on the obverse a beardless head again wearing the bashlik (right-facing like the Seleucid on what seems to be the earliest type, and left-facing thereafter) and on the reverse a bow-holding archer in riding dress facing left on the apparently earliest three types but afterwards right. A Greek legend names Arsaces and occasionally an Aramaic text perhaps mentions the Iranian rank of *krny* (Karen) or 'general'. These coins are possibly to be assigned to the last years of Arsaces I (*c.* 220–215 BC, types 1–4, struck perhaps at Nisa) and the first of Arsaces II (*c.* 215–209 BC, types 5–6, struck possibly at Hecatompylus).[9]

### The second century BC

Despite political changes, work in Greek style continued across western Asia. Grid-plan cities were still being laid out, most notably by the Indo-Greeks (or Indo-Bactrians), with their foundation in north-west India of 'Lotus City' (Pushkalâvati) around 150 BC. Very possibly the great capital of Taxila (Fig. 9) also dates from this period, although the precise sequence of events and foundation date of the grid-plan city on the Sirkap Mound are as yet uncertain, and it remains a

9. Parthian coins: Abgarians and Sellwood 1971. Failaka terracottas: Mathiesen 1982.

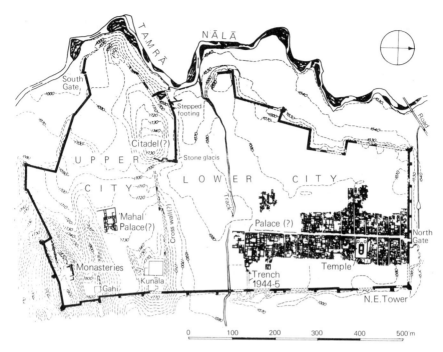

Fig. 9 Taxila, Pakistan: plan of the Sirkap mound with grid-plan streets, c. 50 BC–AD 150 [From R. E. M. Wheeler, *Flames over Persepolis*, London 1968, 113]

possibility that it was carried out by the nomadic Indo-Scythians under their king Azes I, who apparently supplanted the last Greek king in Taxila around 57 BC. Elsewhere, another usurper, Hyspaosines of the southern Babylonian kingdom of Characene, refounded an Antioch about 140–120 BC on the same lines as his capital Spasinu Charax. To the south of Characene, on Failaka, the north wall of the fort was pushed forward, before occupation ceased around 100 BC. At Seleucia-Tigris, there was work on cult buildings perhaps in the decades following the Parthian takeover in 141 BC. Two basically similar shrines were built: 'Temple A' and 'Temple B', each an open-air enclosure with a small theatre attached, and A had a covered ambularium inside the outer wall. The linking of religious building and theatre was a phenomenon particularly characteristic of hellenistic and Roman Syria (but contrast Millar, above pp. 117–8). The Greeks of Seleucia-Tigris still lived in houses of Greek type, with a two-column porch (*prodomos*) facing an interior court. At Dura-Europus, the open-air enclosure of the goddess Artemis with its cut-stone work and Doric colonnade may have originated at this time, if not earlier. The first phase of the temple of Zeus Megistos may also belong to this century; the form of the temple itself is unclear, but the ashlar sanctuary wall and Doric columned gateway were Greek. At Antioch-Orontes the main street was surfaced with stones, and shops with strong walls and rectangular rooms were built. At Ai Khanum a new building phase of the palace incorporated some Greek features: more of the blind arcading in relief introduced as wall decoration in the previous century, standard Corinthian column capitals, and the earliest known example of the kind of colonnaded court called the 'Rhodian' peristyle, in which one row of columns is higher than the others, all datable before *c.* 150 BC.

Greek artefacts continued to be popular and influential. There was considerable importation of various items. Some sculpture has been found in west Iran: at Tal-i Zohak a small female head was discovered allegedly of Parian marble and apparently representing Aphrodite, and at Malamir a less than life-size white marble (divine?) female torso attired in a revealing chiton, the technique of which with its careful chiselling and abrading and fairly sparing use of the drill suggests a later hellenistic date. Fragments of large bronze heads from a mountain shrine at Shami, a female and a male portrait head, were found along with fragments of a gold diadem and therefore perhaps belonged to a king (*CAH* VII.I² 21, pl. 19). Greek statuettes, particularly of bronze, have been found at a number of dispersed sites, especially at Greek foundations. There is a group from Laodicea (Nihavand) in west Iran comprising the deities Zeus, Apollo, Athena, a gilded Eros, a rider figure and Isis in her Egyptian headdress (a solar disc between two ears of corn, surmounted by two plumes), perhaps associated with some sanctuary (Plate IV). A bronze Heracles was found at Ai Khanum and another at Pushkalâvati (Charsada).

Greek items were also imported by the Parthians. The building that seems to have functioned as the Treasury of the Parthian central Asian capital at Nisa yielded a whole group of Greek figurines of this period: silver gilt figures of Athena, Eros, a siren, centaur, sphinx and eagle, marble statuettes of draped and semi-nude females, presumably goddesses (Plate VII), and a marble arm holding a satyr's head. Monarchs of the period may well have patronised Greek artists for portraits, if identifications of sculptures in the round based on coin profiles are correct; these include a scowling marble head in Rome identified as Euthydemus I of Bactria (*c.* 200 BC: Plate V) and a bronze figurine and standing nude statue identified as the Seleucid king Demetrius I (162–151/0 BC).

Seleucid and other rulers continued to mint in quantity, with striking portrait heads in profile on the obverse and divine or other subjects on the reverse together with their name, on the Attic standard and in a remarkably pure Greek style throughout (Colledge 1977, pl. 38d). The silver issues remained the most important, with gold and bronze less so (Colledge 1977, pl. 39gg). These high standards of crafts-manship were maintained by the Greek rulers of Bactria and India. The Bactrians used the Attic standard (Colledge 1977, pl. 39i). Around 150 BC king Eucratides I struck the largest gold coin of antiquity, a twenty-stater piece, shortly before his realm was overwhelmed by central Asian nomads. The Indo-Greeks (or Indo-Bactrians) of north India sometimes also issued coins on this standard, and *c.* 120 BC (?) Amyntas produced the largest silver coin of the ancient world, a twenty-drachm medallion, in this series. Doubtless these Attic-standard pieces were normally for trading north of the Hindu Kush, for most Indo-Greek issues were of a lighter, Indian weight, including many of circular Greek silver drachm, tetradrachm or occasionally hemi-drachm denominations, and some bronze pieces, in varied designs (Colledge 1977, pl. 39k,m). Parthian issues, too, were essentially Greek in style (especially those issued from Seleucia-Tigris after its capture in 141 BC), at least until the time of Mithridates I (*c.* 171–138 BC), but used Iranian iconography and so, strictly, fall into my category of 'hybrid' production.

Scattered small finds indicate further activity of Greek character. At Uruk and Seleucia-Tigris seal-impressions on clay *bullae* were from gems carved with divinities, heads and animals. At the Parthian capital of Nisa, a semicircular altar had painted garlands as decoration, and in the Treasury there were ivory couch legs of Greek design. The palace at Ai Khanum was brought reasonably up to date in its interior bathroom design by the application of a red wash on the walls and by the laying of competently executed pebble floor mosaics with various designs, figured and otherwise, including a sea-monster, all characteristic of Greece. The pebble technique was one still in use in the Greek cities during the hellenistic period, but being ousted by the cut-stone cube or *tessera* (Dunbabin 1979).

But what is of special interest at Ai Khanum are the great wall reliefs, executed in a very particular technique. On a framework of wood and cloth figured compositions were built up in a combination of clay and stucco, in a new development of techniques used in the Greek cities and then painted. Room 9 of the palace boasted wall reliefs which included at least fifteen persons on four different scales from half to fully life-size, and room 6 a huge equestrian group, two to three times life-size. Equally notable is the recurrence of wall reliefs of this type at the Parthian capital of Nisa, where in the building complex known as Old Nisa the walls of the Square and Round Halls were decorated with niches, in each of which stood an over life-size figure done in this technique; a standing female in excellent Greek style survives (Plate VIII). Perhaps these were executed for the Parthian court by artisans from Bactria. Sculpture was also represented by some noteworthy pieces in local limestone from Ai

Khanum such as a bearded head on a rectangular pillar ('herm': Plate VI) from the gymnasium, with realistic features (perhaps the Denavar fragments should be dated here as well: see above p. 145), and from a mausoleum the gravestone of a nude youth with upturned gaze. Thus in the second century BC Greek craftsmanship in western Asia remained active and innovative, at least in those genres familiar to Greeks, such as their own building forms, and sculpture, mosaic and coins.

Work drawing on the various local traditions continued to be produced. This was reflected architecturally in various ways. Some city-foundations may be cited. Around 150 BC, shortly before being overrun by central Asian nomads, the Bactrians founded a town whose ancient name is unknown at the site of Dilberdjin, some 40 kilometres north-west of Bactra. But this was no grid-plan layout. A huge, square enclosure was protected by a great mud-brick wall with towers and gates, the largest of which faced southwards towards the capital; the structures which arose both inside and outside were in only the roughest alignment. At the centre of the complex was a great circular building with stamped earth walls and numerous internal rooms, reminiscent of earlier and contemporary fortresses of central Asia such as Koi-Krylgan-Kala, although less organised than the latter. Circular again was the layout c. 140 BC of the Parthian refoundation of the Babylonian village, Ctesiphon, sited close to the recently conquered Seleucia-Tigris with a plan that was not of Hippodamian design. At Hecatompylus (Shahr-i Qumis), in north-east Iran, by then under Parthian control, a large fortified residence on site VI with rooms surrounded by corridors opening on to a great court, probably of central Asian inspiration, was constructed around this time.

Religious structures also perpetuated and developed earlier traditions. In Uruk, the ziggurat, the Bit Reš sanctuary of Anu and Antum and the Irrigal sanctuary of Ishtar and Nana were functioning well after the Parthian conquest of c. 140 BC, as is now revealed by the discovery of new texts (Kessler 1984b). It is possible that part of the mound at Seleucia-Tigris (see n. 4) called Tell 'Umar once was the site of a structure of ziggurat type, and that it was first constructed in this period. At the same date the Mesopotamian 'broad-room' type indented temple and temple outside the walls at Ai Khanum were still being utilised. Another 'broad-room' temple 'of the Dioscuri' was built c. 150 BC at the new Bactrian foundation of Dilberdjin (Kruglikova 1977), with Iranian corridors (and so overall an example of my 'hybrid' category). The open-air terrace with enclosure wall was represented by examples in west Iran: the one at Shami had an internal portico and statuary (see below for Khurha and Kangavar). At the Parthian capital, (Old) Nisa, more cult buildings were erected. Within a large fortified complex, whether a palace-fortress or a religious enclosure, some buildings look like temples. A solid 'Square Temple', surrounded by slim corridors of Iranian variety, might well have been a fire tower of some sort. Close by was a 'Square Hall', a 'centralised square' design with the usual four central columns derived from Achaemenid architecture, embellished with Greek decorative forms and Graeco-Bactrian-style wall reliefs comprising over life-size figures standing in niches, which may have functioned either as a reception hall, or as a dynastic shrine (Colledge 1977, 38 fig. 10; Plate I). An ancient tomb type, the *hypogeum*, entered down steps and with burial slots either side of a central corridor (found in the Neo-Assyrian period) occurred in examples datable to around 150 BC at towns as far apart as Palmyra (Colledge 1976, 58–9, with no. 169), Susa and Ai Khanum. Local Babylonian house types remained in use throughout Mesopotamia.

Traditional pottery types and figurines were still being produced: in particular, examples of the Mesopotamian stiff nude goddess figurine turned up not only in Mesopotamia, but also in west Iran and at Ai Khanum. Achaemenid art styles also inspired some activity. In the Treasury at (Old) Nisa, along with Greek items, were ivory couch legs of Achaemenid design. A Parthian king, almost certainly Mithridates II (c. 124/3–87 BC), commissioned a great rock relief at Bisitun in west Iran, overlooking a main highway (Plate XI). It is now damaged, but a seventeenth-century drawing of it when in a better state is helpful. To the right, in left-facing profile, stands the king; before him, also in profile, pose four nobles, named above in Greek like the king and with a small figure of victory personified (Nike) hovering over them. Perhaps Mithridates II is handing out fiefs to selected nobles. What is particularly noteworthy is the evocation of Achaemenid imperial style, for the relief is placed, surely deliberately, below the famous triumphal relief of Darius the Great, and this all accords with Mithridates' publication of a claim to be descended from a member of the Achaemenid house. So the choice of this Achaemenid-style representation (itself derived from a much earlier relief nearby) may have been deliberate and politically calculated. In the second century, therefore, Mesopotamian and Iranian architecture and art remained enormously influential.

There is ever more evidence of work intermingling Mesopotamian, Iranian and Greek traditions. The Mesopotamian 'broad room' temple type seems to have been adapted at Seleucia-Tigris for a rebuilding in baked brick of the supposed Heroon around 140–100 BC. At Dilberdjin it formed the basic element in a mud-brick temple built c. 150 BC and dedicated, to judge from wall-paintings, to the Greek Dioscuri, but with Iranian corridors around the inner chamber (cella), and thus anticipating in its form the cella of the great dynastic shrine of the Kushan king Kanishka of some three centuries later at Surkh

Kotal. Other structures mixed traditional elements with Greek. At Babylon, houses of Mesopotamian plan *very* occasionally incorporate a Greek columned (peristyle) court. The open Greek market place (agora) at Dura Europus, after the Parthian takeover (by *c.* 113 BC), was gradually filled with little, densely packed shops, and so became more like a covered market. In west Iran, the basically open-air religious terraces of Khurha and Kangavar, perhaps of this period, acquired some notable features (Fig. 8). The Khurha enclosure had a limestone colonnade, ostensibly Ionic with a taper (*entasis*) in the columns, but with Persian bases comprising two steps surmounted by a circular torus moulding, a shaft thin by Greek standards, and 'watchspring' capitals (Fig. 8B; Plate II). That at Kangavar, again in local limestone, boasted a grand double-entry staircase in imposing masonry of Persepolitan grandeur; around the platform ran a colonnade in the Doric Greek order, but with Persian square bases – a double solecism from the standard Greek viewpoint, as Doric columns should have no bases at all – and mouldings misplaced according to the Greek canon (Fig. 8A).

At Ai Khanum, were further examples of both the juxtaposition of Near Eastern and Greek cultural elements, and their blending. The indented temple, combining 'broad-room' plan with Greek wall reliefs, remained in use. In the palace, the Persian type column-base with two steps and *torus* was used for limestone columns otherwise in the Greek Ionic and Corinthian orders. The treasury, built *c.* 150 BC, had long, narrow rooms that recall both an Achaemenid antecedent at Persepolis and contemporary parallels at the Parthian capital Nisa. The Ai Khanum gymnasium was reminiscent of Greek types, but with prominent corridors recalling those of the Persian tradition and a puzzling central rotunda with two side rooms and a corridor of unknown purpose in the south court (see n. 7). The rich lived in grand houses which blended Greek courtyard types with Iranian rectangular arrangements and corridors, like the mansion in the south quarter (Fig. 6C). A strikingly similar house was erected in about 150 BC at the new foundation of Dilberdjin.

Other mixed structures characterised the city of Nisa. A Round Hall, perhaps originally with a wooden, pyramidal roof, has reminded some observers of circular Greek structures such as circular temples (*tholoi*) and the Arsinoeion on Samothrace (*c.* 280 BC). Indeed its decoration included (terracotta) metopes and Corinthian capitals of Greek type, as well as arched niches as found at Ai Khanum. But the overall square plan and surrounding straight, narrow corridors seem more reminiscent of the Iranian 'centralised square' design (Colledge 1977, 38, fig. 10A). The Square House, later definitely used as a Treasury, with a square, open colonnaded court surrounded by long, narrow rooms, recalls Greek exercise buildings (*palaestrae*) and closed porticos (stoas), as well as arrangements in Neo-Assyrian and Neo-Babylonian palaces and the Treasury at Persepolis.

Some artistic production falls into the category of subjects or items appropriate to one culture expressed in the style of another (usually Greek). Thus Parthian monarchs issued coins with Parthian subject matter but in various Greek styles – the profile, now usually left-facing male head on the obverse, and commonly a seated archer figure on the reverse (Colledge 1977, pl. 38h,hh). The Greek style is purest on the coins issued by Mithridates after his capture of Seleucia in 141 BC (doubtless a result of his use of die-cutters there: Colledge 1977, pl. 38j, jj) and most linear on those of Mithridates II (*c.* 124/3–87 BC: Colledge 1977, pl. 38k,kk). Similarly, the Indo-Greek kings minted issues, most of which were 'Indianised' on a light Indian standard. The coins had Prakrit legends on the reverse (and Greek on the obverse) and frequently idiosyncratic or Indian subject matter. The shapes were circular mainly for silver issues, but square commonly for copper and bronze, in imitation of Indian currency. Despite this they were always in Greek style (Colledge 1977, pl. 39k–p). The series of nude goddess figurines in Babylonia, Mesopotamian in conception but Greek in execution, continued. So, very probably, did the series of 'Bactrian' silver and bronze vessels with their rich ornamentation.

A further dramatic illustration of this process came to light in the Treasury of Nisa: the fragments of sixty or more ivory drinking horns (rhytons) with rich figured decoration comprising reliefs of Bacchic scenes, sacrifice, heads and animals, and ending in the foreparts (*protomai*) of a horse, griffin, centaur or female. They are Iranian in form and subject matter, cf. the row of heads, but Greek in execution, as is shown both by the style and by the labelling of a goddess, Hestia, in Greek (Plate XII). Were these perhaps a commission by the Parthian kings from the neighbouring Bactrians, a further link between the two realms, or the Parthian kings patronising local crafts-men? An example of the reverse, an item essentially Greek but in non-Greek guise, is provided by pottery, in which from around 150 BC a revival of an ancient technique of coloured glazes may be seen, used on both local and Greek shapes.

At the new Bactrian town of Dilberdjin the temple was decorated with wall-paintings (in a somewhat linear Greek style) of the two Dioscuri with white horses beneath what might be a *palaestra* scene. Other examples in which Greek and non-Greek elements are blended occur in sculpture. Figurines from Babylonia and Failaka are of this kind (see n.9), as is a little serpentine head perhaps of a Parthian ruler, possibly of the second or first century BC, from north Mesopotamia. At Ai Khanum, the limestone statuette of a standing woman is basically Greek in execution but there is some non-Greek linearity in the style (Plate IX). Particularly noteworthy is another rock relief overlooking the highway at Bisitun. Heracles reclines, holding a bowl in a standard Greek pose, before a niche (Plate X). Helpfully, a Greek inscription informs us that it was put up by a high Seleucid official in June 148 BC; a second inscription, in Aramaic is unfinished (see Sherwin-White, above p. 23). Significantly for an official Seleucid work, the style is poised midway between Greek and Iranian; rounded forms are rendered in a slightly stiff way, and the sculptor's technique makes much use of flat and claw chisels in the Greek way but without the drill or abrasives, leaving a crisp finish (Colledge 1979, 228–9, 237–40, figs. 8–10). Thus the various categories of new styles, combining Greek and non-Greek elements ('hybrid') flourished at this time.

## The first century BC

The output of purely Greek work had now diminished enormously. Little Greek art was imported into western Asia – primarily coins, and a late hellenistic statuette possibly of Aphrodite at what was now Parthian Dura Europus. The Seleucid, and occasionally the Indo-Greek monarchs, still minted Greek coins.

What may be regarded as work based on traditional local non-Greek styles had also decreased. At Dura-Europus the old Greek market place had now been filled with shops; *c.* 75–50 BC the temple of Zeus Megistos, and in 40–32 BC the temple of Artemis, were rebuilt as shrines incorporating a 'broad-room' cella (Downey, see n.5). But such architectural ornament as survives from these later 'broad-room' temples often includes Greek elements, and so they should rather be considered as of my 'hybrid' category. The small quantity of art bearing no traces of Greek influence includes impressions from seals on clay items made for official purposes found at Nisa and Hecatompylus (Shahr-i Qumis), gems carved in the central Asian 'Animal Style', and colourful 'nomad' jewellery from Taxila.

Instead, what had now blossomed right across western Asia was 'hybrid' work, in which Greek and various locally derived styles mingled. Architectural examples proliferated, particularly from the mid-century. At Palmyra, from *c.* 50 BC, local limestone began to be employed for building and art: Aramaic inscriptions were given Greek mouldings, architectural decoration of Graeco-Iranian types emerged, and the first of its long succession of splendid, soaring cut-stone funerary towers were raised, radiating outwards from the increasingly monumental inhabited quarters. At Seia (Si'), the temple of the god Ba'alshamin (33–32 BC) used both the Persian 'centralised square' and Greek forms. In the kingdom of Commagene, Antiochus I (*c.* 69–31 BC) raised a whole series of monuments of grandiose proportions. There were sanctuaries devoted to the king's cult, and in addition what was called the *hierothesion*, royal tomb and sanctuary combined, for the worship of the king, his ancestors and divinities. The royal cult took many forms – rock-cut tombs, reliefs on bases above processional ways, a mound surrounded by groups of columns bearing statuary and reliefs (Colledge 1977, 46 fig. 17), and most impressively of all the colossal hilltop tumulus of Nemrud Dağ, 150 metres high, dominating on either side a great terrace with reliefs and colossal seated statues. As part of his programme of dynastic art, Antiochus covered his realm with statuary and reliefs depicting himself, his family, ancestors and patron deities (Plate XIII). The style is a blend of Persian and Greek. Art forms and the iconographical repertoire mix such ancient Anatolian items as the rock relief and dado relief with Persian elements like the figures of Achaemenid kings from whom Antiochus claimed descent. Contemporary Anatolian and Iranian costume is employed, and Greek forms such as the statue on a column or scenes like the handclasp (or *dexiôsis*, here between Antiochus and selected deities). A lion relief illustrates his horoscope.

At Nisa the 'centralised' Square Hall was apparently rebuilt at this time, with Doric 'quadrilobate' columns on square bases. At Khaltchayan, in central Asia, a building datable to *c.* 50 BC–AD 50 – perhaps a reception hall – was built. It contained a six-column portico, a central hall entered (like a 'broad-room' shrine) through its long side, and a ('centralised'?) square inner chamber with two central columns, enclosed by corridors, but with roof edge ornaments (antefixes) and terracotta roof tiles of Greek type (Fig. 10). At Taxila temples were constructed, perhaps under the Indo-Scythians. One at Mohrâ Maliârân had an Ionic columned porch. Another, better known, on the Jandial site mixed Greek proportions and Ionic portico order with Iranian square cella, tower and corridors, and a covering outside of a special Indian stucco using crushed shells (Fig. 11).

Some art is of the kind where the style of one culture (in every case, Greek) is used for items characteristic of another culture. The 'Indianised' coin issues of the Indo-Greeks were of this sort, in both their circular and their square forms, as were Elymaean coins (Colledge 1977, pl. 38f and 39a,c), and Parthian issues until *c.* 50 BC (Colledge 1977, pl. 38l,mm; see ibid. pl. 39j,k–s, for coins of Indian rulers), after which the different styles were blended. The same appears to be true of the 'Bactrian' silver and bronze bowls and plates which might be datable to this period. Especially striking are two apparently late hellenistic heads from west Iran, in a marble that is white but with blue-grey streaks and thus most likely from south-west Anatolia: so it may have been imported. The technique is Greek. One, from the open-air shrine at Shami, shows a bearded Parthian prince. The other, from Susa, is female and Greek in all its details

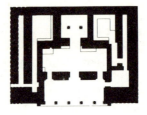

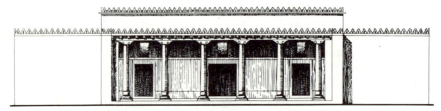

Fig. 10 Khaltchayan, north Bactria, USSR: 'reception hall', plan and front facade, probably c. 50 BC – AD 50 [From G. A. Pugachenkova, *Skulptura Khaltchayana*, Moscow 1971, 16–17]

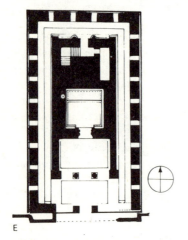

Fig. 11 Taxila, Pakistan: plan of the 'Jandial' temple, Indo-Scythian period, probably first century BC [From A. U. Pope (ed.), *A Survey of Persian Art*, Oxford 1938, I]

E

apart from a city-wall crown with merlon ornament. This suggests that the subject is the Good Fortune (Tyche) of a city (Susa?).

But most hybrid art is of the fully blended variety. This was true of Parthian coinage after about 50 BC (Colledge 1977, pl. 38n,o), and of associated coinages such as those of Armenia and Commagene (ibid. pl. 39e,r–u). It was true of other small items, such as pottery (for instance at Ai Khanum), or seal impressions of horsemen with lions and of suppliants from Nisa and Hecatompylus (Shahr-i Qumis), as well as, in all probability, circular schist and steatite 'toilet trays' from Taxila. The latter had reliefs of satyr and nymph, couples, reclining figures or animals. From the Mesopotamian town of Assur come two limestone gravestones with profile male figures in Parthian dress, one bearing an Aramaic text and date that may be read as 89/88 BC or AD 12/13; the Greek heritage is visible in a certain rounding of forms. Traces of wall-painting including a head in the vestibule of the Khaltchayan 'reception hall' (*c.* 50 BC–AD 50) show a continuation of the style seen at Dilberdjin. The main reception chamber in the Khaltchayan hall was decorated with splendid wall reliefs in clay and stucco on a wooden frame – in other words in the 'Bactrian' method seen earlier at Ai Khanum and Parthian Nisa – picked out in vivid colours (Fig. 12). In the centre of the main wall sat a royal couple

A

B

C

Fig. 12 Khaltchayan, north Bactria, USSR: 'reception hall', reconstruction of three wall-compositions in painted clay and stucco. (A) Central group: a royal couple with high-ranking persons; (B) North part of main wall: a seated noble, high-ranking clansmen and a goddess on a chariot; (C) South wall: mounted central Asian archers [From G. A. Pugachenkova, *Skulptura Khaltchayana*, Moscow 1971, 51, 61, 71]

flanked by attendants; on the north side were further nobles, and a goddess on a chariot, while on the south were central Asian archers. Above the whole ensemble ran a garland frieze, held up by Erotes. Most characteristic of this blended style is the great bronze statue of a Parthian grandee from the Shami sanctuary, variously dated *c.* 50 BC–AD 150; although Iranian in subject, the figure exhibits a Greek naturalism (Plate XIV). Thus in this period the hybrid has become completely predominant; and within the possibilities offered by this development, one has emerged pre-eminent: that in which different styles are completely blended.[10]

Grateful acknowledgment is made to the following for supplying photographs and giving permission to reproduce them: Mrs C. M. Bradford: Plates II, XI; Trustees of the British Museum, London: Plate III; Délegation archéologique française en Afghanistan, Kabul and Paris: Plates VI, IX; Dr. F. K. Dörner (photo Klemens Rintelen, Münster): Plate XIII; German Archaeological Institute Rome (neg. 33–24), and Museo Torlonia, Villa Albani: Plate V; Professor G. A. Pugachenkova: Plate VIII; Service Photographique, Muzeh-e Iran-e Bastan, Teheran: Plates IV, XIV; K. V. Trever (1940), *Pamiatniki Greko-Baktriiskogo Isskustva*, Moscow: *Union Soviétique*, December 1954: Plates VII, XII.

10. Shami head: Colledge 1977, 82, pl. 8b; id. 1979, 226–7, fig. 5. Susa head: id., 1977, 84, pl. 9c; 1979, 225–6, fig. 4. Taxila trays: Francfort 1979. Commagene: Colledge 1977, 229, fig. 11.

# Abbreviations

AA = *Archäologischer Anzeiger*
AA(A)S = *Annales Archéologiques (Arabes) de Syrie*
AASOR = Annual of the American Schools of Oriental Research
AB = Siglum for cuneiform texts in Bodleian Library, Oxford (now in Ashmolean Museum)
AC = *L'Antiquité Classique*
*Acta Antiqua* = *Acta Antiqua Academiae Scientiarum Hungaricae*
*Acta Ir.* = *Acta Iranica*
*ADAJ* = *Annual of the Department of Antiquities of Jordan*
ADFU = Ausgrabungen der Deutsche Forschungsgemeinschaft in Uruk-Warka
*AfO* = *Archiv für Orientforschung*
*AHw* = W. von Soden 1965–1981 *Akkadisches Handwörterbuch*, Wiesbaden
*AJA* = *American Journal of Archaeology*
*AJAH* = *American Journal of Ancient History*
*AJBA* = *Australian Journal of Biblical Archaeology*
*AJP* = *American Journal of Philology*
*AJSL* = *American Journal of Semitic Languages and Literature*
*AMI* = *Archäologische Mitteilungen aus Iran*
*Annales ESC* = *Annales. Economies, sociétés, civilisations*
*ANRW* = H. Temporini, W. Haase (eds.) *Aufstieg und Niedergang der Römischen Welt: Geschichte und Kultur Roms im Spiegel der neueren Forschung* Berlin
ANS = American Numismatic Society
*Anth. Pal.* = *Anthologia Palatina*
AOAT = Alter Orient und Altes Testament
*AOF* = *Altorientalische Forschungen*
*Ar. Or.* = *Archiv Orientalní*
*BaM* = *Baghdader Mitteilungen*
BAR = British Archaeological Record
*BASOR* = *Bulletin of the American Schools of Oriental Research*
*BCH* = *Bulletin de Correspondance Hellénique*
BE = J. Robert, L. Robert, *Bulletin Epigraphique*
BE VIII = A. T. Clay: *Legal and Commercial Transactions dated in the Assyrian, Neo-Babylonian and Persian Periods* Philadelphia 1908.
*BiOr* = *Bibliotheca Orientalis*
*BJ* = *Bonner Jahrbücher des Rheinischen Landesmuseum*
*BOR* = *The Babylonian and Oriental Record*
BRM I = *Babylonian Records in the Library of J. Pierpont Morgan* I: A. T. Clay *Babylonian Business Transactions of the First Millennium* BC New York 1912
BRM II = *Babylonian Records in the Library of J. Pierpont Morgan* II:

A. T. Clay *Legal Documents from Erech dated in the Seleucid Era (312–65 BC)* New York 1913

*CAD = Chicago Assyrian Dictionary*

*CP = Classical Philology*

*CPJ = Corpus Papyrorum Judaicarum* ed. V. A. Tcherikover, A. Fuks, Cambridge, Mass. 1957–1964 (3 vols.)

*CQ = Classical Quarterly*

*CRAI = Comptes Rendus de l'Académie des Inscriptions*

*CT* 49 = *Cuneiform Texts from Babylonian Tablets in the British Museum*: D. A. Kennedy, *Late-Babylonian Economic Texts* London 1968

*CT* 55–57 = *Cuneiform Texts from Babylonian Tablets in the British Museum*: T. G. Pinches *Neo-Babylonian and Achaemenid Economic Texts* London 1982

*DHA = Dialogues d'Histoire Ancienne*

Diels = *Die Fragmente der Vorsokratiker* by H. Diels edited by W. Kranz (6th ed.) Berlin 1951

*EI = Epigraphica Indica*

*FGrHist. = Die Fragmente der griechischen Historiker* by F. Jacoby (Berlin, Leiden)

*FuB = Forschungen und Berichte der Staatlichen Museen zu Berlin*

*GGM = Geographi Graeci Minores* ed. C. Müller

*GM = Göttinger Miszellen*

*ID = Inscriptions de Délos* ed. F. Durrbach 1926–9; and P. Roussell 1935, Paris

*IEJ = Israel Exploration Journal*

*IG = Inscriptiones Graecae*

*IGLS = Inscriptions grecques et latines de la Syrie* ed. L. Jalabert, R. Mouterde, J. P. Rey-Coquais (Paris)

*Ir. Ant. = Iranica Antiqua*

*JA = Journal Asiatique*

*JAOS = Journal of the American Oriental Society*

*JCS = Journal of Cuneiform Studies*

*JEA = Journal of Egyptian Archaeology*

*JHS = Journal of Hellenic Studies*

*JJS = Journal of Jewish Studies*

*JNES = Journal of Near Eastern Studies*

*JRAS = Journal of the Royal Asiatic Society*

*Der Kleine Pauly = Lexikon der Antike in fünf Bänden* Munich

*LBAT = Late Babylonian Astronomical and Related Texts* copied by T. G. Pinches and J. N. Strassmaier; prep. for pub. by A. J. Sachs with the co-operation of J. Schaumberger (Providence, R. I., 1955)

Liddell and Scott = H. G. Liddell, R. Scott 1940 *A Greek–English Lexicon* 9th ed. Oxford

*LCM = Liverpool Classical Monthly*

*Nbn. =* J. N. Strassmaier 1889 *Inschriften von Nabonidus, König von Babylon (555–538 v. Chr.)* Leipzig (Babylonische Texte, Heft I–IV)

*NC = Numismatic Chronicle*

NCBT = Siglum for Newell Collection of Babylonian Tablets, New Haven

n.f. = Neue Folge

n.r. = Nieuwe Reeks

n.s. = Nova Series

*OA = Oriens Antiquus*

*OECT* IX = G. J. P. McEwan 1982 *Texts from Hellenistic Babylonia in the Ashmolean Museum* Oxford (Oxford Editions of Cuneiform Texts IX)

*OGIS* = W. Dittenberger (ed.) 1903–5 *Orientalis Graeci Inscriptiones Selectae* 2 vols. Leipzig

*OLZ* = *Orientalistische Literaturzeitung*

*Or* = *Orientalia*

*PCZ* = C. C. Edgar 1925–31 *Zenon Papyri* 4 vols Cairo

*PDura* = *The Excavations at Dura–Europos . . . Final Report* V Pt. 1 *The Parchments and Papyri* ed. C. B. Welles, R. O. Fink, J. F. Gillam New Haven 1959

*PEQ* = *Palestine Exploration Quarterly*

*Proc. Camb. Phil. Soc.* = *Proceedings of the Cambridge Philological Society*

*PSAS* = *Proceedings of the Seminar for Arabian Studies*

*PZenon* = *Zenon Papyri: Business papers of the 3rd century* BC ed. W. C. Westermann and E. S. Hasenoehrl New York 1934–40

*RB* = *Revue Biblique*

*RE* = *Pauly's Realenzyklopädie der classischen Altertumswissenschaft* hrsg. G. Wissowa Stuttgart 1894–

*REA* = *Revue des Etudes Anciennes*

*REG* = *Revue des Etudes Grecques*

*RLA* = *Reallexikon der Assyriologie* Berlin 1928–

*RN* = *Revue Numismatique*

*RPh* = *Revue Philologique*

*RTP* = P. Briant 1982 *Rois, Tributs et Paysans: études sur les formations tributaires du Moyen-Orient ancien* Besançon (Centre de Recherches d'Histoire Ancienne 43)

*SDB* = *Supplément au Dictionnaire de la Bible*

*SEG* = *Supplementum Epigraphicum Graecum*

*TAPhA* = *Transactions and Proceedings of the American Philological Association*

*TAPhS* = *Transactions of the American Philosophical Society*

*TBER* = J.-M. Durand 1981 *Textes Babyloniens d'Epoque Récente* Paris (Recherches sur les grandes civilisations: études assyriologiques – cahier no.6)

*TCL* VI = F. Thureau-Dangin 1922 *Tablettes d'Uruk à l'usage des prêtres du temple d'Anu au temps des Séleucides* Paris (Textes Cunéiformes de Louvre 6)

*TCL* XII = G. Contenau 1927 *Contrats néo-babyloniens I (de Téglath-phalasar à Nabonide)* Paris (Textes Cunéiformes de Louvre 12)

*TCS* = Texts from Cuneiform Sources

*TMO* = Travaux de la Maison de l'Orient

*UAE Arch.* = *Archaeology in the United Arab Emirates*

*UVB* = *Vorläufiger Bericht über die von dem Deutschen Archäologischen Institut und der Deutschen Orientgesellschaft aus Mitteln der Deutschen Forschungsgemeinschaft unternommenen Ausgrabungen in Uruk-Warka*

*VAB* = Vorderasiatische Bibliothek

*VDI* = *Vestnik drevnej istorii*

*WVDOG* = Wissenschaftliche Veröffentlichungen der Deutschen Orientgesellschaft

*YBC* = Siglum of Yale Babylonian Collection, New Haven

*YCS* = *Yale Classical Studies*

*YOS* I = A. T. Clay 1915 *Miscellaneous Inscriptions in the Yale Babylonian Collection*, New Haven (Yale Oriental Series, Babylonian Texts 1)

*ZA* = *Zeitschrift für Assyriologie und verwandte Gebiete*

*ZPE* = *Zeitschrift für Papyrologie und Epigraphik*

# Bibliography

Names formed with the elements *de, van* or *von* are listed under 'D' and 'V' respectively. Arabic names with the prefix *al-* are listed under the main name, e.g. al-Qaisy appears under 'Q'.

Abgarians M. T., Sellwood D. G. 1971 'A hoard of early Parthian drachms', *NC* (7th series) 11, 103–19 and pls. 20–3

Abou Assaf A., Bordreuil P., Millard A. R. 1982 *La Statue de Tell Fekherye et son inscription bilingue assyro-araméenne* Paris (Recherches sur les civilisations 7 (10): Etudes assyriologiques)

Adams R. McC. 1981 *Heartland of Cities: surveys of ancient settlement and land use in the central floodplain of the Euphrates* Chicago

Adams R. McC., Nissen H.-J. 1972 *The Uruk Countryside: the natural setting of urban societies* Chicago

Akurgal E. 1961 *Die Kunst Anatoliens von Homer bis Alexander* Berlin

Albrectsen E. 1958 'Alexander the Great's visiting card' *Kuml*, 172–91

Allen R. E. 1983 *The Attalid Kingdom: a constitutional history* Oxford

Altheim F. 1948 *Weltgeschichte Asiens im griechischen Zeitalter II* Halle

André-Leicknam B. in press 'The inscriptions' *Catalogue of the Bahrain National Museum*

Austin M. M. 1981 *The Hellenistic World from Alexander to the Roman Conquest: a selection of ancient sources in translation* Cambridge

Avi-Yohah M. 1959 'Syrian Gods at Ptolemais-Accho' *IEJ* 9, 1–12

————— 1972 *The Holy Land* London

Aymard A. 1938 'Une ville de la Babylonie Séleucide' *REA* 40, 5–42 (= id. 1967 *Etudes d'Histoire Ancienne* Paris, 178–211)

Bailey C. 1947 *Lucretius,* de rerum natura 3 vols. Oxford

Baines J., Eyre C. J. 1983 'Four notes on literacy' *GM* 61, 65–96

Balsdon J. P. V. D. 1979 *Romans and Aliens* London

Balty J. 1981 'L'oracle d'Apamée' *AC* 50, 5–14

Balty J., Balty J. C. 1977 'Apamée de Syrie, archéologie et histoire I. Des origines à la Tetrarchie' *ANRW* II/8, 103–34

Balty J. C. 1971 'Nouvelles données topographiques et chronologiques à Apamée de Syrie' *AAAS* 21, 131–5

Baroni B. 1984 'I terreni e i privilegi del tempio di Zeus a Baitokaike (*IGLS* VII 4028)' in Virgilio B. (ed.) *Studi Ellenistici* I Pisa (Bibl. di studi antichi 48), 135–67

Bawden G., Edens C., Miller R. 1980 'The Archaeological Resources of ancient Taymā: preliminary archaeological investigations at Taymā' *Atlal* 4, 69–106

Beaucamp J., Robin C. 1983 'L'evéché nestorien de Mashmahig dans l'archipel d'al-Bahrayn' in Potts 1983b, 171–96

Bellinger A. R. 1963 *Essays in the Coinage of Alexander the Great* New York (ANS Numismatic Studies 11)

Bengtson H. 1951 'Die Bedeutung der Eingeborenenbevölkerung in den hellenistischen Oststaaten' *Welt als Geschichte* 11, 135–42 (= *Kleine Schriften zur alten Geschichte* Munich 1974, 293–303)

―――― 1952 *Die Strategie in der hellenistischen Zeit* Munich

Benveniste E. 1964 'Edits d'Asoka en traduction grecque' *JA* 252, 137–57

Bernard P. 1969 'Quatrième campagne de fouilles à Aï Khanoum (Bactriane)' *CRAI*, 313–35

―――― 1970 'Campagne de fouilles 1969 à Aï Khanoum en Afghanistan' *CRAI*, 301–49

―――― 1971 'La campagne de fouilles de 1970 à Aï Khanoum (Afghanistan)' *CRAI*, 385–452

―――― 1973 *Aï Khanoum* I Paris

―――― 1976a 'Campagne de fouilles 1975 à Aï Khanoum' *CRAI*, 287–322

―――― 1976b 'Les traditions orientales dans l'architecture Gréco-Bactrienne' *JA* 264, 245–75

―――― 1978 'Campagne de fouilles 1976–1977 à Aï Khanoum' *CRAI*, 421–63

―――― 1980a 'Campagne de fouilles 1978 à Aï Khanoum' *CRAI*, 435–59

―――― 1980b 'Heracles, les grottes de Karafto et le sanctuaire du mont Sambulos en Iran' *Studia Iranica* 9, 301–24

Bertrand J. M. 1982 'Sur l'inscription d'Hefzibah' *ZPE* 46, 167–74

Bibby G. 1957 'The Hundred-Meters section' *Kuml*, 128–64

―――― 1965 'Arabian Gulf Archaeology' *Kuml*, 133–52

―――― 1966 'Arabian Gulf Archaeology' *Kuml*, 75–95

―――― 1972 *Looking for Dilmun* Harmondsworth

―――― 1973 *Preliminary Survey in East Arabia 1968* Copenhagen (Danish Archaeological Expedition to the Arabian Gulf, Reports 2: Jutland Archaeological Society Publications XII)

Bickermann E. 1937 *Der Gott der Makkabäer: Untersuchungen über Sinn und Ursprung der makkabäischen Erhebung* Berlin (= trans. *The God of the Maccabees: Studies on the meaning and origin of the Maccabean revolt*) Leiden 1979 (Studies in Judaism in Late Antiquity 32)

―――― 1938 *Institutions des Séleucides* Paris

―――― 1939a 'La cité grecque dans les monarchies hellénistiques' (review of Heuss 1937) *RPh* 13, 335–49

―――― 1939b 'Sur une inscription de Sidon' *Mélanges Syriens offerts à Monsieur René Dussaud par ses amis et élèves* Paris, 91–9

―――― 1976a 'The Septuagint as a translation' in id. 1976b, 167–200

―――― 1976b *Studies in Jewish and Christian History* I Leiden

Bidez J. 1935 'Les écoles chaldéennes sous Alexandre et les Séleucides' *Annuaire de l'Institut de Philologie et d'Histoire Orientales* 3, 41–89

Biran A. 1977 'Chronique Archéologique: Tell Dan' *RB* 84, 256–63

Bivar A. D. 1978 'The Aramaic Summary' in Stronach 1978, 161–2

Boardman J. 1970 *Greek Gems and Finger Rings* London

Börker C. 1974 'Griechische Amphorenstempel vom Tell Halaf bis zum Persischen Golf' *BaM* 7, 31–49

Boucharlat R. 1984 'Les périodes pré-islamiques aux Emirats Arabes Unis' in Boucharlat, Salles 1984, 189–99

―――― 1986 'Some notes about Qala'at al-Bahrain during the Hellenistic period' in al-Khalifa, Rice 1986, 435–44

Boucharlat R., Daglongeville R., Hesse A., Sanlaville P. 1984 *Survey in Sharjah Emirate, UAE First Report (March 5–14 1984)* Lyon (mimeo GS Maison de l'Orient)

Boucharlat R., Salles J.-F. 1981 'The history and archaeology of the Gulf from the fifth century BC to the seventh century AD: a review of the evidence' *PSAS* 11, 65–94

Boucharlat R., Salles J.-F. (eds) 1984 *Arabie Orientale, Mésopotamie et Iran méridionale de l'age de fer au début de l'époque islamique* Paris

Boucharlat R., Salles J.-F. in press 'Bahrain in the Hellenistic period' *Catalogue of the Bahrain National Museum*

Bouché-Leclerq A. 1899 *L'Astrologie Grecque* Paris

Bowersock G. W. 1983a 'Antipater Chaldaeus' *CQ* 33, 491

———— 1983b *Roman Arabia* Cambridge, Mass.

———— 1986 'Bahrain, Tylos and Tyre: in the Greco-Roman World' in al-Khalifa, Rice 1986, 399–406

Bowman R. A. 1939 'Anu-uballit Kefalon' *AJSL* 56, 231–43

Briant P. 1976 '"Brigandage", dissidence et conquête en Asie achéménide et hellénistique' *DHA* 2, 163–258; 273–9

———— 1977 *Alexandre le Grand* (2nd rev. ed.) Paris

———— 1982a 'D'Alexandre le Grand aux Diadoques: le cas d'Eumène de Kardia' *RTP*, 13–93 (orig. pub. *REA* 1972, 32–73; 1973, 43–81)

———— 1982b 'Colonisation hellénistique et populations indigènes: la phase d'installation' *RTP*, 227–62 (orig. pub. *Klio* 60 (1978), 57–92)

———— 1982c 'Communautés rurales, forces productives et mode de production tributaire' *RTP*, 405–30 (orig. pub. *Zamân* 1980, 76–100)

———— 1982d 'Contrainte militaire, dépendance rurale et exploitation des territoires en Asie achéménide' *RTP*, 175–225 (orig. pub. *Index* 8 (1978/9), 48–98)

———— 1982e *Etat et pasteurs au Moyen-Orient ancien* Cambridge, Paris (Coll. Production pastorale et société)

———— 1982f 'Remarques sur "laoi" et esclaves ruraux en Asie Mineure hellénistique' *RTP*, 95–135 (orig. pub. *Actes du Colloque 1971 sur l'esclavage* Paris 1973, 93–133)

———— 1984 'La Perse avant l'Empire (un état de la question)' *Ir. Ant.* 19, 71–118

———— 1985 'Les Iraniens d'Asie Mineure après la chute de l'empire achéménide' *DHA* 11, 167–95

———— 1987 'Pouvoir central et polycentrisme culturel dans l'empire achéménide' in Sancisi-Weerdenburg, H. W. A. M. (ed.) *Achaemenid History I: sources, structures, synthesis* Leiden, 1–31

Brinkman J. A. 1968 *A Political History of Post-Kassite Babylonia 1158–722 BC* Rome (Analecta Orientalia 43)

Bruneau P. 1970 *Recherches sur les cultes de Délos à l'époque hellénistique et à l'époque impériale* Paris (Bibl. des écoles françaises d'Athènes et de Rome 217)

———— 1982 '"Les Israélites de Délos" et la juiverie délienne' *BCH* 106, 465–504

Bunge J. G. 1976 'Die Feiern Antiochus IV. Epiphanes in Daphne 166 BC' *Chiron* 6, 53–71

Burn A. R. 1951 *Alexander and the Hellenistic Empires* (2nd ed.) London

Burney C. A. 1977 *From Village to Empire* Oxford

Burstein S. M. 1978 *The Babyloniaca of Berossus* Malibu, Calif. (Sources from the Ancient Near East 1.5)

Callot O. 1984 'Les monnaies' in Salles 1984c, 157–67

Callot O., Marcillet-Jaubert J. 1984 'Hauts-lieux de la Syrie du Nord' *Temples et Sanctuaires* Lyon, 185ff (TMO 7)

Calvet Y. 1984a 'Ikaros: Testimonia' in Salles 1984c, 21–9

————— 1984b 'Tylos et Arados' in Boucharlat, Salles 1984, 341–6

Calvet Y., Caubet A., Salles J.-F. 1984 'French excavations at Failaka, 1983' *PSAS* 14, 9–20

————— 1985 'French excavations at Failaka, 1984' *PSAS* 15, 11–26

Cameron A. 1969–1970 'Agathias on the Sassanians' *Dumbarton Oaks Papers* 23–4, 69–183

Carratelli G. P. 1966 'Greek inscriptions of the Middle East' *East and West* 16, 31–6

Casson L. 1980 'Rome's trade with the East: the sea voyage to Africa and India' *TAPhS* 110, 31–5

Caubet A., Salles J.-F. 1984 'Le sanctuaire hellénistique B6' in Salles 1984c, 73–156

Childs W. A. P. 1978 *The City-Reliefs of Lycia* Princeton, N.J.

Christensen A. P., Johansen C. F. 1971 *Hama. Fouilles et recherches 1931–1938 III.2: Les potéries hellénistiques et les terres sigillées orientales* Copenhagen

Clanchy M. T. 1979 *From Memory to Written Record: England 1066–1307* London

Cleuziou S. 1978/1979 'The second and third seasons of excavations at Hili 8' *UAE Arch* II–III, 30–69

Cohen G. M. 1978 *The Seleucid Colonies* Wiesbaden (Historia Einzelschriften 30)

Colledge M. A. R. 1976 *The Art of Palmyra* London

————— 1977 *Parthian Art* London

————— 1979 'Sculptors' stone-carving techniques in Seleucid and Parthian Iran' *East and West* 29, 221–40 and figs. 1–19

Coogan M. D. 1974 'Life in the diaspora: Jews at Nippur in the fifth century BC' *Biblical Archaeologist* 37, 6–12

————— 1976 *West Semitic Personal Names in the Murašû Documents* (Harvard Semitic Monographs 7) Cambridge, Mass.

Cook J. M. 1983 *The Persian Empire* London

Coulton J. J. 1977 *Greek Architects at Work* London

Cross F. M. 1969 'Papyri of the fourth century BC from Dâliyeh' in Freedman D. N., Greenfield J. C. (eds.) *New Directions in Biblical Archaeology* Garden City N.Y., 45–69

————— 1981 'An Aramaic ostracon of the third century BC from Jerusalem' *Eretz-Israel* 15, 67ff

Crowfoot J. W., Kenyon K. M., Sukenik E. L. 1942 *Samaria-Sebaste I: The Buildings* London

Crowfoot J. W., Crowfoot G. M., Kenyon K. M. 1957 *Samaria-Sebaste I: The Objects* London

Cumont F. 1927 'La Patrie de Séleucos de Séleucie' *Syria* 8, 83–4

Dalley S. 1984 'The cuneiform tablet from Tell Tawilan' *Levant* 16, 19–22

Dandamaev M. A. 1981 'The Neo-Babylonian citizens' *Klio* 63, 45–9

Debord P. 1982 *Aspects sociaux et économiques de la vie religieuse dans l'Anatolie gréco-romaine* Leiden

de Cardi D. B. 1978 *Qatar Archaeological Report: excavations 1973* Oxford

de Franciscis A. 1963 *Il Museo Nazionale di Napoli* Naples

Dentzer J.-M., Dentzer J. 1981 'Les fouilles de Si' et la phase hellénistique en Syrie du sud' *CRAI*, 78–102

Diakonov I. M. 1965 'A Babylonian political pamphlet from about 700 BC' in Güterbock H. G., Jacobsen T. (eds.) *Studies in Honor of Benno Landsberger on his seventy-fifth birthday April 21, 1965* Chicago, 343–9

Dohrn T. 1960 *Die Tyche von Antiochia* Berlin

Donner F. M. 1981 *The Early Islamic Conquest* Princeton, N.J.

Donner H., Röllig W. 1964–1968 *Kanaanäische und aramäische Inschriften* 3 vols. (2nd ed.) Wiesbaden

Dossin G. 1971 'La glose Sarachéro d'Hesychios' *Bull. de la classe de lettres et sciences morales et politiques, Académie royale de Belgique* sér. 5,5, 389–99

Doty L. T. 1977 *Cuneiform Archives from Hellenistic Uruk* Ann Arbor, Mich. (diss.)

——— 1978/9 'A cuneiform tablet from Tell 'Umar' *Mesopotamia* 13/14, 91–8

——— 1979 'An official seal of the Seleucid period' *JNES* 38, 195–7

——— 1980 'The archive of the Nanâ-iddin family from Uruk' *JCS* 30, 65–89

Dougherty R. P. 1932 'The names of two Aramean scribes stamped on clay *bullae*' in Rostovtzeff 1932, 94–7

Downey G. 1961 *A History of Antioch in Syria from Seleucus to the Arab Conquest* Princeton N.J.

Downey S. B. forthcoming *Later Mesopotamian Religious Architecture* Princeton N.J.

Drews R. 1975 'The Babylonian chronicles and Berossus' *Iraq* 37, 39–55

Drijvers H. J. W. 1972 *Old Syriac (Edessean) Inscriptions* (Semitic Study Series n.s. III) Leiden

——— 1977 'Hatra, Palmyra, und Edessa: die Städte der syrisch-mesopotamischen Wüste in politischer, kulturgeschichtlicher und religionsgeschichtlicher Bedeutung' *ANRW* II.8, 799–906

Dunbabin K. M. D. 1979 'Technique and materials of Hellenistic mosaics' *AJA* 83, 266–77

Dupont-Sommer A. 1964 'Quatre inscriptions araméennes inédites provenant d'Iran' *CRAI*, 283–7

During-Caspers E. C. L. (ed.) in press *Beatrice de Cardi Felicitation Volume* Amsterdam

Dussaud R. 1955 *La pénétration des Arabes en Syrie avant l'Islam* Paris

Eddy S. K. 1961 *The King is Dead: studies in the Near Eastern resistance to hellenism 334–31 BC* Lincoln, Nebraska

Ehrenberg V. 1969 *The Greek State* (2nd ed.) London

Eichler F. 1950 *Die Reliefs des Heroon von Gjölbaschi-Trysa* Vienna

Eissfeldt O. 1965 *The Old Testament: an introduction* (trans.) Oxford

Ellis R. S. 1968 *Foundation Deposits in Ancient Mesopotamia* New Haven, Conn. (Yale Near Eastern Researches 2)

Errington R. M. 1970 'From Babylon to Triparadeisos, *JHS* 90, 49ff

Fales F. M. 1973 'Remarks on the Neirab Texts' *OA* 12, 131–42

Falkenstein A. 1941 *Topographie von Uruk, I. Teil: Uruk zur Seleukidenzeit* Leipzig (ADFU 3)

Farkas A. 1974 *Achaemenid Sculpture* Istanbul

Fellmann R. 1970 *Le sanctuaire de Balshamin à Palmyre V: Die Grabanlage* Neuchâtel (Bibliotheca Helvetica Romana 10:5)

Filliozat, J. 1961–62 'Graeco-Aramaic inscription of Asoka near Kandahar' *EI* 34, 1–8

Finkel I. L. 1980 'Bilingual Chronicle Fragments' *JCS* 32, 65–80

Fischer T. 1979 'Zur Seleukideninschrift von Hafzibah' *ZPE* 33, 131–8

Francfort H. P. 1979 *Les palettes du Gandhara* Paris (Mémoires de la Délégation Archéologique Français en Afghanistan XXIII)

Francis E. D., Vickers M. 1985 'Greek Geometric Pottery at Hama and its implications for Near Eastern chronology' *Levant* 17, 131ff

Frankfort H. 1970 *The Art and Architecture of the Ancient Orient* Harmondsworth (Pelican History of Art, 4th ed.)

Fraser P. M. 1972 *Ptolemaic Alexandria* 3 vols. Oxford

Frézouls E. 1954/5 'Recherches historiques et archéologiques sur la ville de Cyrrhus' *AAS* 4/5, 89–128

———— 1959 'Recherches sur les théatres de l'Orient syrien' *Syria* 36, 202–27

———— 1977 'Cyrrhus et la Cyrrhestique jusqu'a la fin du Haut-Empire' *ANRW* II.8, 164–97

———— 1978 'La toponymie de l'Orient syrien et l'apport des éléments macédoniens' in *La toponymie antique: actes de colloque de Strassbourg 1975* Leiden (Travaux Centre de recherche sur le Proche-Orient et la Grèce antique 4), 219–48

Frye R. 1982 'The "Aramaic" inscription on the tomb of Darius' *Ir.Ant.* 17, 85–90

Fugman E. 1958 *Hama: fouilles et recherches de la Fondation Carlsberg 1931–1938, II: architecture des périodes pré-hellénistique* Copenhagen

Funck B. 1984 *Uruk zur Seleukidenzeit* Berlin (Schriften zur Geschichte und Kultur des alten Orients 16)

Fussman G. 1982 'Pouvoir central et regions dans l'Inde ancienne' *Annales ESC* 37, 621–47

Garlan Y. 1983 'Le commerce des amphores grecques' in Garnsey, Whittaker 1983, 37–44

Garnsey P., Whittaker C. R. (eds.) 1983 *Trade and Famine in Classical Antiquity* Cambridge

Gauthier P. 1985 *Les cités grecques et leurs bienfaiteurs (IVe–Ier siècle avant J.-C.): contribution à l'histoire des institutions* Paris (*BCH* Suppl. XII)

*Gazeteer of Arabia* 1979, Scoville S.A. (ed.) Graz

Geraty L. T. 1975 'The Khirbet el-Kôm bilingual ostracon' *BASOR* 220, 55–61

Gibson McG., Biggs R. D. (eds.) 1977 *Seals and Sealing in the Ancient Near East* Malibu (Bibliotheca Mesopotamica 6)

Glassner J.-J. 1984 'Inscriptions cunéiformes de Failaka' in Salles 1984c, 31–50

Goossens G. 1943 *Hiérapolis de Syrie: essai de monographie historique* Louvain

Gow A. S. F., Page D. L. 1965 *The Greek Anthology, Hellenistic Epigrams* Cambridge

Grayson A. K. 1975a *Assyrian and Babylonian Chronicles* Locust Valley, N.Y. (TCS 5)

—————— 1975b *Babylonian Historical-Literary Texts* Toronto (Toronto Semitic Texts and Studies 3)

Groom N. 1981 *Frankincense and Myrrh* London

Grosjean F. 1982 *Life with Two Languages: an introduction to bilingualism* Cambridge, Mass.

Habicht C. 1958 'Die herrschende Gesellschaft in den hellenistischen Monarchien' *Vierteljahrschrift für Soziologie und Wirtschaftsgeschichte* 45, 1–16

Hallock R. T. 1977 'The use of seals on the Persepolis fortification tablets' in Gibson, Biggs 1977, 123–33

Hamilton J. R. 1973 *Alexander the Great* London

Hannestad L. 1983 *Ikaros – The Hellenistic Settlements vol. 2: Pottery from Failaka, with a survey of Hellenistic pottery in the Near East* Copenhagen (Jutland Archaeological Publications XVI/2)

—————— 1984a 'Danish excavations on Failaka' in Boucharlat, Salles 1984, 59–66

—————— 1984b 'The pottery from the Hellenistic settlements on Failaka' in Boucharlat, Salles 1984, 67–83

Hardy-Guilbert C. 1984 'Fouilles archéologiques à Murwab, Qatar' in Boucharlat, Salles 1984, 169–88

Hengel M. 1974 *Judaism and Hellenism: studies in their encounter in Palestine during the early Hellenistic period* vols. 1–2 (trans.) London

—————— 1980 *Jews, Greeks and Barbarians: aspects of the hellenization of Judaism* (trans.) London

Herbert S. 1981 'Tel Anafa: the 1981 season' *Muse* 15, 23ff

Heuss A. 1937 *Stadt und Herrscher des Hellenismus in ihren staats- und völkerrechtlichen Beziehungen* Berlin (Klio Beiheft 39) (repr. 1963 with Nachwort, Wiesbaden)

Hornblower J. 1981 *Hieronymus of Cardia* Oxford

Hornblower S. 1982 *Mausolus* Oxford

Horowitz G. 1980 'Town planning in hellenistic Marisa: reappraisal of the excavations after eighty years' *PEQ* 112, 93–111

Horsley G. H. R. 1981 *New Documents Illustrating Early Christianity, 1: a review of the Greek inscriptions and papyri published in 1976* North Ryde‾

Humphries J. 1974 'Some late prehistoric sites in the Sultanate of Oman. Haward Archaeological Survey in Oman' *PSAS* 4, 49–77

Ikida Y. 1979 'Royal cities and fortified cities' *Iraq* 41, 75–84

Invernizzi A. 1968 'Bullae from Seleucia' *Mesopotamia* 3/4, 69–124

—————— 1976 'Ten years research in the Al-Mada in the area of Seleucia and Ctesiphon' *Sumer* 32, 166ff

Jakob-Rost L., Freydank H. 1972 'Spätbabylonische Rechtsurkunden aus Babylon mit aramäischen Beischriften' *FuB* 14, 7–35

Jenkins G. K. 1972 *Ancient Greek Coins* London

Jeppesen K. 1960 'A royal message to Ikaros' *Kuml*, 153–204

—————— 1963 'A Hellenistic fortress on the island of Ikaros (Failaka) in the Persian Gulf' *VIIIe Congrès d'Archéologie Classique: Le rayonnement des civilisations grecque et romaine sur les cultures peripheriques* Paris, 541–44

Jeremias J. 1962 *Jerusalem zur Zeit Jesu* (3rd ed.) Göttingen (=1969 *Jerusalem in the Time of Jesus: an investigation into economic and social conditions during the New Testament period* (rev.ed.; trans.) London)

Joannès F. 1979–1980 'Les successeurs d'Alexandre le Grand en Babylonie' *Anatolica* 7, 99–116

———— 1982 *Textes Economiques de la Babylonie Récente (Etude des textes de TBER-cahier no.6)* Paris (Etudes Assyriologiques no.5)

Jones A. H. M. 1940 *The Greek City from Alexander to Justinian* Oxford

Karst J. 1911 *Die Chronik. Eusebius Werke 5* Leipzig

Kervran M. 1984 'A la recherche de Suhar: état de la question' in Boucharlat, Salles 1984, 241–70

———— 1986 'Qala'at al-Bahrain: a strategic position from the Hellenistic period to modern times' in al-Khalifa, Rice 1986, 462–9

Kessler K. 1984a 'Duplikate und Fragmente aus Uruk. Teil II' *BaM* 15, 261–72

———— 1984b 'Eine arsakidenzeitliche Urkunde aus Warka' *BaM* 15, 273–81

al-Khalifa, Haya Ali and Rice, M. (eds.) 1986 *Bahrain through the Ages: the archaeology* London

Khouri F. I. 1980 *Tribe and State in Bahrain* Chicago

Kleiss W. 1970 'Zur Topographie des "Partherhanges" in Bisitun' *AMI* (n.f.) 3, 133–68

Köhler U. 1900 'Zwei Inschriften aus der Zeit Antiochus IV. Epiphanes' *Sitzungsbericht der Akademie der Wissenschaften Berlin* 51, 1100–8

Koldewey R. 1913 *Das wiedererstehende Babylon* Leipzig

Komoróczy G. 1973 'Berossos and the Mesopotamian Literature' *Acta Antiqua* 21, 125–52

Kraeling C. H. 1964 'A new Greek inscription from Antioch on the Orontes' *AJA* 68, 178ff (and pl. 60)

Kreissig H. 1978 *Wirtschaft und Gesellschaft im Seleukidenreich: die Eigentums- und die Abhängigkeitsverhältnisse* Berlin (Schriften zur Geschichte und Kultur der Antike 16)

Krückmann O. 1931 *Babylonische Rechts- und Verwaltungsurkunden aus der Zeit Alexanders und der Diadochen* Weimar

Kruglikova I. 1977 'Les fouilles de la mission soviéto-afghane sur le site gréco-kushan de Dilberdjin en Bactriane' *CRAI*, 407–27

Kuhrt A. 1982 'Assyrian and Babylonian traditions in classical authors: a critical synthesis' in Nissen H.-J., Renger J. (Hrsg.) *Mesopotamien und seine Nachbarn: politische und kulturelle Wechselbeziehungen im alten Vorderasien vom 4. bis 1. Jahrtausend v. Chr.* Berlin, 539–53 (Berliner Beiträge zum Vorderen Orient 1)

———— 1983 'A brief guide to some recent work on the Achaemenid empire' *LCM* 8/10 December, 146ff

———— 1987a 'Survey of written sources available for the history of Babylonia under the later Achaemenids' in Sancisi-Weerdenburg H. W. A. M. (ed.) *Achaemenid History I: sources, structures, synthesis* Leiden, 147–57

———— 1987b 'Usurpation, conquest and ceremonial: from Babylon to Persia' in Cannadine D. N., Price S. R. F. (eds.) *Rituals of Royalty: Power and Ceremonial in Traditional Societies* Cambridge (Past and Present Publications), 20–55

———— forthcoming 'Nabonidus and the priesthood' in Beard M., North J. (eds.) *Pagan Priests* London

Kuhrt A., Sherwin-White S. M. 1987 'Xerxes' destruction of Babylonian temples' in Sancisi-Weerdenburg H. W. A. M., Kuhrt A. (eds.) *Achaemenid History II: the Greek sources* Leiden

Lambert W. G. 1960 *Babylonian Wisdom Literature* Oxford

————— 1976 'Berossus and Babylonian Eschatology' *Iraq* 38, 171–3

————— 1978 *The Background of Jewish Apocalyptic* London (The Ethel M. Wood Lecture delivered before the University of London on 22 February 1977)

Landau Y. H. 1966 'A Greek inscription found near Hefzibah' *IEJ* 16, 54–70

Landsberger B. 1965 *Brief eines Bischofs von Esagila an König Asarhaddon* Amsterdam (Mededeelingen der Koninglijken Akademie van Wetenschapen n.r. 28/VI)

Lane Fox R. 1973 *Alexander the Great* London

Langdon S. 1924 'The Babylonian and Persian Sacaea' *JRAS*, 65–72

Langdon S., Watelin L. C. 1930 *Excavations at Kish* III Paris

Lapp P. W., Lapp N. (eds) 1974 *Discoveries in the Wadi ed-Daliyeh* Cambridge, Mass. (AASOR 41)

Larsen C. 1983 *Life and Land Use on the Bahrain Islands: the geoarchaeology of an ancient society* Chicago

Lassus J. 1972 *Antioch-on-the-Orontes Publications: les portiques d'Antioche* Princeton, N.J.

Lawrence A. W. 1972 *Greek and Roman Sculpture* London

————— 1973 *Greek Architecture* Harmondsworth (Pelican History of Art, 3rd ed.)

Leemans W. F. 1946 '*Kidinnu*: un symbole de droit divin babylonien' in David M., van Groningen B. A., Meijers E. M. (eds.) *Symbolae ad Ius et Historiam Antiquitatis Pertinentes Julio Christiano van Oven dedicatae* Leiden, 36–61

Legrain L. 1951 *Ur Excavations vol. X: seal cylinders* London

Lehmann-Haupt C. F. 1892 'Noch einmal die *Kaššû: Kissioi*, nicht *Kossaioi*' *ZA* 7, 328–34

————— 1937 'Berossos' *RLA* II, 1b–17b

Lenger M.-T. 1980 *Corpus des ordonnances des Ptolémées* (2nd ed.) Brussels (Académie royale de Belgique mém. classe des lettres 8. 2e série, 64.2)

Lenzen S. 1974 'Bemerkungen über einige spätzeitliche Anlagen' in Lenzen S., Nissen H.-J. *UVB* 25, 23

Leriche P. 1982 'La fouille de la ville hellénistique d'Ibn Hani: bilan provisoire 1981' in Yon M. (ed.) *Archéologie au Levant: recueil à la mémoire de Roger Saidah* Lyon, 271ff

Le Rider G. 1965 *Suse sous les Séleucides et les Parthes: les trouvailles monétaires et l'histoire de la ville* Paris (Mission archéologique en Iran XXXVIII)

Levine I. M. 1978 'Cos versus Cnidos and the historians' *History of Science* 16, 42–75; 77–92

Lewis B. 1982 *The Muslim Discovery of Europe* London

Lewis D. M. 1978 'The Seleucid inscription' in Stronach 1978, 159–61

Livingstone A., Spail B., Ibrahim M., Kamal M., Taimani S. 1983 'Taima: recent soundings and new inscribed material' *Atlal* 7, 102ff

Lloyd G. A. 1979 *Magic, Reason and Experience* Cambridge

Lloyd-Jones H. 1982 *Classical Survivals* London

Lombard P. 1985 *L'Arabie Orientale à l'Age du Fer* 2 vols. Paris (Thèse: Université de Paris I)

Lombard P., Salles J.-F. 1984 *La Nécropole de Janussan* Lyon (TMO 6)

Lowick N. 1974 'Trade patterns on the Persian Gulf in the light of recent coin evidence' in Konymjian D. (ed.) *Near Eastern Numismatics, Iconography, Epigraphy and History: studies in honour of George C. Miles* Beirut, 319–33

Maass E. 1958 *Commentariorum in Aratum Reliquiae* Berlin

Madhloom T. 1974 'Excavations of the Iraqi Mission at Mleihah, Sharjah, UAE' *Sumer* 30, 149–58

Magie D. 1950 *Roman Rule in Asia Minor to the end of the third century after Christ* 2 vols. Princeton N.J.

Mathiesen H. E. 1982 *Ikaros – The Hellenistic Settlements I: the terracotta figurines* Copenhagen (Jutland Archaeological Publications XVI.1)

Mazar B. 1957 'The Tobiads' *IEJ* 7, 137–45; 229–38

Mendels D. 1981 'The Five Empires: a note on a propagandistic topos' *AJP* 102, 330–7

Meuleau M. 1968 'Mesopotamia under the Seleucids' in Grimal P. (ed.) *Hellenism and the Rise of Rome* (trans.) London, 266–89

Milik J. T. 1967 'Les papyrus araméens d'Hermopolis et les cultes syrophéniciens en Egypte perse' *Biblica* 48, 546ff

Millar F. G. B. 1978 'The background to the Maccabean Revolution: reflections on Martin Hengel's "Judaism and Hellenism"' *JJS* 29, 1–21

———— 1983 'The Phoenician cities: a case-study of hellenisation' *Proc. Camb. Phil. Soc.* 209, 55–71

Momigliano A. D. 1934 'Su una battiglia tra Assiri e Greci' *Athenaeum* (n.s.) 12, 412–16

———— 1975 *Alien Wisdom: the limits of hellenization* Cambridge

Moorey P. R. S. 1975 'Iranian troops at Deve Hüyük in the fifth century BC' *Levant* 7, 108–17

———— 1980 *Cemeteries of the First Millennium BC at Deve Hüyük* Oxford (BAR International Series 87)

Morel J.-P. 1983 'La céramique comme indice du commerce antique' in Garnsey, Whittaker 1983, 66–74

Mørkholm O. 1960 'Greek coins from Failaka' *Kuml*, 199–207

———— 1972 'A Hellenistic coin hoard from Bahrain' *Kuml*, 195–202

———— 1979 'New coin finds from Failaka' *Kuml*, 219–36

Murray O. 1970 'Hecataeus of Abdera and Pharaonic Kingship' *JEA* 56, 141–71

———— 1972 'Herodotos and Hellenistic culture' *CQ* 22, 200–13

Musti D. 1977 'I Regni del Medio Oriente' in Bardinelli R. B. (ed.) *La Società Ellenistica Quadro Politico* Bompiano, 192ff (Storia e Civiltà dei Greci 7)

———— 1984 'Syria and the East' in Walbank F. W., Astin A. E., Frederiksen M. W., Ogilvie R. M. (eds.) *The Cambridge Ancient History* (2nd ed.) 7.1: *The Hellenistic World* Cambridge, 175–220

McDowell R. H. 1935 *Stamped and Incised Objects from Seleucia on the Tigris* Ann Arbor, Mich. (University of Michigan Studies, Humanistic Series 36)

McEwan G. J. P. 1981a 'Arsacid Temple Records' *Iraq* 43, 131–43

———— 1981b *Priest and Temple in Hellenistic Babylonia* Wiesbaden (Freiburger Altorientalische Studien 4)

———— 1982 'An official Seleucid seal reconsidered' *JNES* 41, 51–3

Naveh J. 1973 'The Aramaic Ostracon' in Aharoni Y. (ed.) *Beer-Sheba I: Excavations at Tel Beer-Sheba 1969–71 Seasons* Tel Aviv, 79–82 (Tel Aviv: Publications of the Institute of Archaeology 2)

———— 1981 'The Aramaic Ostraca from Tell Arad' in Aharoni Y. *Arad Inscriptions* Jerusalem, 153–76 (Judaean Desert Studies)

Naveh J., Greenfield J. C. 1984 'Hebrew and Aramaic in the Persian Period' in Davies W. D., Finkelstein L. (eds.) *The Cambridge History of Judaism I: Introduction; The Persian Period* Cambridge, 115–29

Neugebauer O. 1957 *The Exact Sciences in Antiquity* (2nd ed.) Providence, R. I.

Newell E. T. 1938 *The Coinage of the Eastern Seleucid Mints* New York

———— 1941 *The Coinage of the Western Seleucid Mints from Seleucus I to Antiochus III* New York (ANS Numismatic Studies 4)

Nodelman S. A. 1960 'A preliminary history of Characene' *Berytus* 12, 83–121

North R. 1957 'The status of the Warka excavations' *Or.* (n.s.) 26, 185–256

*Nouveau Choix d'Inscriptions Grecques* 1971 *Textes, traductions, commentaires* par l'Institut Fernand-Courby, Paris

Nylander C. 1970 *Ionians in Pasargadae: studies in Old Persian architecture* Uppsala (Boreas: Uppsala Studies in Ancient Mediterranean and Near Eastern Civilisation 1)

Oelsner J. 1971 'Review of: *Cuneiform Texts from Babylonian Tablets in the British Museum XLIX: Late-Babylonian Economic Texts* by D. A. Kennedy, London 1968' *ZA* 61, 159–70

———— 1974 'Keilschriftliche Beiträge zur politischen Geschichte Babyloniens in den ersten Jahrzehnten der griechischen Herrschaft (331–305)' *AOF* 1, 129–51

———— 1975–6 'Zwischen Xerxes und Alexander: babylonische Rechtsurkunden und Wirtschaftstexte aus der späten Achämenidenzeit' *Welt des Orients* 8, 310–18

———— 1976 'Erwägungen zum Gesellschaftsaufbau Babyloniens von der neubabylonischen bis zur achämenidischen Zeit (7.-4. Jh. v.u.Z.)' *AOF* 4, 131–49

———— 1978 'Kontinuität und Wandel in Gesellschaft und Kultur Babyloniens in hellenistischer Zeit' *Klio* 60, 101–16

———— 1981 'Gesellschaft und Wirtschaft des seleukidischen Babyloniens: einige Beobachtungen in den Keilschrifttexten aus Uruk' *Klio* 63, 39–44

———— forthcoming *Materialien zur babylonischen Gesellschaft und Kultur in hellenistischer Zeit* Budapest

Oppenheim A. L. 1949 'Akk. *arad ekalli* = "Builder"' *Ar.Or.* 17 (= *Festschrift B. Hrozny*), 227–35

Orth W. 1977 *Königlicher Machtanspruch und städtische Freiheit: Untersuchungen zu den politischen Beziehungen zwischen den ersten Seleukidenherrschern (Seleukos I, Antiochos I, Antiochos II) und den Städten des westlichen Kleinasien* Munich (Münchener Beiträge zur Papyrusforschung und antiken Rechtsgeschichte 71)

Otto W. 1928 'Beiträge zur Seleukidengeschichte des 3. Jahrhunderts v. Chr.' *Abhandlungen der bayerischen Akademie der Wissenschaften, phil.-hist. Klasse* 34/1, 1–98

Pallis, S. A. 1956 *The Antiquity of Iraq* Copenhagen

Parker R. A. 1959 *A Vienna Demotic Papyrus on Eclipse- and Lunar-Omina* Providence, R.I. (Brown University Egyptological Studies 2)

Parlasca K. 1982 *Syrische Grabreliefs hellenistischer und römischer Zeit. Fundgruppen und Probleme* Mainz (3. Trierer Winckelmannprogramm, 1981)

Parpola S. 1983 *Letters from Assyrian Scholars to the kings Esarhaddon and Assurbanipal. Part II: Introduction and appendices* Kevelaer, Neukirchen-Vluyn (AOAT 5/II)

Pedech P. 1984 *Historiens Compagnons d'Alexandre* Paris

Peremans W. 1982 'Sur le bilinguisme dans l'Egypte des Lagides' in Quaeg-
ebeur J. (ed.) *Studia Paulo Naster Oblata II: Orientalia Antiqua* Louvain,
142–54 (Orientalia Lovaniensia Analecta)

Perkins A. 1973 *The Art of Dura-Europus* Oxford

Peters F. E. 1972 *The Harvest of Hellenism* London

Pidaev P. 1974 *Drevnjaja Bactrija* Leningrad

Piggott S. 1976 *Ruins in a Landscape: essays in antiquarianism* Edinburgh

Pinches T. G. 1890 'A Babylonian tablet dated in the reign of Aspasinē' *BOR*
4, 131–5

————— 1902 *The Old Testament in the Light of the Historical Records and
Legends of Assyria and Babylonia* London

Pirenne J. 1963 'Aux origines de la graphie syriaque' *Syria* 40, 101–37

Polotsky H. J. 1932 'Aramäische *prš* and das *Huzvaresch*' *Le Muséon* 45,
273–83

Porada E. 1960 'Greek coin impressions from Ur' *Iraq* 22, 228–34 (and pl.
XXXI) (= Mallowan M., Wiseman D. J. (eds.) *Ur in Retrospect*)

Porter R. K. 1821–22 *Travels in Georgia, Persia, Armenia, Ancient Babylonia
. . . during the years 1817, 1818, 1819, and 1820*, I–II, London

Postgate J. N. 1976 *Fifty Neo-Assyrian Legal Documents* Warminster

Potts D. 1983a 'Archaeological perspectives on the historical geography of the
Arabian Peninsula' *Münstersche Beiträge zur antiken Handelsgeschichte* II/
2, 113–24

————— (ed.) 1983b *Dilmun: new studies in the archaeology and early history
of Bahrain* Berlin

————— 1984a 'Northeastern Arabia in the later pre-Islamic era' in Boucharlat, Salles 1984, 85–144

————— 1984b 'Thaj and the location of Gerrha' *PSAS* 14, 91–7

————— 1985 'A preliminary report on coins of Seleucid date from North-
eastern Arabia in the Morris collection', *PSAS* (in press)

Potts, D., Mughannum I., Frye J., Sanders G. 1978 'Comprehensive Archaeological Survey Program: preliminary report on the second phase of the
Eastern Province Survey, 1397/1977' *Atlal* 2, 7–27

Préaux C. 1939 *L'Economie Royale des Lagides* Paris

————— 1954 'Les villes hellénistiques principalement en Orient' *Recueils de
la Societé Jean Bodin* 6, 69–134

Preisigke F. 1931 *Wörterbuch der griechischen Papyrusurkunden* III Berlin

Pritchard J. B. 1969 *Ancient Near Eastern Texts relating to the Old Testament*
(3rd rev. ed.) Princeton, N.J.

al-Qaisy R. 1975 'Archaeological investigations and excavations at the State
of the United Arab Emirates-Arabian Gulf' *Sumer* 31, 57–157 (in Arabic)

Rainey A. F. 1969 'The satrapy beyond the river' *AJBA*, 51–78

Rajak T. 1983 *Josephus: the historian and his society* London (Classical Life
and Letters)

Rappaport K. 1970 'Gaza and Ascalon in the Persian and Hellenistic periods
in relation to their coins' *IEJ* 20, 75ff

Raschke G. 1978 'New studies in Roman commerce with the East' *ANRW* II.9/
2, 605–1361

Reiner E. 1961 'The etiological myth of the "Seven Sages"' *Or.* 30, 1–11

Rémondon R. 1964 'Problèmes de bilinguisme dans l'Egypte lagide (*UPZ I*,
148)' *Chronique d'Egypte* 39, 126–46

Renger J. 1977 'Legal aspects of sealing in ancient Mesopotamia' in Gibson, Biggs 1977, 75–88

Rey-Coquais J.-P. 1973 'Inscriptions grecques d'Apamée' *AAAS* 23, 39–84

───── 1978 'Inscription grecque découverte à Ras Ibn Hani: stèle de mercénaires lagides sur la côte syrienne' *Syria* 55, 313–25

Richter G. M. A. 1946 'Greeks in Persia' *AJA* 50, 6–14

───── 1965 *The Portraits of the Greeks* I–III London

Rigsby K. J. 1980 'Seleucid notes' *TAPhA* 110, 233–54

Ringren H. 1983 'Akkadian apocalypses' in Hellholm D. (ed.) *Apocalypticism in the Mediterranean World and the Near East* (Proceedings of the International Colloquium on Apocalypticism, Uppsala, August 12–17, 1979) Tübingen, 379ff

Roaf M. 1980 'Texts about the sculptures and sculptors at Persepolis' *Iran* 18, 65–74

Robert J., Robert L. 1954 *La Carie* II Paris

───── 1983 *Fouilles d'Amyzon en Carie I: exploration, histoire, monnaies et inscriptions* Paris

───── 1984 'Pline VI 49, Démodamas de Milet et la reine Apamée' *BCH* 108, 467–72

Robert L. 1963 'Review of: *Samothrace. Excavations conducted by the Institute of Fine Arts, New York*, edited by Karl Lehmann. *Vol. 2, part 1: The inscriptions on stone* by P. M. Fraser, New York 1960' *Gnomon* 35, 50–79

Robertson C. M. 1975 *A History of Greek Art* Cambridge

Robin C. 1974 'Monnaies provenant de l'Arabie du Nord-Est' *Semitica* 24, 84–125

Root M. C. 1979 *The King and Kingship in Achaemenid Art: essays on the creation of an iconography of empire* Leiden (Acta Iranica 3e série, Textes et Mémoires vol. IX)

Roschinski H. P. 1980 'Sprachen, Schriften und Inschriften in Nordwestarabien' *BJ* 180, 151ff

Rostovtzeff M. 1923 'Notes on the economic policy of the Pergamene kings' in Buckler W. H., Calder W. M. (eds.) *Anatolian Studies presented to Sir William Mitchell Ramsay* Manchester, 359–90

───── 1928 'Syria and the East' *Cambridge Ancient History* VII, Cambridge, 155–95 (= ch.5)

───── 1932 'Seleucid Babylonia: bullae and seals of clay with Greek inscriptions' *YCS* 3, 1–114

───── 1933 'L'hellénisme en Mesopotamie' *Scientia*, 1–15

───── 1951 *The Social and Economic History of the Hellenistic World* (2nd ed.) Oxford

Roueché C., Sherwin-White S. M. 1985 'Some aspects of the Seleucid empire: the Greek inscription from Failaka in the Arabian Gulf' *Chiron* 15, 1–39

Rougeulle A. 1982 'Des "étuves" à dattes à Bahrain et en Oman . . .' *Paléorient* 8/2, 67–77

Roussell A. 1958 'A Hellenistic terracotta workshop in the Persian Gulf' *Kuml*, 191–200

Rutten M. 1935 *Contrats de l'époque Seleucide conservées au Musée du Louvre* Paris (Babyloniaca 15)

Sachs A. J. 1952 'Babylonian horoscopes' *JCS* 6, 49–75

───── 1977 'Achaemenid Royal Names in Babylonian astronomical texts' *AJAH* 2/2, 129–47

Sachs A. J., Wiseman D. J. 1954 'A Babylonian king list of the hellenistic period' *Iraq* 16, 202–11

Said E. W. 1978 *Orientalism* New York

Salles J.-F. 1978/1979 'Note sur l'archéologie des Emirats Arabes Unis aux periodes hellénistique et romaine' *UAE Arch.* II–III, 74–91

————— 1980 'Monnaies d'Arabie orientale: éléments pour l'histoire des Emirats Arabes Unis à l'époque historique' *PSAS* 10, 97–109

————— 1984a 'Bahrain hellénistique, données et problèmes' in Boucharlat, Salles 1984, 151–63

————— 1984b 'Céramiques de surface à ed-Dour, Emirats Arabes Unis' in Boucharlat, Salles 1984, 241–70

————— 1984c *Failaka: Fouilles Françaises 1983* Lyon (TMO 9)

————— 1986 'The Janussan necropolis and late 1st millennium BC burial customs in Bahrain' in al-Khalifa, Rice 1986, 445–61

————— in press 'Le Golfe entre l'Extrême et le Proche Orient à l'époque hellénistique' in During-Caspers in press

Samuel A. E. 1970 'The Greek element in the Ptolemaic bureaucracy' *Proceedings of the 12th International Papyrological Congress = American Studies in Papyrology* 7, 443ff

————— 1983 *From Athens to Alexandria: hellenism and social goals in Ptolemaic Egypt* Louvain (Studia Hellenistica 26)

Sancisi-Weerdenburg H. W. A. M. 1983 'Exit Atossa: images of women in Greek historiography in Persia' in Cameron A., Kuhrt A. (eds.) *Images of Women in Antiquity*, London, 20–33

San Nicolò M. 1934 'Parerga Babyloniaca XII: Einiges über Tempelpfründe (*isqu*) und *hemerai leitourgikai* in Eanna' *Ar.Or.* 6, 179–202

————— 1941 *Beiträge zu einer Prosopographie der neubabylonischen Beamten der Zivil- und Tempelverwaltung* (Sitzungsberichte der Bayerischen Akademie der Wissenschaften, phil.-hist. Abt., Jahrgang 1941, Bd. II Heft 2) Munich

Sarkisian G. C. 1952 'Samoupravljajuščijsja gorod Selevkidskoj Vavilonii' *VDI* 1951/1, 68–83

————— 1955 'Častnye klinopinsye kontrakty selevkidskogo vremen: iz sobranija Gosudarstvennogo Ermitaža' *VDI* 1954/5, 136–62 and pls. 1–10

————— 1974a 'Greek Personal Names and the Graeco-Babylonian problem' *Acta Antiqua* 22, 495–503

————— 1974b 'New cuneiform texts from Uruk of the Seleucid period in the Staatliche Museen zu Berlin' *FuB* 16, 15–76

————— 1982 'Zum Problem des Herrschertitels im Uruk der Seleukidenzeit' in Dandamayev M. A., Gershevitch I., Klengel H., Komoroczy G., Larsen M. T., Postgate J. N. (eds.) *Societies and Languages of the Ancient Near East: studies in honour of I. M. Diakonoff* Warminster, 333–5

Sauvaget J. 1941 *Alep: Essai sur le développement d'une grande ville syrienne des origines au milieu du XIXe siècle* Paris

Schachermeyr F. 1966 'Die letzten Pläne Alexanders des Grossen' in Griffith G. T. (ed.) *Alexander the Great: the main problems* Cambridge, 322–44

————— 1970 *Alexander in Babylon und die Reichsordnung nach seinem Tode* Vienna (Sitzungsbericht der österreichischen Akademie der Wissenschaften, phil.-hist. Klasse 268, 3)

Schiwek H. 1962 'Der persische Golf als Schiffahrts- und Seehandels-route in achämenidischer Zeit und in der Zeit Alexanders des Grossen' *BJ* 162, 5–97

Schlumberger D., Robert L., Dupont-Sommer A., Benveniste E. 1958 'Une bilingue Gréco-Araméenne d'Asoka' *JA*, 1–48

Schmidt E. 1941 'Die Griechen in Babylon und das Weiterleben ihrer Kultur' *AA* 56, 786–844

Schmidt E. F. 1953–70 *Persepolis* I–III Chicago

Schmitt H. 1964 *Untersuchungen zu Antiochos dem Grossen und seiner Zeit* Wiesbaden

Schnabel P. 1923 *Berossos und die babylonisch-hellenistische Literatur* Berlin

Schober L. 1984 *Untersuchungen zur Geschichte Babyloniens und der Oberen Satrapien von 323–303 v. Chr.* (Europäische Hochschulschriften III/Bd. 147) Frankfurt-am-Main

Schoff W. (ed.) 1974 *The Periplus of the Erythraean Sea* (2nd ed.) New Delhi

Scholz B. 1983 'Die Verwandtschaft des Anu-uballit-Kephalōn' in Seybold I. (ed.) *Festschrift G. Molin* Graz, 315–21

Schürer E. 1973; 1979; 1986 *History of the Jewish People in the time of Jesus Christ, 175 BC–AD 135* I–III (ed. G. Vermes and F. G. B. Millar) Oxford

Schwartz E. 1897 'Berossos 4' *RE* III/1, Sp.309–16

Segal J. B. 1970 *Edessa: the Blessed City* Oxford

Seibert J. 1967 *Historische Beiträge zu den dynastischen Verbindungen in hellenistischer Zeit* Wiesbaden (Historia Einzelschriften 10)

———— 1983 *Das Zeitalter der Diadochen* Darmstadt (Erträge der Forschung 185)

Seirafi E., Kirichian A. 1965 'Recherches archéologiques à Ayin Dara au N–O d'Alep' *AAS* 15/2, 3–20

Seyrig, H. 1946 'Inscriptions grecques de l'agora de Palmyre' *Antiquités Syriennes* III Paris, 188–235 ( = *Syria* 22 (1941) 'Antiquités Syriennes 38', 223–70

———— 1951 'Antiquités Syriennes, 48: Arados et Baetocaece' *Syria* 28, 191–206

———— 1959 'Antiquités Syriennes, 76: Caractères de l'histoire d'Emèse' *Syria* 36, 184–92

———— 1970a 'Antiquités Syriennes, 89: Les dieux armés et les Arabes en Syrie' *Syria* 47, 77–100

———— 1970b 'Antiquités Syriennes, 92: Séleucus I et la fondation de la monarchie syrienne' *Syria* 47, 290–311 (= slightly earlier version in English: 'Seleucus I and the foundation of Hellenistic Syria' in Ward W. A. (ed.) 1968 *The Role of the Phoenicians in the Interaction of Mediterranean Civilization* (Papers presented to the Archaeological Symposium at the American University of Beirut, March 1967) Beirut, 53–63)

———— 1971a 'Antiquités Syriennes, 95: Le culte du Soleil en Syrie à l'époque romaine' *Syria* 48, 337–66

———— 1971b 'Le monnayage de Hiérapolis de Syrie à l'époque d'Alexandre' *RN* 13, 1–21

Shahbazi A. S. 1975 *Irano-Lycian Monuments: the principal antiquities of Xanthos and its region as evidence for Iranian aspects of Achaemenid Lycia* Teheran

———— 1976 *Persepolis Illustrated* Persepolis

Shahîd I. 1984 *Rome and the Arabs* Washington (Dumbarton Oaks Publications)

Sherwin-White S. M. 1980 'Review of Cohen 1978' *JHS* 100, 259–60

_____ 1982 'A Greek ostrakon from Babylon of the early third century BC' *ZPE* 47, 51–70

_____ 1983a 'Aristeas Ardibeltaios: some aspects of the use of double names in Seleucid Babylonia' *ZPE* 50, 209–21

_____ 1983b 'Babylonian Chronicle Fragments as a source for Seleucid history' *JNES* 42, 265–70

_____ 1983c 'Ritual for a Seleucid king at Babylon' *JHS* 103, 156–9

Smelik K. A. D. 1979 'The "omina mortis" in the histories of Alexander the Great' *Talanta* 10–11, 92–111

Smith R. H. 1982 'Preliminary report of the 1981 season of the Sydney/ Wooster Joint Expedition to Pella' *ADAJ* 26, 323ff

Smith S. 1924 *Babylonian Historical Texts relating to the Capture and Downfall of Babylon* London

Speleers L. 1925 *Recueil des Inscriptions de l'Asie Antérieure des Musées Royaux du Cinquantenaire à Bruxelles: Textes sumériens, babyloniens et assyriens* Brussels

Spoerri W. 1959 *Späthellenistische Berichte über Welt, Kultur und Götter* Basle (diss.)

_____ 1975 'Beros(s)os' *Der Kleine Pauly* I Munich, 1548 (Nachträge)

Starcky J. 1966 'Pétra et la Nabatène' *SDB* 7, 886–1017

_____ 1975/6 'Stèle d'Elahagabal' *Mélanges Université St.-Joseph* 49, 501ff

Stern E. 1982 *The Material Culture of the Land of the Bible in the Persian Period* Warminster, Jerusalem

Stewart A. 1979 *Attika: Studies in Athenian Sculpture of the Hellenistic Age* London (Society for the Promotion of Hellenistic Studies Supplementary Papers 14)

Strommenger E. 1964 'Grabformen in Babylon' *BaM* 3, 157–73

Stronach D. 1978 *Pasargadae* Oxford

Stucky R. A. 1976 'Prêtres Syriens II: Hiérapolis' *Syria* 53, 127–40

_____ 1983 *Ras Shamra – Leukos Limen: Die nach-ugaritische Besiedlung von Ras Shamra* Paris

Sullivan R. D. 1977 'The dynasty of Emesa' *ANRW* II.8, 198–219

Swain J. W. 1940 'The theory of the four monarchies: opposition history under the Roman empire' *CP* 35, 1–21

Tadmor H. 1981 'Addendum' to Mendels 1981 *AJP* 102, 338–9

al-Takriti, Y. 1985 *PSAS* 17 (in press)

Tarn W. W. 1929 'Ptolemy II and Arabia' *JEA* 15, 9ff

_____ 1951 *The Greeks in Bactria and India* (2nd ed.) Cambridge

Tarn W. W., Griffith G. T. 1952 *Hellenistic Civilisation* (3rd rev. ed.) London

Taylor J. 1983 *Seleucid Rule in Palestine* Ann Arbor, Mich. (diss.)

Tcherikover V. 1927 *Die hellenistischen Städtegründungen von Alexander dem Grossen bis auf die Römerzeit* Leipzig

_____ 1937 'Palestine under the Ptolemies (a contribution to the study of the Zenon Papyri)' *Mizraim* 4/5, 9–90

Teixidor J. 1977 *The Pagan God: popular religion in the Ancient Near East* Princeton, N.J.

_____ 1981 'L'hellénisme et les "Barbares": l'exemple syrien' *Le temps de la réflexion*, 257–274

_____ 1984 *Un Port Romain du Desert: Palmyre* Paris (Semitica 34)

Thapar R. 1966 *A History of India 1* Harmondsworth

———— 1981 'The state as empire' in Claessen H. J. M., Skalník P. (eds.) *The Study of the State* The Hague, 409–26

Thompson M. 1982 'The coinage of Philip II and Alexander III' in Barr-Sharrar B. (ed.) *Macedonia and Greece in Late Classical and Early Hellenistic Times* Washington, 113–21 (National Gallery of Art, Washington, Studies in the History of Art 10, Symposium Series I)

Tilia A. B. 1968 'A study on the methods of working and restoring stone and on the parts left unfinished in Achaemenian architecture and sculpture' *East and West* 18, 67–95

Tosi, M. 1983 'The relevance of prehistoric non-farming economies in the formative process of Central Asian civilizations' *Journal of Central Asia* 6

———— 1986 'Early maritime cultures of the Arabian Gulf and the Indian Ocean' in al-Khalifa, Rice 1986, 94–107

Vaggi G. 1937 'Siria e Siri nei documenti dell'Egitto greco-romano' *Aegyptus* 17, 29–51

Van Beek W. G. 1958 'Frankincense and myrrh in ancient South Arabia' *JAOS* 78, 141–51

Van der Spek R. J. 1980 'Review of *Die antiken und die alt-orientalischen Komponente im Hellenismus. Beiträge des Kolloquiums Hartenstein, 30.3.–1.4. 1976* (= *Klio* 60/1 (1978))' *BiOr* 37, 253–9

———— 1981 'Review of Kreissig 1978' *BiOr* 38, 212–19

———— 1985 'The Babylonian temple during the Macedonian and Parthian domination' *BiOr* 42, cols. 541–562

———— 1986 *Grundbezit in het Seleucidische Rijk* (with English summary) Amsterdam (diss.)

Van Dijk J. 1962 'Die Tontafeln aus dem Reš-Heiligtum' *UVB* 18, 44–52

Van Dijk J., Mayer W. R. 1980 *Texte aus dem Reš-Heiligtum in Uruk-Warka* Berlin (*BaM* Beihefte 2)

Van Driel G. 1987 'Continuity or decay in the late Achaemenid period: evidence from southern Mesopotamia' in Sancisi–Weerdenburg, H. W. A. M. (ed.) *Achaemenid History I: sources, structures, synthesis* Leiden, 159–81

Versnel H. S. 1978 *De Tyrannie verdrijven? Een las in historische ambiguiteit* Leiden

Veyne P. 1976 *Le pain et le cirque* Paris

Vogt B. 1984 '1st millennium BC graves in the Samad area' in Boucharlat, Salles 1984, 271–84

Voigtlander E. von 1963 *A Survey of Neo-Babylonian History* Ann Arbor, Mich. (diss.)

von Gerkan A. 1937 'Die Entwicklung des grossen Tempels von Baalbek' *Corolla Ludwig Curtius zum 60. Geburtstag dargebracht*, 55ff (= Boehringer E. (ed.) 1959 *Von antiker Architektur und Topographie: gesammelte Aufsätze* Stuttgart, 267–71)

von Soden W. 1975 'Review of *CAD* vol. 8:K, 1971' *OLZ* 70, 459–62

———— 1977 'Aramäische Wörter in neuassyrischen, und neu- und spätbabylonischen Texten. Ein Vorbericht. III' *Or* 46, 183–97

Wachtel N. 1977 *The Vision of the Vanquished: the Spanish Conquest of Peru through Indian eyes, 1530–1570* (trans.) Brighton

Wagner J. 1983 'Dynastie und Herrscherkult in Kommagene: Forschungsgeschichte und neuere Funde' *Istanbuler Mitteilungen* 33, 177ff

Wagner J., Petzl G. 1976 'Eine neue Temenos-Stele des Königs Antiochos I von Kommagene' *ZPE* 20, 201–23

Walbank F. W. 1967 *A Historical Commentary on Polybius* I Oxford
———— 1981 *The Hellenistic World* London
Waldmann H. 1973 *Die kommagenischen Kultreformen unter König Mithridates I Kallinikos und seinem Sohne Antiochos I* Leiden (Etudes préliminaires aux religions orientales dans l'empire romain 34)
Waywell G. B. 1978 *The Freestanding Sculptures of the Mausoleum of Halicarnassos in the British Museum: a catalogue* London
Weidner E. F. 1941/4; 1954/6; 1968/9 'Die astrologische Serie Enûma Anu Enlil' *AfO* 14, 172–95; 308–18; 17, 71–89; 22, 65–75
Weisgerber G. 1980 '. . . und Kupfer in Oman' *Der Anschnitt* 32, 62–110
———— 1981 'Mehr als Kupfer in Oman' *Der Anschnitt* 33, 174–263
Weissbach F. H. 1911 *Die Keilinschriften der Achämeniden* Leipzig (VAB 3)
Welles C. B. 1934 *Royal Correspondence in the Hellenistic Age* (repr. 1966) New Haven, Conn.
———— 1956 'The Greek city' in *Studi in Onore di Aristide Calderini e Roberto Paribeni* I Milan, 81–99
———— 1970 'The Role of Egyptians under the first Ptolemies' *Proceedings of the 12th International Papyrological Congress = American Studies in Papyrology* 7, 505ff
Welwei K. W. 1979 'Abhängige Landbevölkerung auf "Tempelterritorien" im hellenistischen Kleinasien und Syrien' *Ancient Society* 10, 97–118.
Wetzel F., Schmidt E., Mallwitz A. 1957 *Das Babylon der Spätzeit* Berlin
Will E. 1962 'Les premières années du regne d'Antiochos III' *REG* 75, 72–129
———— 1979–1982 *Histoire Politique du Monde Hellénistique* I–II (2nd ed.) Nancy
———— 1983 'Le développement urbain de Palmyre: temoignages épigraphiques anciens et nouveaux' *Syria* 60, 69–81
———— 1984 'The Succession to Alexander' in Walbank F. W., Astin A. E., Frederiksen M. W., Ogilvie R. M. (eds.) *The Cambridge Ancient History* (2nd ed.) 7.1: *The Hellenistic World* Cambridge, 23–61.
Williamson A. 1973 *Sohar and Oman Seafaring in the Indian Ocean* Muscat
Winnett F. V., Reed W. L. 1970 *Ancient Records from North Arabia* Toronto.
al-Wohaibi F. 1980 *Studio storico-archeologico della costa occidentale del Golfo Arabico in età ellenistica* Rome
Wolski J. 1974 'Arsace Ier, fondateur de l'état parthe' *Acta Ir.* 3, 159–99
———— 1976 'Untersuchungen zur frühen parthischen Geschichte' *Klio* 58, 440–57
———— 1977 'L'Iran dans la politique des Séleucides' *Acta Antiqua* 25, 149–56
———— 1982 'Le problème de la fondation de l'état gréco-bactrien' *Ir. Ant.* 17, 131–46
———— 1984 'Les Séleucides et l'heritage d'Alexandre le Grand en Iran' in Virgilio B. (ed.) *Studi Ellenistici* I Pisa, 9–20
Wolley C. L. 1932 'Excavations at Ur, 1931–2' *Antiquaries Journal* 12, 355–92
———— 1962 *Ur Excavations vol. IX: The Neo-Babylonian and Persian Periods* London
Yassine K. 1983 'Tell el-Mazar, Field I. Preliminary report of Area G.H.L. and M: the summit' *ADAJ* 27, 495ff
Young R. 1956 'The campaign of 1955 at Gordion: preliminary report' *AJA* 60, 249–66
———— 1962 'The 1961 campaign at Gordion' *AJA* 66, 153–68

Zadok R. 1979 'On some non-Semitic names in cuneiform' *Beiträge zur Namen-forschung* (n.f.) 14, 294–301

Zarins J., Ibrahim M., Potts D., Edens C. 1979 'Comprehensive archaeological survey program: preliminary report on the survey of the Central Province, 1978' *Atlal* 3, 9–42

Zarins J., Whalen N., Ibrahim M., Morad A., Khan M. 1980 'Comprehensive archaeological survey program: preliminary report on the Central and South-Western Provinces survey' *Atlal* 4, 9–36

# General Index